EGYPT

THE ELUSIVE
ARAB SPRING

EGYPT

THE ELUSIVE ARAB SPRING

DR WAFIK MOUSTAFA

GILGAMESH
PUBLISHING LTD

EGYPT – THE ELUSIVE ARAB SPRING

Published by Gilgamesh Publishing in 2014
Email: info@gilgamesh-publishing.co.uk
www.gilgamesh-publishing.co.uk

ISBN:
(paperback) 978-1-908531-41-4
(hardback) 978-1-908531-46-9

CIP Data: A catalogue for this book is
available from the British Library

CONTENTS

Foreword by Michael Binyon of *The Times*

Perhaps nowhere were the hopes for the Arab Spring higher than in Egypt. The poor hoped for higher wages and better jobs, the middle classes wanted freedom and the whole country demanded dignity. And no other country has seen such disappointment. After the fall of Mubarak, Egypt found itself adrift. The elderly generals who took charge were inexperienced in government, suspicious of outsiders and unsure what to do. The subsequent elections gave victory to the Muslim Brotherhood, and Egyptians were optimistic that President Morsi, the first leader elected in free and fair elections for 60 years, would bring prosperity, jobs, order and opportunity, cleaning up corruption and rising above his sectarian background to govern in the interests of all Egyptians. They were soon to be bitterly disillusioned.

Few governments have proved so inept or fallen so fast in popularity. Emerging from persecution and hiding, the Brotherhood proved utterly inexperienced, incapable of halting the economy's collapse, interested only in Islamising Egyptian society as rapidly as possible and intent on pushing through a constitution that marginalised swaths of the population: the liberals, secularists, technocrats, women and the large Christian minority.

The ousting of the Morsi Government by the Armed Forces in June 2013 – seen almost everywhere outside Egypt as a military coup – brought huge initial relief to the millions who had thronged the streets to demand *Tamurod* (Rebellion). But change came at a bloody cost: an immediate curfew, almost a thousand people killed in the shoot-outs with

Morsi supporters encamped in the centre of Cairo, a growing clamp-down on the press, a ban on demonstrations and the arbitrary arrest of hundreds of people thought to be secret Brotherhood supporters, sometimes on the flimsiest of evidence. With the Muslim Brotherhood banned and General Abdel Fattah el-Sisi, the head of the Armed Forces, now seen as the frontrunner to become President, Egypt seems to be returning to where it was three years ago. So what has become of the Arab Spring?

In a courageous assessment of what has gone wrong, Wafik Moustafa looks fair and square not just at the past three years, or even the final stagnant years of Mubarak's long period in office. He looks much further back, to the Free Officers coup of 1952 which forced King Farouk from the throne and brought the Army into Egyptian politics – a place it has occupied ever since. And he tells some devastating home truths. He demolishes the claims of the 1952 Revolution, and exposes the brutal costs, in democratic freedoms, economic competence and foreign policy of Gamal Adel Nasser, the charismatic colonel hailed as the victor of Suez and leader of the Arab world, who turned Egypt into a totalitarian state and destroyed its once solid reputation as a centre of liberal learning.

He looks also at the Egyptian press, and the Arab press in general, and pours scorn on its pretensions, its one-sided attitudes, its censorship and self-censorship and its naïve tendency to blame outsiders, especially America and the West, for all Egypt's ills. The press, he says, is little more than political propaganda put out by one faction or the other, both giving rise to, and perpetuating, the myths that Arab governments have concocted to explain away their failures.

He looks too at Arab attitudes to Israel, and though no apologist for the Jewish state, he exposes some of the disinformation and the historical inaccuracies put out by Arab governments over the years. Exploiting Arab and Muslim anger over the fate of the Palestinians, politicians have found Israel a convenient target to divert public opinion from more pressing issues at home.

The bulk of Dr Moustafa's analysis, however, and his most searing comments, are reserved for political Islam. Egypt was the cradle of the Muslim Brotherhood, the place where Islamism began as an ideology more than 80 years ago. Men such as Hassan Al-Banna and Sayyid Qutb were the founders of a movement that was essentially anti-intellectual, anti-Western and antithetical to liberalism and modernity.

He traces the manoeuvrings of the politicians to suppress, pre-empt or co-opt the Islamists, whose power has steadily grown over the years despite unrelenting pressure on them from the British, the Nasser Government and President Mubarak, who rounded up thousands of Islamists after the assassination of Anwar Sadat. In detailed and well chosen examples, Dr Moustafa shows the baleful influence of the Islamists on Egyptian learning, culture and liberal thought Reactionary and intolerant rulings by the Islamists, including those outside the country, have gradually reduced intellectual freedoms and changed the social climate so that, as he says, "Egypt has become a deeply conservative, closed and often xenophobic society".

All this has come at the expense of liberal, Western-educated or secular Egyptians, who have been unable to produce convincing counter-arguments or overcome the association with Western ideals and values that are now so deeply out of fashion across the Middle East. Dr Moustafa makes no secret of his dismay at this trend. He himself – a liberal long-time resident of Britain who is now chairman of the Conservative Arab Network – admires the humanity and tolerance of the towering figures of the Egyptian literary and cultural scene in the 1920s and 30s: men such as the writers Taha Hussein and Naguib Mahfouz or Huda Shaarawi, the brave woman who founded the first institute for female education in Egypt. And in a useful chapter he traces the revival of learning in Egypt, much of it inspired by France, since Napoleon's invasion in 1798 and the beginnings of Islamic modernism at the turn of the last century. This, he fears, has now been thrown into jeopardy by the present climate of intolerance and growing extremism.

His account is bracing, sharp and, to many, controversial. He says things that many Arab politicians and opinion-makers would rather not hear said. "The political culture in many Arab states is blighted by an inferiority complex and an overarching conspiratorial narrative, defined by colonial subjugation." He knows his history, and his clear exposition of how sharia – Islamic law – has evolved over the centuries is a lot more nuanced than the simplistic pronouncements of today's would-be Islamist authorities. His criticisms of modern Egypt, a country he still holds dear for all its current difficulties, are those that any politician ought to heed:

the slow deterioration in standards of education, the failings of the health service, the way the liberalisation of the economy under Sadat and Mubarak was exploited by unscrupulous businessmen to create a rich elite, out of touch with the harsh world of most ordinary people and dependent on cronyism and connections with the political establishment.

Given all this, the overinflated expectations of the Arab Spring were bound to fall short – not only in Egypt but in those other Arab countries where dictatorships have been replaced not with democracy but with turbulence and power struggles between Islamists, militias and those idealistic young people who had hoped their social network revolution would lead to greater freedom and opportunity.

The strength of his analysis, however, is his honesty in admitting the failings of even those whom he admires and whose hopes he shares. The United States, though often unjustly maligned by conspiracy theorists, has to accept blame for some policies that have been harmful to Arab interests. Men such as the liberal Mohamed ElBaradei, the former head of the UN's International Atomic Energy Agency, were unable to engage either with the Supreme Council of the Armed Forces, the post-Mubarak ruling junta, or with the mass of ordinary Egyptians. Turkey, which could have been a model for the Arab Spring, has recently lost its sure touch, largely due to Prime Minister Erdogan's "problematic" conservatism.

Dr Moustafa tells us a lot about the forces that have shaped Egypt today. And his widespread contacts with the leading figures in the country's social, intellectual and political life give him a clear-sighted vantage point to warn his countrymen, as they approach fresh elections, that, unless they are very careful and learn the lessons of recent history, many of their hopes may turn out, yet again, to be disappointments.

Author's introduction

This book has been many years in the making. It is probably fair to say that it was conceived in response to my experiences when I stood for the Egyptian presidency. My candidacy was not driven by any real expectation that I would be running Egypt, but I did want to draw attention to the thinking of the large communities of Egyptians living in the West. Theirs is generally a liberal agenda, benefitting from international experience, but sadly overlooked by successive Egyptian governments more caught up on domestic issues.

It was a trying experience. I filled in the forms. I was examined by an overtly hostile panel calling themselves the electoral committee and I was interviewed by the Egyptian media. At the end of the interviews I was asked if I felt I would like to express my gratitude to Mubarak for having an open political process. I obliged. That note of thanks was the sole clip from my interview which was broadcast. To the public, it seemed I was simply unreservedly endorsing the nation's leader.

Everywhere I went, I was followed by plain clothes police. The Nile Hilton, where I stayed on this trip, as on others, became suddenly oddly assiduous in the housekeeping. My room was thoroughly "serviced" any time I was not in it – altogether a different level of service from my earlier visits.

As it turns out, Mubarak's cosmetic opening of the presidential contest in response to relentless pressure from George W Bush was probably the start in the countdown to his demise.

For my own part, my five seconds of fame were soon past, but the experience motivated me to find another way to give voice to the sort of thinking that exists among Egyptians who are not directly caught up in the circles of government: a vision for how things ought to be run, and a hope for the country's future. This book seeks to clarify some of this thinking, supported by hard facts and joined with little bits of my own personal experience.

A great many people have been incredibly helpful in putting this book together – too many for me to thank here. I would like to thank all the authors and journalists whose work I have drawn upon, as referenced in the text or shown in bibliography. Foremost I must certainly thank Michael Binyon – ever a distinguished and authoritative commentator on world events – who was good enough to cast and eye over the text and write a foreword. For the editorial support from the book's earliest drafts I must thank Catherine Frisina and Alex Webster. Especial thanks are also due to my brother, Morsi El-Sheikh, for his insights into the systemic rigging of parliamentary elections in Egypt. Last but not least, I would specifically like to thank Max Scott and Charles Powell and their colleagues at Gilgamesh Publishing for their continuous support during the editing of the work, made particularly fiddlesome by the need to keep pace with the fast changing developments in Egypt. *Egypt – the Elusive Arab Spring* was started under Mubarak, edited under Morsi, and launched under Sisi. Hopefully a close reading of the text will arm the reader for what to expect as the Egyptian political system continues to evolve.

Chronology

331 BC – Alexander the Great founds the city of Alexandria and the Great Library.

AD 330 – Emperor Constantine founds the new capital of the Roman Empire, Constantinople.

c. 570 – Birth of Mohammed in Mecca.

619 – Persians invade Egypt for a short period of 10 years.

632–650 – The period of the "Rightly Guided Caliphs" or successors to Mohammed, in effect rulers of the Arab empire, centred in Medina and Mecca.

641 – Muslims conquer Egypt taking over Alexandria (under Omar, the second caliph) and ending the Byzantine presence in Egypt.

680 – Tragedy of Karbala (in modern Iraq): Troops from Umayyad Caliph Yazid I (645-683) murder Husain, the son of Ali, the fourth of the first Rightly Guided Caliphs (c. 626-680). Ali's followers formed a religious party called Shi'ites and insist that only descendants of Ali deserve the title of caliph or deserve any authority over Muslims. The opposing party, the Sunnis, insist on the customs of the historical evolution of the Caliphate rather than a hereditary descent of spiritual authority, and continue through the Umayyad and subsequently Abbasid Caliphates.

691 – The Dome of the Rock shrine built on the Temple Mount in the Old City of Jerusalem. patterned in size, and style after the Church of the Holy Sepulchre, as an alternative to Kaaba, at the order of Umayyad Caliph Abd al-Malik, the dome was the first work of Islamic architecture.

692 – Khalif Abd al-Malik ibn Marwan, sent his General Al-Hajjaj ibn Yusuf to renite the Islamic empire. Hajjaj army destroyed Kaaba, defeated and killed Mecca Khalif Ibn Zubayr, beheading him and crucifying his body, reestablishing Umayyad power over a vast Islamic Empire including Kaaba.

696 – Arabic was declared the official language of Islam.

717–718 – Muslims attempt to conquer Constantinople, capital of the Byzantine Empire. They also advance in Western Europe as far as France (Franks stop their advance).

722 – The Hadith (Tradition), an elaborate system of validating religious theories and Quranic commentaries by linking them to oral traditions about or from Muhammad and his followers, began to develop.

750 – Abbasids become rulers of Muslim Empire with Baghdad as centre; the Golden Age of Islam begins.

810 – The *Book of the Authentic Collection* (90 volumes) is written by Muhammad ibn Isma'il al-Bukhari, gathering the sayings of the prophet Muhammad from various sources.

868 – Ahmed ibn Tulun founds Tulunid dynasty.

900 – The Fatimids of Egypt conquered north Africa and included this territory as an extension of Egypt until 972 CE.

970 – Fatimids found the great mosque of Al-Azhar.

1100 – Arabs establish regular trade caravans from across northern Africa; they gradually extend routes across the Sahara desert into the West African kingdoms of Mali and Ghana for the gold and salt trade. Arab trade network becomes very prosperous and facilitates the exchange of ideas and technologies among societies with which they trade.

1118 – Crusaders launch their first yet unsuccessful attack on Egypt.

1250 – Shagaret El-Dorr ascends power to be de facto ruler - the first and only female in Egypt's Islamic history. 80 days into her rule she marries a Mamluk marking the beginning of a new era of Mamluk rule.

1257 – Shagaret El-Dorr has her husband Aybak killed. She, herself, gets killed by Aybak's fellow Mamluks.

1258 – Monguls led by Hulegu destroy Baghdad, kill the caliph and end the Abbasid Caliphate on their way to fight Mamluks of Egypt.

1291 – End of Crusades: Muslims defeat Christians and regain in Holy Lands.

1348 – The Black Death hits Egypt, decimating much of the population.

1453 – Ottoman Turks conquer Constantinople under the rule of Muhammad II, ending the Byzantine Empire. The city is renamed Istanbul, and becomes the capital of the Ottoman Empire.

1488 – Route of Cape of Good Hope discovered. Egypt starts to lose tolls levied on convoys passing through Egyptian lands.

1520–1566 – Suleyman the Magnificent rules as Sultan of the Ottoman Empire and increases its territory. The Empire reaches its peak in culture, art, literature, architecture, and laws. The Ottoman Empire exists until the end of World War I (1918).

1798 – Napoleon Bonaparte invades Egypt, British Admiral Nelson sinks the French fleet anchored in Abu Kibir bay. The French capitulate to the British.

1801 – French troops evacuate from Egypt ending the French expedition.

1805 – Muhammad Ali, an Albanian soldier who has risen to head of the police, is installed as Wali of Egypt and becomes the father of modern Egypt.

1811 – Muhammad Ali eliminates threat of Mamluks, slaughtering 470 in the Citadel.

1818 – Ibrahim Pasha, son of Muhammad Ali, defeats Wahhabi movement in the Arabian Peninsula and seizes most of Arabia (modern day Saudi Arabia).

1831 – Muhammad Ali begins military campaign directed against the Ottoman Porte.

1841 – "Treaty of London" clinched between Western powers to protect the ailing Ottoman Empire, provinces are taken away from Mohamed Ali's control with severe restriction on size of Egypt's military down to only 20,000 soldiers.

1848 – Abbas succeeds his grandfather, Muhammad Ali, as ruler, and one year later Muhammad Ali dies.

1863 – Said Pasha who ruled since 1854 dies, succeeded by Ismail.

1867 – Title of Egypt's viceroy changes to "Khedive," a Persian word meaning ruler.

1869 – Suez Canal inaugurated in a splendid ceremony. Egypt's finances descend into chaos and the country slides into bankruptcy.

1879 – Ottoman Sultan deposes Khedive Ismail under pressure from the European powers his son Tawfik replaces him in post.

1882 11 July – Unrest in Alexandria, many Europeans killed, British fleet bombards Alexandria.

1882 14 September – Cairo falls to the British forces, one day after the defeat of nationalist Ahmed Orabi in El-Tal El-Kebir battle. Lord Cromer becomes the de facto governor of Egypt. He stabilises the country's finances and establishes a governance system.

1892 – Khedive Tawfik dies suddenly, succeeded by his son Abbas II Helmy who had been a student in Vienna.

1908 – The Egyptian nationalist, Mustafa Kamel, dies of tuberculosis, after forming the Nationalist Party a year earlier.

1914 – In preparations for World War I, Britain overthrows Khedive Abbas Helmy, who had been establishing links with the German and Ottoman axis forces, and installs his uncle Hussein Kamel.

1917 – King Fuad, a former Italian army officer, comes to power after the death of his brother Sultan Hussein.

1919 March – Egyptians revolt over deportation of nationalist Saad Zagloul.

1922 – Egypt gains independence from Britain and the first secular constitution for Egypt is declared.

1923 – Turkey declared secular Republic. The Latin alphabet replaces the Arabic alphabet.

1932 – The founding of Saudi Arabia by Abdelaziz Ibn Saud.

1936 April – King Fuad, the first constitutional King, dies from lung ailment, and is succeeded by his son Farouk, just 16 years old.

1936 – Nahas Pasha agrees a treaty with Britain reducing the British forces in Egypt.

1946 – The independence and foundation of Syria as a Republic.

1948 – The state of Israel announced. Arab countries led by Egypt attack newly born state of Israel, suffering defeat, widely known as the "Nakba", the catastrophe. British troops withdraw from the cities and maintain their only presence in the Suez Canal zone.

1952 July – Coup d'état by the colonels, deposing King Farouk, and proclaiming his infant son Fuad II as the new King of Egypt.

1953 June – Egypt proclaimed republic under General Neguib.

1954 – British forces speed up the evacuation from Egypt.

1956 – Gamal Abdel Nasser Nasser becomes President and nationalises Suez Canal.

1956 October – Britain, France and Israel launch the Tripartite invasion in retaliation over Nasser's Suez Canal nationalisation, the famous 'Suez Crisis', ending in humiliating withdrawal once it became clear the plan was not supported by the US.

1958 – Union between Syria and Egypt, which is to last only three year.

1963 – Yemen War: Egypt commits up to 80,000 soldiers to support the Republican side.

1967 6 June – Israel launches the Six-Day War, seizing Sinai, West Bank, Gaza and Golan Heights.

1970 September – President Nasser dies, apparently of a sudden and unexpected heart attack, and is succeeded by his Vice-President, Anwar Sadat.

1971 – Treaty of Friendship between Egypt and the Soviet Union is signed. President Anwar Sadat signed a peace deal with Israel.

1971 – Egypt's new constitution is introduced and the country is renamed the Arab Republic of Egypt.

1971 – The Aswan High Dam is completed. It proves to have a huge impact on irrigation, agriculture and industry in Egypt.

1973 October – Yom Kippur War: Egypt and Syria go to war with Israel during Israel's celebration of Yom Kippur to reclaim the land they lost in 1967. Egypt begins negotiations for the return of Sinai after the war. Here begins the era of shuttle diplomacy, with US Secretary of State, Henry Kissinger embarking on a series of meetings in Israel and Egypt, culminating in the Camp David Accords.

1975 June – The Suez Canal, closed since the 1967 war, is re-opened.

1975-1990 – Lebanon civil war.

1978 September – Camp David Accords for peace with Israel are signed. Israeli forces withdraw from Sinai.

1979 March – The peace treaty between Egypt and Israel is signed. Egypt is then condemned by other Arab nations and excluded from the Arab League.

1981 6 October – Anwar Sadat is assassinated by an Islamist officer during a military parade. A national referendum approves Hosni Mubarak as the new President.

1989 – Egypt rejoins the Arab League and the headquarters are relocated to Cairo from Tunis.

1995 June – Mubarak is the target of an assassination attempt in Addis Ababa, Ethiopia, upon his arrival at a summit of the Organisation of African Unity.

1997 – Fifty-eight tourists are killed by gunmen in front of the Temple of Hatshepsut near Luxor. It is alleged that Egypt's Islamic Group (Jema'a Islamiya) is responsible.

2004 October – Bomb attacks target Israeli tourists on Sinai peninsula; 34 people are killed.

2004 November – Funeral of Palestinian leader Yasser Arafat is held in Cairo.

2005 May – Following anti-government demonstrations and under pressure from US President G W Bush, a referendum vote backs a constitutional amendment that will allow multiple candidates to stand in presidential elections.

2008 April – Military courts sentence 25 leading Muslim Brotherhood members to jail terms in crackdown targeting the organisation's funding. More than 800 arrested over a month. Brotherhood boycotted municipal elections after only 20 candidates allowed to stand.

2009 June – US President Barack Obama makes key speech in Cairo calling for a new beginning between the United States and the Muslim world.

2010 February – Former UN nuclear chief Mohamed ElBaradei returns to Egypt and, together with opposition figures and activists, forms a coalition for political change. ElBaradei says he might run in presidential election scheduled for 2011.

2011 January – Anti-government demonstrations, apparently encouraged by Tunisian street protests which prompted sudden departure of President Ben Ali. President Mubarak reshuffles his cabinet but fails to placate demonstrators, whose calls for his resignation grow louder. Days later he promises to step down in September.

2011 February – President Mubarak loses power and the army council takes control of the country.

2011 March – Egyptians approve package of constitutional reforms aimed at paving the way for new elections.

2011 April – Former President Mubarak and his sons, Alaa and Gamal, are arrested on suspicion of corruption.

2011 August – Former President Mubarak goes on trial in Cairo, charged with ordering the killing of demonstrators earlier in the year.

2011 October – Clashes between Coptic Christians and security forces kill 24 people.

2011 November – Violence in Cairo's Tahrir Square as security forces clash with protesters accusing the military of trying to keep their grip on power. Prime Minister Essam Sharaf resigns in response to the unrest. Start of parliamentary elections.

2011 December – National unity government headed by new Prime Minister Kamal al-Ganzouri takes office.

2012 May – Muslim Brotherhood candidate Mohammed Morsi tops the first round of voting in first free presidential elections, narrowly ahead of Mubarak-era Prime Minister Ahmed Shafiq. Official media put turnout at a low 43%. Military leaders announce the end of the state of emergency in place since Anwar Sadat's assassination in 1981.

2012 June – Muslim Brotherhood candidate Mohammed Morsi narrowly wins the second round presidential election. Court sentences ex-President Mubarak to life in prison for complicity in the killing of protesters during the 2011 uprising.

2012 August – New Prime Minister Hisham Qandil appoints a cabinet dominated by figures from the outgoing government, technocrats and Islamists, excluding secular and liberal forces. In the course of a military power struggle Defence Minister Tantawi and Chief of Staff Sami Anan stand down and General El Sisi takes the role of head of the armed forces and Minister of Defence.

2012 September – President Morsi issues a decree stripping the judiciary of the right to challenge his decisions, but rescinds it in the face of popular protests.

2012 December – Islamist-dominated constituent assembly approves draft constitution that boosts the role of Islam and restricts freedoms. Public approve it in a referendum, prompting extensive protest by secular opposition leaders, Christians and women's groups in a campaign of civil disobedience encouraged by the military. Government paralysis weakens the currency and delays a $4.8bn (£3bn) IMF loan.

2013 January – More than 50 people are killed during days of violent street protests. The army chief warns that political strife is pushing the state to the brink of collapse.

2013 June – President Morsi appoints Islamist allies as regional leaders in 13 of Egypt's 27 governorates. Most controversially he appoints a member of a former Islamist armed group linked to a massacre of tourists in Luxor in 1997. This prompts further protests and the Luxor governor subsequently resigns.

2013 July – The military removes President Morsi in response to mass demonstrations calling for his resignation. General El Sisi becomes de facto ruler of Egypt, appointing Adly Mansour as civilian interim President.

2013 August – More than a thousand are killed as security forces storm protest camps in Cairo set up by supporters of Mr Morsi. State of emergency declared and curfews imposed.

2013 September – Court bans Muslim Brotherhood from carrying out any activity in Egypt and orders confiscation of its assets. Unrest continues...

2014 January – Morsi appears in cage, and later a soundproof glass box, in a series of trials.

CHAPTER 1

EGYPT AND THE ARAB SPRING

The Arab Spring came about because the people of many Arab countries across the region had reached a tipping point. For generations, the Arabs had been denied their basic right to dignity and liberty. Notions of equality under the law and self determination were abstract concepts which successive Middle Eastern governments declared inapplicable to their countries. Forced to defer to state and religious authorities for almost everything, the Arabs were also bereft of their personal rights, which George Orwell articulated as, "the liberty to have a home of your own, to do what you like in your spare time, to choose your amusements instead of having them chosen for you from above." Though Orwell was writing about another people in another time, he may as well have been talking of the Arabs of the 20th century.

The unrest began in Tunisia in December 2010 when a 26 year old man named Mohammed Bouazizi had his cart, from which he sold fruit, confiscated by the police. Fed up with the constant harassment, extortion and humiliation, Bouazizi set himself alight in the middle of a busy road outside the local governor's office. Protests erupted within hours, and within days had turned to mass demonstrations and, in some cases, furious riots.

As the protests rapidly spread across the country, President Ben Ali panicked, swallowed his pride and paid a visit to the dying fruit-seller, whose self-immolation had been the catalyst for the unrest. Though the president was photographed standing over the young man's hospital bed, the gesture did little to calm public anger. Unable to escape public fury, the president fled, ending up in Saudi Arabia and Tunisia's government collapsed. The events in Tunisia were swiftly followed by mass civil unrest in several other Arab countries in North Africa and Arabia, and ultimately cost thousands of lives across the region.

As the protests began in Egypt, President Mubarak and his close circle of advisors, ministers and family were initially in denial that what had happened in Tunisia could happen there. Those at the top of government did not even show the basic curiosity about what was going on in the streets of Cairo.

For many years, Egyptian society had been afflicted by injustice presided over by the government. Poverty, intimidation by the police and economic hopelessness created two parallel societies in Egypt; one was an entrenched political class which hoarded the nation's wealth and power, and the other consisted of everyone else.

The Mubarak regime was largely unconcerned by the spread of democracy in the third world from the 1980s, which had led to democratic reform in South America, East Asia and some parts of Africa. Egypt was not alone in resisting such a global paradigm shift. Democratic transformation bypassed the Arab and Muslim world, its effects numbed by the oil bonanza that the Gulf monarchies had enjoyed since the 1970s.

The international community (the United Nations, international NGOs and the major western powers) had repeatedly suggested that their undemocratic allies in the region should perhaps introduce democratic reform, since Arab countries were often found lurking at the bottom of global democracy indices. However, aside from maintaining rubber-stamp parliaments and holding cursory elections, these concerns were brushed aside; the regimes knew that the international community would not force their hand in their internal affairs.

Conversely, when the Arab Spring uprisings did begin, it was complicated by the interplay of regional and international interests. Iran, Saudi Arabia and especially Qatar were significant players through their funding of Islamist organisations and their sponsorship of certain politicians and parties through their state owned media outlets. The major powers were largely sidelined, restricted mainly to the formalities of UN resolutions and some logistical support, with the notable exception of the military intervention in Libya. The success of the Libyan campaign has hampered the prospects of any further military intervention in the region for the time being, as Russia and China will not want to see any more Arab regimes fall. Aside from the resistance of both these countries to foreign intervention in principle (with the exception of their own intervention in their neighbours' affairs) both countries have strong bilateral relationships with certain Arab countries which they do not want lost.

Through popular uprising alone there has been partial success in effecting political change in Tunisia and Egypt. Elsewhere the situation is more complicated.

There are examples of Muslim countries making the transition to democracy after popular uprisings, such as Albania. More generally, countries such as Poland went through democratic transformation with little loss of life. However, unlike the collapse of the Soviet Union, there have been few practical attempts to reach political resolution, such as the famous roundtable discussions in Poland. During the Arab uprisings, the opposition and incumbent regimes have sought the political, sometimes physical, annihilation of each other.

The actual concept of a forum for open discussion between political rivals currently does not exist in the Arab mindset, where politics is a zero sum game. Unlike the experience of the Eastern bloc in the late 80s and early 90s, the Arab public opposition is diffuse and directed through a myriad of smaller groups, social media, satellite television and religious communities, rather than through political leadership. Despite being hailed as the unique enabler of the Arab Spring, the role of social media has consistently been overstated in the news. Other, more traditional factors have proved pivotal, such as the abandonment of the dictators by foreign allies and, perhaps most crucially, the refusal of the military to take orders from their own regimes. In the Middle East, very few credible political reformers who have the ability to mobilise the public have emerged. When the Eastern bloc collapsed, there were well known opposition leaders and nationwide political groups to handle negotiations with old regimes and then step into government. This was similarly the case in South Africa and Burma. Unfortunately there is no Mandela or Suu Kyi on the horizon in the Middle East.

From the outset of the Arab Spring, many commentators made the same comparisons between the Arab countries and those of Eastern

Europe. However, the social fabric of the Arab world is so different to that with which we are familiar in the West, and making such comparisons is naive. Far from delivering peace and prosperity, the Arab Spring has left many countries in political turmoil. As a result, the Arab world may have to embrace a consequent 'Islamic Spring' and base their political systems on retrograde cultural notions and archaic legal concepts.

A common misunderstanding is that the Arab world is a unified cultural entity. Rather, each Arab country exists within a confluence of competing sub-cultures, ethnic identities and historical backgrounds. As such, each country has responded to this wave of change differently.

LIBYA

The military undertaking in Libya is testimony of the West's resolve to support popular uprising in the region. Libya is a vast land mass without large human resources, though its significant hydrocarbon reserves justified the urgency of decisive action to uproot the Gaddafi regime. After the uprising there were regrettable acts on the part of the victors, including the mutilation of Gaddafi's corpse and numerous extrajudicial executions. The subsequent public display of the late dictator's body, accompanied by parents taking photographs of their children posing next to the corpse was hardly conducive to a new dawn of democracy. Gruesome murders of former leaders have become all too common in the Arab world in the recent past. The modern practice began in 1958 with the murder, mutilation and public display of the Iraqi royal family.

YEMEN

Yemen is a deeply divided society, with a social structure based around a centuries-old tribal system, of which it is still some generations away from liberating itself. The army in Yemen is largely confined to the cities, and is itself subdivided by tribal elites. Yemen is frequently subject to civil unrest; for example, in 2005 a cut in subsidised petrol ignited protests that left 42 people dead across the country. The president, Ali Abdullah Saleh had been in power since 1978 and had earned a reputation as a competent crisis manager, seeing his country through reunification with the South and a civil war.

The Yemeni protests began soon after the Tunisian uprising, as Yemenis vented their frustration at their corrupt and dictatorial government. The Gulf Cooperation Council had been mediating between the president and the opposition, organised around the tribes. The Gulf Co-operation Council (GCC) drafted a deal for transition of power, which the president spurned. In June 2011, an assassination attempt (widely believed to have been carried out by a rogue faction of the army) forced him out of the country. The injured president was forced to concede power in November 2011. The net result of the uprising was essentially one faction of the regime assuming power from another, with the blessing of their powerful neighbour to the north, Saudi Arabia.

The influence of the former president, Ali Abdullah Saleh, still pervades Yemeni politics. His brother commands the elite Republican Guard, the strongest division in the Yemeni army and he still has allies throughout the government.

For some time, certain pockets of Yemen have declared themselves Sharia compliant zones, and have been witness to vigilante beheadings and amputations of limbs carried out on the pretext of upholding Sharia law. These areas are also those over which the US drones fly, hunting fighters and ideologues loyal to Al Qaeda in the Arabian Peninsula (AQAP), the local organisation adhering to the Al Qaeda ideology. Should the control of the central government decline further, it is likely these areas will assert greater autonomy. Yemen also has to deal with persistent separatist movements in the South, which was a separate country until 1990, and the Houthi rebellion in the North, instigated by a rebel group who adhere to a form of Shiite Islam.

BAHRAIN

The Bahrain 'spring' continues to simmer on the small island where Saudi Arabia provides the backbone of the internal security and the United States bases its fifth fleet. The country has been ruled by the Sunni Al Khalifa dynasty for nearly 200 years, albeit with long periods of Ottoman and British supervision. Iran seeks to support the discontented Shiite majority, hoping to win popular support among the people.

Bahrain is under enormous pressure from Saudi Arabia, and to lesser extent, the United States, both of which are terrified of the prospect of an Iranian client state in the Gulf. Though that prospect is extremely unlikely, Saudi Arabia sent troops into Bahrain in March 2011, warning the government that they would remove the protesters from the Pearl Roundabout in Manama, the capital, if the Bahraini government did not. On 16 March 2011, the demonstrations were violently ended by the government. The government has since been roundly accused of brutality and widespread human rights abuses.

In an effort to mitigate international criticism the government has embarked on a multi-faceted public relations campaign. They have continued the practice of appointing retired American and British police and military officers to mentor their security forces, and contracted western companies to monitor dissident internet activity. They have also made several conspicuous appointments, such as that of a Jewish woman as ambassador to the United States and a Christian woman as their ambassador to the United Kingdom. The government have, however, made virtually no concessions to the protesters, aside from opening a national dialogue in which they have taken no part.

THE GULF

The authority of the Gulf monarchies is waning though they have not yet witnessed the violent confrontations that have occurred in Bahrain. This is partly due to the distribution of income from hydrocarbon exports, in addition to guaranteed employment for their populations. However, the presence of American, non-Muslim, military bases in the Arabian Peninsula continues to serve as a flashpoint for opposition.

The GCC which consists of Saudi Arabia, Kuwait, Qatar, Oman and the United Arab Emirates, have all acted to stabilise their fellow GCC member, Bahrain. These states, particularly Saudi Arabia, are deeply concerned that unrest may spread to within their borders. Saudi Arabia also contains a substantial Shiite minority which has often complained of discrimination.

Qatar has enthusiastically encouraged the popular movements in the Arab republics. They arguably possess the most potent weapon of soft power in the region, the Al Jazeera satellite news channel. Qatar has sought for many years to increase its influence internationally and is reacting to the Arab Spring in accordance with that aim, using its considerable financial resources in the process.

ALGERIA AND NORTH AFRICA

The Algerian leadership is trying hard to balance its position. The civil war of the 1990s claimed the lives of over 100,000 citizens; however, it largely saw the end of the militant Islamic movement within the country. It recently asserted its international credibility by hosting a friendly visit by President Francois Hollande of France and former Secretary of State Hillary Clinton. However, at 75 years of age, President Bouteflika shows no signs of ceding power.

Almost all Algerians are ethnic Berbers, not Arabs. The actual Arabic language content of Algerian Arabic is one of the lowest in the Arab world. In spite of post-colonial efforts to rid the country of French, the language is still widely used by government and media. Algeria also practises a significant degree of social liberalism. Women have equal civic and social rights and polygamy is almost non-existent. Algeria is one of few countries in the Islamic world in which it is not unusual to find female judges, or for that matter, bus drivers.

Islamist militants are still active inside Algeria, as was proved by the 2013 occupation of the In Amenas gas plant. The attack was led by an organisation loyal to the veteran Algerian Islamist fighter, Mokhtar Belmokhtar, rather than by the more active regional terror group, Al Qaeda in the Islamic Maghreb, based in Mali.

The conflict in Mali that began in 2012 and continued through 2013 was a spin-off of the Arab Spring, partly coming about as Mali was flooded with excess heavy weaponry as a result of the conflict in Libya. The rebellion, instigated by the nomadic Tuareg people in the North of the country, was one of a series of rebellions that had been fought by the Tuareg for the best part of a century. However, the arms that they had acquired, and the return of thousands of unemployed Tuareg from Libya in the wake of the Gaddafi regime's collapse enabled them to unleash a ferocious armed campaign which caught the Malian government off guard. Had it not been for French military intervention at the behest of the Malian government the state of Mali would have disintegrated.

SUDAN

Sudan is the forgotten entity of the Middle East. Two decades of civil war have left it a divided and failed state. Moreover, a second civil war is still raging in Darfur. The conflict has been overlooked by the states of the

Arab League and the world at large. It is more likely than not that this festering conflict, partly the result of a cultural clash between the Arabs and Black Africans will lead to further fragmentation of the country. The conflict, which is rarely reported in Arabic media, has cost some two million lives and resulted in four million displaced persons. Like the Syrian civil war, outside states have got involved, creating a proxy war. In this case, the foreign actors are primarily Ethiopia and Uganda.

At present, it is a totally dysfunctional state. The army's territorial control is restricted to certain areas and cities, whilst the rest of the country is ruled by local, often separatist, militia. It possesses few resources, and lacks the economic capacity to evolve into modernity. The 23-year long rule of Colonel Omar Hassan al Bashir, who is wanted by the International Criminal Court in The Hague for crimes against humanity, looks unlikely to end soon.

As an African nation, Sudan fits oddly in the Arab world system and gains little of practical benefit from it, if any. Harbouring Osama Bin Laden back in the early 1990s did not enhance its domestic or international standing. The introduction of Sharia law into the Sudan in 1991, by President Numeri, further divided the country. Harsh punishments, amputations of hands and stonings to death have taken place.

SYRIA

The Syrian leg of the Arab Spring is a catastrophe, a wound that will continue to bleed for the foreseeable future. Syrian society is deeply factionalised, tens of thousands are dead, and two and a half million are internally displaced. Its infrastructure is in ruins and more than two million Syrian refugees have fled to neighbouring countries. At the moment, there is no possibility that a peaceful settlement can be reached; each side is bent on the total destruction of the other.

From its inception as a modern state after the First World War, Syria was forced to become a state of 27 religious and ethnic groups. It is an artificially created entity pieced together by Britain and France in the years following the First World War, its boundaries drawn up from dismembered administrative districts of the Ottoman Empire.

As the conflict in Syria continues to deteriorate, its mosaic population is beginning to fragment. The Arab League proved unimportant in the region's political calculations. Many observers see the conflict as a proxy war between Iran and its Sunni Arab rivals in the region, or perhaps even between Iran and the United States.

Without international consensus, the major powers have been hesitant to intervene militarily in the conflict. Saudi Arabia, Qatar, Turkey and to a lesser extent other Sunni countries in the Middle East are believed to be sending arms to the opposition. The United States is providing only non-lethal aid and humanitarian assistance. Iran and Lebanon-based Hezbollah, another Shiite ally, support the Assad regime. The Assad family, which has governed Syria since 1970, is Alawite, a form of Shiite Islam, one of the minorities in a country that is nearly three-quarters Sunni. Like his father before him, Bashar filled key positions in his government and military with members of his extended family. The Alawites make up about 12 per cent of the country's population. Many of the country's Christians (who make up about 10 per cent of Syrians) also back Assad, preferring his secular rule to an Islamist alternative.

Syria's President Bashar al Assad has been in power since 2000, when he succeeded his father who had ruled the country as a dictator for 30 years. When Bashar took office at the age of 34, Western nations had hopes that he might be more moderate than his father, a hard-line nationalist who had allied his country with the Islamic Republic of Iran and the Soviet Union. Bashar was young, secular and Western-educated. However, the opposition has denied any real change in Syria and has labelled his reforms both cursory and gimmicky.

The unrest began in Deraa in March 2011, after a group of teenagers were arrested for writing anti-Assad political graffiti. Protests erupted, inspired by the success of the movements in Tunisia and Egypt. Dozens of people were killed when security forces cracked down on protesters. Demonstrators soon called for Assad to leave office, following in the footsteps of Mubarak and Ben Ali. Assad promised to make changes, and lifted the country's decades old state-of-emergency law.

Meanwhile, battalions of troops moved into Deraa and began to crack down on protesters. As anti-regime demonstrations gradually turned more violent in the summer of 2011 soldiers began to defect to the protesters' side. These officers and soldiers eventually formed the nucleus of the Free Syrian Army, the main armed group opposed to Assad. What began as street protests eventually developed into a full-scale civil war –

financed, with funds mostly coming via the Gulf oil states. It is both better organised and better armed than it was at the start of the uprising. Many of the fighters are ex-soldiers, mainly Sunnis, who defected from the military, although civilians have also taken up arms against the regime. Islamist death squads have also become a feature of the civil war. Jabhat al-Nusra (the Nusra Front), an adherent to the Al Qaeda ideology, has claimed responsibility for suicide bombings on Syrian government targets, raising fears of growing Islamic extremism among the opposition. In December 2012, the United States declared Jadhat al-Nusra a terrorist group as part of an effort to blunt the influence of extremists within the Syrian opposition, which was by then receiving tacit support from both the US and the EU.

There were numerous reports that a 'frustrated' and 'desperate' Assad used deadly chemical weapons against the population. A full-scale attack on a country's civilians would be an ending perhaps too gruesome to imagine. The Assad regime subsequently claimed that the rebels were guilty of chemical attacks – claims that were echoed by Russia's ambassador to the UN. In September 2013 the US and Russia agreed a deal to put Assad's stockpile of chemical weapons under international control.

The removal of Assad at this stage may precipitate the break-up of Syria and widespread anarchy. Syria has already deteriorated into a humanitarian crisis. A United Nations report on the crisis conceded insurgent responsibility, however the report lays most of the responsibility on the government, saying, "cities, towns and villages have been, and are continuing to be, devastated by aerial attacks, shelling, tank fire, bomb attacks and street-to-street fighting."

By November 2012, the diffuse collection of Syrian opposition groups declared that they had formed a unified opposition movement in Qatar, the Syrian National Coalition for Opposition and Revolutionary Forces. By bringing together the different religious and political groupings, the Syrian opposition could present a united front to the world, and most importantly, receive money from Western governments.

Mouaz al Khatib, a softly spoken former imam of the Umayyad mosque in Damascus was chosen as its first president. Khatib, a moderate Islamist, could not claim any significant public support within Syria, and stepped down barely five months after assuming leadership. The group also appointed communists and Christians to senior positions in an attempt to prove to the international community that it was a secular group. The SNC has been largely ineffectual as it does not represent Syria on the ground, and therefore can't function as a credible alternative to the Syrian government. At the same time, the Syrian public has become exhausted as radical Islamists have infiltrated the country. The increasingly brutal opposition have shifted the responsibility for the violence away from the regime.

The West had been far more reluctant to intervene in Syria than in Libya, one of the main reasons being that Russia and China will not stand for a further violation of another country's internal affairs. However, American military personnel were deployed in Turkey near the Syrian border in early 2013, ostensibly to man missile batteries, though it was widely speculated that they were there as a contingency for future military intervention. Such planning is also the result of the conflict spilling out beyond its borders. In June 2012, Syrian forces shot down a Turkish fighter jet near the shared border. The Syrian government maintained that the flight had violated its airspace, an accusation which Turkey denied. Cross-border tensions escalated in October 2012 when a Syrian mortar shell landed in a Turkish village just across the border and killed five people. Turkey has repeatedly stated that it will not hesitate to use force in defence of its interests, and knows it can count on the backing of its NATO allies.

EGYPT

There had been calls for reform in Egypt for many years. Even Mubarak used to talk about democracy to assuage his Western benefactors, though he never ceded any real power to the people. When the uprising began, Mubarak was under a great deal of pressure from different quarters, both inside and outside the country, with the United States being the main international concern. The President was further pressed by his ambitious younger son, Gamal, his anointed successor. Gamal ran the country by proxy, filling the cabinet with slick but inexperienced ministers. These ministers, many of whom possessed expensive postgraduate degrees from Europe were dubbed by the public 'Gamal's cabinet.' Despite his attempts at control, Gamal was extremely unpopular with the Egyptian public, and the prospect of his presidency was growing nearer as his father entered his eighties, retreating from public life. However, the regime reached a point of no return, becoming incapable of sharing power or developing a democracy. The economy was in trouble, unemployment rose to around 15%, poverty rose and many Egyptians experienced daily indignities at the hands of corrupt state authorities.

The government was in such a state of disarray that, when protests began seeking to emulate the success of the Tunisian uprising, it made a series of bad judgments. The rallying call behind the protests was initially the fraudulent parliamentary election of 2010 which resulted in the absolute domination of Mubarak's National Democratic Party. The protests quickly evolved into a general call for Mubarak to leave office immediately. None of the concessions the government offered could distract the demonstrators from this goal. The protesters were certain that the government would attempt to thwart democratic transition if it remained in power. These demonstrations quickly spread, and led to a general breakdown in law and order. Shops were looted and police stations set alight and crowds continued to mass in Tahrir Square, in the heart of Cairo.

In the end, the Egyptian army played a crucial buffering role in containing the rioting and violence, preventing the collapse of the country. The Generals were restrained enough not to turn on either the protesters, or the government, and compelled Mubarak to step down. In the months that followed Mubarak's downfall, the United States maintained political pressure on the ruling Supreme Council of Armed Forces, known as the SCAF in Egypt. At the same time, the US continued providing the SCAF with military aid. The US strategy in the Middle East is largely dependent on Egyptian stability, to preserve the peace treaty with Israel and combat radicalism.

Both the government and the protesters lacked any cogent plan for political resolution. The Generals, though disciplined and professional, were not intellectuals and lacked a certain degree of political awareness. They remained largely unaware of the workings of modern democratic systems, aside from free elections, and few of them paid attention to the Western media or foreign political theory. They were reluctant to work with Egyptians well-versed in Western democratic politics. Egyptian liberals argue that their intellectual understanding and political outlook is actually comparable to that of the Islamists, hence it was easier for them to cut a deal with them, rather than the more 'complicated' liberals and scholars.

Mohamed ElBaradei, the Nobel Prize laureate, had the most promise as a potential post Mubarak President of Egypt, being well-regarded by many right across Egyptian society. He could have emulated the success of fellow Nobel laureate, Lech Walesa, leader of Solidarity and Poland's first democratic President. However, despite his qualities, ElBaradei rapidly lost the respect of the public, partly due to a persistent negative state media campaign. His physical appearance was lampooned; he was portrayed as a stooge for the West and a bad Muslim. His critics went further to discredit his credentials by pointing to his visits to Israel.

ElBaradei also had his critics amongst the young liberals who spearheaded the protests. The protesters, who desired the complete destruction of the regime, saw the ex-diplomat as too conciliatory, criticising his reluctance to lend his weight to the protests. They also felt that his involvement in Egyptian politics would mitigate the progress made during the uprising, as he would continue to work with elements of the old regime. He also unwisely left the country shortly before the protests were due to begin. It was a misjudgment, and he never recovered from the perception that he was left to chase a bandwagon he had had no part in bringing about.

One of the most bizarre personal attacks made against ElBaradei was the circulation of photographs hacked from his daughter's Facebook account, including images of her in a swimsuit on a beach and with her husband, believed to be a British non-Muslim. The photographs had the desired effect of undermining his standing in Egypt, appealing to conservative Muslim xenophobia and damaging his credentials as a Muslim statesman.

The regime's media repeatedly emphasised that he was an outsider who had not lived in Egypt for many years and had acquired both a European passport and mannerisms. As it happens many of the greatest reformers in modern Egyptian history were educated abroad, such as Khedive Ismail, and King Fuad.

ElBaradei was not tarnished by the corruption of domestic politics. He has a high international profile. He was mild mannered, the right age and was the best-known Egyptian politician after Mubarak. He spoke good English and was in charge of a sizeable UN organisation. He was well aware of the limitations and ambitions of political Islam and it is conceivable that he would have handled the post-Mubarak transition of power more wisely.

However, ElBaradei was unable to form a credible team around himself, and could not present himself as the head of a 'government in waiting.' Nor did the military make any serious approaches to him, preferring to deal, if one could call it that, with the Islamists. The Supreme Council of the Armed Forces disliked the idea of working with ElBaradei.

The exclusion of ElBaradei from post-Mubarak Egyptian politics was very much a missed opportunity for Egypt. The generals, especially Field Marshal Tantawi (also a mild-mannered man) would have done well to work with someone like ElBaradei, perhaps to help form a Turkey on the Nile. Unfortunately each of them acted in a vacuum, in fear and suspicion. ElBaradei is now nearing seventy. The opportunity for him to lead his country has passed.

The Egypt of 2011 could have drawn a lesson from the Poland of 1989. Though many miles and decades apart, there were many similarities. The majority populations of both nations were very religious, with a degree of enlightened influence. Both systems were of a totalitarian nature with a high degree of centralisation and had large expanding populations. The Al-Azhar Mosque and the Coptic Church, as moderate religious institutions, could have acted as the Catholic Church did in Poland, using their influence to bring about positive and progressive reform, without violence. However, these bodies have been largely sidelined in recent Egyptian history.

The internal situation was changing by the day. In such political vacuum, the organised and determined groups with strong financial backing stood to gain the most. Consequently the Muslim Brotherhood stood to gain the most out of the situation by taking a bold political gamble.

The Islamists soon realised that the SCAF, though a collection of the most powerful generals in Egypt, was something of a paper tiger. The SCAF lacked political know-how. They did not have their own think-tank or policy unit, nor did they seek help from any advisory bodies, nor were they aware of the importance of such forums in modern world politics. Their default response to political crises was to indulge in old- fashioned rhetoric and attempt to nullify their critics. They did not form a cohesive unit and were easily distracted and influenced by relatively small protests in Tahrir Square. Protesters and agitators were turning out every Friday, making speeches on makeshift platforms erected on the roundabout of the square, draining away the military's energy and gaining further concessions, until it became exhausted and lost the initiative.

The Muslim Brotherhood ultimately intends to install an Islamic state within Egypt. Consequently its members have been conditioned to believe certain things, notably a rejection of secularism, and a suspicion of other religions, particularly Judaism, which is often regarded with outright hatred and bigotry. The language used by President Mohammed Morsi is indicative of this mindset; in a video recording made in 2010 he criticised Zionists as "these bloodsuckers who attack the Palestinians, these warmongers, the descendants of apes and pigs."

In order to project a credible image of government to the outside world, President Morsi has repeatedly denied that his previous remarks and statements are anti-Semitic. For instance, when questioned about them by a delegation of six American senators in January 2013, the President declared that he had respect for all monotheistic religions.

It was a difficult situation for Morsi. Egypt is on the brink of financial collapse and in dire need of international aid. During the Mubarak era, much of Egypt's aid came from the United States, and was contingent on Egypt maintaining regional stability and the 1979 Peace Treaty with Israel. Egypt is also severely lacking in foreign direct investment, as the country no longer seems a safe haven for foreign investment. Since the days of Sadat, much of that foreign investment came from the United States. The United States, however, was reluctant to support an Islamist-led government, particularly one presided over by a man with a history of making anti-Semitic statements.

Morsi is not known to condemn Islamist terrorists and has openly vowed to seek the release of Sheikh Omar Abdul Rahman, the spiritual mentor of the international terror cells that committed the 1993 World Trade Centre bombing and a spate of terror attacks in Egypt that year which killed over a thousand people. Morsi made the gesture clearer still by bringing the family of Omar Abdul Rahman to his side as he took his public oath as President of Egypt in Tahrir Square (which was, incidentally, not a legal requirement). After the 1997 Luxor massacre in which Islamist militants murdered dozens of foreign tourists, mutilated the bodies of the 62 victims and daubed them in leaflets demanding the release of Abdel Rahman. More recently, the hostage takers at the In Amenas gas plant in Algeria in 2013 also demanded the release of Abdel Rahman.

President Morsi and the Muslim Brotherhood at large will not have moderated their Islamist politico-religious ideology. Mohammed Badie, the Supreme Guide of the Muslim Brotherhood and, as such, one of Morsi's ideological mentors, accused Jews of "spreading of corruption on earth." Another senior Brother, Futouh Abd al Nabi Mansour, called upon Allah to "destroy the Jews and their supporters" during a sermon attended by Morsi in 2012.

Many Egyptians feared that Egypt was gradually developing into an Iran by the Nile. The Brotherhood were well funded, with benefactors from all over the Arab world.

Morsi had some success internationally, in particular in brokering a ceasefire to end the 2012 conflict between Hamas and Israel in the Gaza Strip. Morsi also promised to uphold the Camp David Accords with Israel. This placed him in a contradiction, as the Muslim Brotherhood, as an organisation, does not recognise Israel. Consequently, Morsi could not appear to be too conciliatory towards Israel, not only in respect to the Brotherhood but also to the electorate in general who, like many Middle Eastern populations, view Israel with deep suspicion. Despite Egypt's recognition of Israel going back to 1979, Morsi never referred to Israel by name as he would not recognise the country.

In spite of his public commitments to peace with Israel, his anti-Semitic comments indicate that he has not softened his antagonism towards Jews, while his unguarded remarks about President Obama's famous speech in Cairo were a cause for concern in the White House. He has also been sharply critical of the Palestinian Authority, denouncing it in a 2010 interview with Lebanon's Al Quds TV, as "created by the Zionists and American enemies for the sole purpose of opposing the will of the Palestinian people."

In spite of all this, some of Morsi's Islamist opponents accused him of being too receptive to the United States. As primitive as some of the Brotherhood's rhetoric may seem, Morsi was in no place to disagree with the maxim famously coined by President Sadat, that "the United States holds 99% of the cards in the Middle East."

Subsequent events showed that the Egyptian public was not ready for the kind of Islamic government which Morsi represented. However the question remains, how did he get to such a position in the first place? Why did Egypt vote him in, if only to force him out? And, where did his form of government come from? The answers to these questions lie in the rich tapestry that is Egyptian history. For many observers, Egypt's democratic history began in 2011, a Year Zero for Arab politics. The truth is that the events of 2011 and 2013 are part of an ongoing process in the Egyptian state building project, which began with the great *Wali* Muhammad Ali at the beginning of the 19th century. Since then, Egypt has been ruled by a chain of reformers and despots, foreign occupiers and staunch nationalists. Egypt was a leader in politics, society and culture for the Arab world and its affairs were watched carefully by foreign powers. It is in this cauldron, with its myriad different ingredients, that the parallel movements of Egyptian Liberalism and Egyptian Islamism developed into what they are today. As Egypt enters the second decade of the 21st century, in its seventh millennium of recorded civilisation, the two sides are in a pitched battle for its soul and it is not clear which will prevail.

CHAPTER 2

THE MUSLIM BROTHERHOOD
AND ITS IDEOLOGUES

Beginnings

I n the 1930s, Egypt was living through a period of political turbulence, though not as intense as in Europe. Egypt was still nominally under British control, although the nation had been declared independent in 1923 following the 1919 revolution against British rule. While tensions were simmering and Egypt searched for its political and religious identity, a new organisation would arise, coming seemingly out of nowhere to become one of the world's most powerful popular movements: the Muslim Brotherhood.

From its inception until today, the Brotherhood has had one primary aim: the establishment of an Islamic state underpinned by Sharia law. Despite being outlawed for many years within Egypt, it has worked tirelessly towards that aim and established branches in nearly every country in the world with significant Muslim populations, whether they be in the majority or the minority.

In the history of the movement, two Brothers feature more prominently than any other, Hassan al-Banna and Sayyid Qutb. Through sheer willpower they managed to shape the Brotherhood into the multi-faceted international political movement which we know today. Both were born in 1906, both worked as Arabic teachers as young men, as well as authoring books in their spare time. Though they shared similar ambitions and ideas regarding Islam's place in society their influence would be felt decades apart.

Hassan al-Banna had been a primary school teacher. As a boy, he had got involved in Sufism, a kind of Islamic mysticism and he was politically active from his youth, participating in the demonstrations against British rule in 1919. In 1928, he founded a religious and political movement, the "Muslim Society" which the world would later know as the Muslim Brotherhood. It began in the town of Ismailia, providing social services and preaching to the public. When al-Banna moved to Cairo, he found a ready audience for his ideas, attracting more members to his organisation. Only a few members were of his age, the rest were young men. They presumed themselves to be an alternative to the so-called secular politicians, and rejected the values and institutions of 20th century Egypt as having been imposed by foreign powers, particularly the British. al-Banna's idea was simple: Islam provided all the answers one needed to live a moral life, therefore Islam should guide the government, economy and social life of its adherents.

al-Banna was not an intellectual, nor did he ever clarify the form of Islamic government he wanted to implement. In some ways, his greatest political influences were the polemics of the medieval Islamic empire. As a young man, al-Banna was unhappy to see Western influence on the streets of Egypt and concerned by the freedom people had to do as they pleased in modern cities. He was never considered a reformer as such; he simply wanted to purify Islam to return to its old tradition as he understood it. His ideas were similar to those of the Wahhabis of Arabia who fought to return Islam to the glory days of the Muslim Empire, back in the seventh and eighth centuries. They further incorporated an Arab ethnic-national idea into their Islamic movement in order to attract undecided secularists.

By the end of the 1940s the Brotherhood was acquiring a real natural audience, especially at the time of the war over Palestine. At the time, King Farouk was becoming increasingly concerned about the nationalist Wafd Party which was becoming ever more antagonistic towards him. To counteract the influence of the Wafd in the military, the king allowed al-Banna the opportunity to preach in army barracks, where he struck up an acquaintance with a young officer named Anwar Sadat. The two discussed politics, and shared their respective plans for paramilitary opposition to the government. Years later, President Sadat would write that he greatly admired al-Banna.

The Muslim Brotherhood turned more overtly political in the late 1940s. As it became more popular, the government became increasingly concerned about the group and sought to hinder it politically, ensuring that Brotherhood candidates lost the elections in which they were running. The Brotherhood responded with violence. A "secret apparatus" was formed, an underground assassination squad to carry out targeted killings for the Brotherhood. The Brothers also became active militarily, sending volunteers to fight in the 1948 Arab-Israeli war. During the war, the Jews of Cairo were subject to a wave of bomb attacks and the Brotherhood was ultimately found responsible. In spite of this al-Banna publically denied involvement in assassinations and attacks on Jews.

al-Banna was influenced by the fascism and revolutionary nationalist movements affecting Europe at the time. He would later write in one of his essays of his admiration for Adolf Hitler, perhaps the only non-Muslim politician he wrote about in favourable terms (a figure for whom Hajji Amin Al Hussein also expressed admiration).

In the years following the Second World War, the Brothers killed several senior politicians, including Egypt's Prime Minister Nukrashi Pasha in 1948. The government decided on a brutal response to the latter murder. In early 1949, the secret police shot al-Banna as he stood waiting for a taxi. It was hoped that his killing would mean a stop to the recent spate of assassinations. Thirty-two other leading members of the Muslim Brotherhood were arrested and the organisation outlawed.

The death of al-Banna weakened the Brotherhood, though they would soon find an ally in the form of the Free Officers who instigated the coup d'état of 1952. Both were resistant to Western interference in Egypt and both wanted to see the end of the monarchy that ruled the country.

Though Britain declared Egypt independent in 1923, the British retained nominal control over Egyptian affairs. King Farouk, a man then in his 20s and seen both at home and abroad as weak and ineffectual, was perceived as subservient to the British who had forced his hand in government on several occasions. As Britain's influence in the Middle East began to decline in the years following the Second World War, American influence was in the ascendant. The United States, through its agents, was monitoring events closely in Egypt. The CIA's head of

Middle East operations, Kermit Roosevelt, persuaded King Farouk to bribe the Brotherhood to support the monarchy. However, the clumsy tactic had the opposite effect; the Brotherhood used the money to align itself with revolutionary army officers and help overthrow the king.

In 1949 Kermit Roosevelt wrote an essay titled, "Egypt: cake for the fat and onions for the thin." In it, he predicted that the Egyptian monarchy would be overthrown by a popular revolution within the next few years racked by massive inequality between rich and poor. The Free Officers staged a coup d'état in 1952, with the full support of the Muslim Brotherhood.

The Phenomenon of Sayyid Qutb

Qutb was born in 1906, in Asyut, Upper Egypt. He began his career as a teacher, going on to work as a school inspector. He was a deeply religious man, though he never received any formal theological training. Unlike al-Banna, Qutb was something of an intellectual, working as a novelist and literary critic in his spare time.

In 1948, he was sent by the Ministry of Education to study the education system in the United States. He worked in small local colleges in Washington DC and Greely, Colorado, as well as enrolling in Stanford University in California. The trip would have a profound effect on him. The Egyptian schoolteacher from a provincial town in Upper Egypt experienced severe culture shock at what he saw as the loose sexual morals and consumerism of modern American culture. What Qutb could not understand, was how a society such as modern America could have reached the zenith of scientific and industrial achievement, yet embrace a culture which left him intellectually and spiritually bereft.

He saw in the West a deeply insidious evil, a world in which young women wore makeup and short skirts and mixed freely with men. In his writings he would devote many passages to vivid descriptions of seductive female bodies, the ostentatious flouting of which he saw as sinful. He was outraged that Americans had the financial power to create, purchase and consume great works of art, yet they failed to appreciate them or, those who did, remained barely conscious of their artistic meaning. He also equated the liberal social values he witnessed in the

United States with some of its graver social problems, such as racism (which he experienced first-hand) and economic inequality. However, it must be pointed out that he himself made overtly racist references to African Americans when he wrote of his time in the United States. In his article, *On the Arts in America*, he writes of African Americans inventing jazz music in order to "satisfy their primitive inclinations" and "to excite bestial tendencies."

After his experience in the United States, he sought solace in Islam, deciding that only Islam in a political form could resist the encroachment of corrupting Western values. He wrote of the West as an "animal-like society", in opposition to Islam's higher morality and spirituality. The historian Walter Laqueur described Qutb as "a fanatic, a man totally dedicated to the cause he thought right, a person beset with deep psychological difficulties."

Upon his return to Egypt, Qutb joined the Brotherhood and soon became one of its most prominent members, editing its weekly newspapers and overseeing its propaganda output. Initially, his writings were exercises in moralising in which he railed against un-Islamic behaviour and the encroachment of Western culture on the Islamic world.

Qutb was even close to Nasser for a brief period, with the two visiting each other's homes and with Nasser seeking religious advice from Qutb. After Nasser had been in power for a short while however, the relationship turned sour. Though Qutb saw Nasser as the man with power to implement his vision of an Egypt ruled by the Sharia, Nasser made it clear that his government would be secular, not Islamist.

The Free Officers had banned all political parties and movements upon assuming power, with the exception of the Muslim Brotherhood. The Free Officers knew that they could not alienate the Brotherhood straight away. Instead, they formed a new party, the Liberation Rally, in an attempt to prise young Egyptians away from the Brothers and other disbanded parties. The Brotherhood was aware of the regime's plans. Dismayed by the new Egyptian secularism and Nasser's furtive alliance with the United States, they began to organise against the government. Nasser desperately tried to co-opt Qutb into government, offering him any position he wanted, even his own ministry. Qutb refused.

In 1954, Qutb, along with many other prominent Islamists, was arrested and imprisoned by the regime. The crackdown was provoked by an assassination attempt on Nasser, but was also ostensibly an exercise in quelling domestic opposition. Qutb and the other imprisoned Brothers were subject to brutal acts of torture and some did not survive prison. Qutb himself suffered a heart attack after being covered in animal fat and locked in a room with a ravenous attack dog.

Qutb survived the heart attack but it had a profound effect on him. Not only had his bitter experiences further radicalised him, but he had also been personally betrayed by his friend, Nasser.

It was in prison that he completed his magnum opus, a 30 volume commentary on the Quran, which he began in 1951. Qutb interpreted the Quran as explicitly stating that all Christians are destined for hell, as are those who claim to be Muslims but do not uphold the ideals of their religion through deed or action. Qutb came to favour excommunication (Takfeer) of all those Muslims who strayed from the straight path of Islam. Those straying Muslims were initially perceived to be those who worked with Nasser's regime. However, this distinction was then extended to include all Muslims who did not aspire to the Islamic purity as he understood it. As no country in the last several hundred years had properly tried to implement the Sharia no regime could truly call themselves Islamic.

In order to justify jihad against fellow Muslims, Qutb relied on a precedent set by the 12th century Islamic jurist Ibn Taymiyya. When called upon by his Mamluke overlords to bless a military campaign against fellow Muslims in the form of the Mongol rulers of Iran, Taymiyya supplied the requisite judgment, ruling that such an attack was religiously prudent as the Mongols did not adhere to the principles of Islam, in spite of their professions to the contrary. That same justification was adapted by Qutb as a means to oppose the Islamic governments of his day and continues to serve as a doctrine for all Islamists who wage war on fellow Muslims.

Qutb's writings were smuggled out of prison and distributed across Egypt. In 1964, while still in prison, his most popular book was published, *Muallem al Tariq*, or Milestones. The book was his most significant work, a manifesto for political Islam, as fundamental to Islamism as the *Communist Manifesto* is to communism. The book was banned by the Egyptian authorities but its manuscript circulated quickly.

In the book, Qutb is highly critical of Western civilisation and democracy as a viable political system. A system of governance that came from man was always going to be fallible, whereas only legislation derived from the Sharia, which ultimately came from God, could work. Many of the ideas in Milestones bear more than a passing resemblance to European fascist writings of a few decades before. For instance, Qutb writes of the corruption of a society subject to foreign and, in particular, Jewish conspiracies. He also harks back to a perceived Golden Age when Islamic civilisation was dominant. The only way to re-establish such a society was to implement a totalitarian political and cultural system, completely driven and guided by Islam.

Saudi Arabia commissioned millions of free copies of his book to use as weapons in its cold war against Nasser and Arab nationalism. Thus, the book became freely available across the Muslim world, except in Egypt, where it remained banned. Saudi promotion of Qutb's writings marked the beginning of the Saudi policy of exporting its own brand of fundamentalist Islam, Wahhabism, to the rest of the Islamic world. Wahhabism shared many characteristics with Qutbism, although Wahhabism had been preached in Arabia since the 18th century.

The Egyptian government released Qutb in 1964, after lobbying from the Prime Minister of Iraq, Abdal Salam Arif. Arif had read some of Qutb's works while under house arrest and found them to be profound and inspiring. Qutb's influence had also spread to Iraq and Arif believed it necessary to co-opt the middle class Islamist sympathisers there for his own political needs.

After eight months, Qutb was arrested again, as part of a further campaign of repression directed against the Brotherhood. The authorities brutally tortured him and subjected him to a show trial. He was duly found guilty of conspiring against the state and hanged in August 1966. Like al-Banna before him, Qutb had been put to death by the state, thus cementing his status as a martyr for the Muslim Brotherhood and Islamists around the world.

The execution of Qutb provoked a schism within political Islam. Some revolutionary young men interpreted Qutb's teachings to mean that it was imperative for all Muslims to revolt against their *jahiliyya* regimes, including the Egyptian government. However, the mainstream Muslim Brotherhood continued to advocate the use of social programmes and education as a means of spreading the message of political Islam. With

Qutb dead he could no longer clarify what he meant to the masses who eagerly devoured his writings.

Omar Telmisani, Supreme Guide of the Muslim Brotherhood in the 1980s, asserted that Qutb's writings did not represent the Muslim Brotherhood, only "Qutb's personal views." Within the Brotherhood itself, there were camps both supportive of and opposed to Qutb and his writings, though publicly almost all Brothers refer to him as their martyred spiritual guide. One of Sayyid Qutb's main successes in Egypt was in marginalising the Ulema of Al-Azhar Mosque. He portrayed them as the lapdogs of the regime, only interested in preserving their positions. In doing so, he created an environment in which the popular Islamists, often without the Ulema's years of training in Islamic theology, set the parameters for Islamic politics in Egypt and the Middle East. Today, some of the most famous Egyptians are televangelists, who never attended Al-Azhar, although their programmes reach millions of households. They are direct descendants of Qutb.

The Militants

Nasser's crackdown on the group in the mid 1960s failed to destroy the Brotherhood. Thousands were arrested with dozens killed in custody. Qutb was not the only one sentenced to death. He was tried with six others who faced the same penalty. The devastating defeat in the 1967 Six Day War with Israel severely weakened Nasser's position. He could no longer continue to expend the considerable resources required to repress the organisation, so began to ease off. Quietly and under pressure from King Faisal, he allowed many Brothers to leave the country. Many of them were awarded lucrative jobs in the oil-exporting Arab states, especially in Saudi Arabia.

Nasser's sudden death in 1970 was a lifeline for the Muslim Brotherhood. Nasser's successor, Anwar Sadat, was much more sympathetic to the group. Sadat sought to co-opt the Brotherhood in his battle against leftists and the remaining Nasserists who represented the most potent challenge to his authority. Sadat never lifted the ban on the organisation but he did release Brothers from his prisons and quietly tolerated them in public life.

Al Gama'a Al Islamiyya, or The Islamic Group, an offshoot of the Brotherhood, was formed in the 1970s as a result of the schism in Islamist ranks. Those who favoured a violent Islamic uprising and the overthrow of the state helped form the new organisation. It was able to rely on broad support from the start, acting as an umbrella group for the militant Islamist offshoots of the Brotherhood which had been sprouting in Egypt's university campuses in the early 1970s. The new movement was formed with the blessing of Sadat because student politics at the time were dominated by leftists and Nasserists.

The movement spread quickly and by the late 1970s completely dominated student politics in Egypt, pushing its secular competitors underground. It was during this period that many prominent Egyptian Islamists active today first began organising politically, including Ayman al Zawahiri, Mohammed Morsi and Essem el Erian.

The Islamists turned against Sadat following his peace with Israel. In many ways, the Islamist revival defined itself against the state of Israel, and consequently, any normalisation of relations with Israel was seen by the Islamists as heresy. This was particularly true in the case of Sadat, though his early successes in the 1973 war against Israel made him something of a hero. Aside from what was seen as his capitulation to Zionism, Sadat had also opened up the Egyptian economy to large amounts of Western investment and welcomed a multitude of foreign, frequently Western, corporations to Egypt. This led to the appearance of the Western-style consumer culture which Sayyid Qutb had warned against two decades before. At the same time, Sadat restructured Egypt's economy which led to poverty and the famous bread riots of 1977, caused by the revocation of subsidies on basic foodstuffs. Thousands of Egyptians flocked to join the Brotherhood and its revolutionary younger sibling, Al Gama'a Al Islamiyya.

In 1981, Sadat was assassinated at a military parade. The killing was carried out by members of a militant group, Egyptian Islamic Jihad, acting in conspiracy with Al Gama'a Al Islamiyya. The assassination led to the rounding up of thousands of Islamists, but it did not provoke the Islamist uprising that its perpetrators had hoped.

At around this time the revolutionary Islamists found another unlikely ally. The Russians invaded Afghanistan in 1979, and the United States committed itself to a proxy war, supporting Afghan insurgents, known as the mujahedeen (those engaged in jihad) then fighting against the occupying Russians. When the mujahedeen ideologues and their supporters portrayed the conflict as a Holy War, the United States realised it could count on the tacit, or even active, support of radical Islamists worldwide.

Egypt, Saudi Arabia and other Arab states quietly released their Islamist prisoners, on condition that they go and fight the new jihad in Afghanistan against the Soviet Union. It was hoped that they would not return. Some of them ended up using weaponry provided by the CIA which was not concerned about the flood of Arab Islamists into Afghanistan through Pakistan. Later on, some found their way to Europe as political refugees.

Hardline radicals such as Ayman al Zawahiri and Omar Abdul Rahman were released by the early Mubarak regime and found their way to Afghanistan. Zawahiri had been a member of the Muslim Brotherhood from his early teens. Following the execution of Sayyid Qutb he decided to put his energies towards revolutionary Islamism which was, as he saw it, the only way to implement Qutb's vision for an Islamic utopia. Zawahiri's underground group eventually merged with others to form Egyptian Islamic Jihad, one of the world's most active terror groups. In the late 1980s, command of EIJ passed to Zawahiri, who at that time was a close associate of Osama Bin Laden, to whom he had attached himself in Afghanistan. The EIJ members, led by Zawahiri in Afghanistan, came to be known as "the Egyptians," being known for their influence over Bin Laden, who was a funder and organiser of jihadi activity in Afghanistan at the time.

Omar Abdul Rahman was another adherent of Qutbism. Born in 1938, Abdul Rahman's outspoken criticism of the government landed him in prison soon after graduating from Al-Azhar University. In the 1970s, Abdul Rahman acted as a spiritual mentor to the radical students who would form the next generation of militant Islamist groups, including Egyptian Islamic Jihad. By the 1980s, he was the leader of Al Gama'a Al Islamiyya. After Afghanistan, Abdul Rahman made his way to the USA via Sudan. His easy entry into the USA was never adequately explained, given the fact that it was not easy for an Egyptian to get a visa for the United States, and especially since his name was on a State Department terrorist watch list. Three years later, after preaching throughout the USA and Canada that holy war against the United States was a religious necessity, Rahman was arrested and charged in connection with the 1993 World Trade Centre bombing. He was sentenced to life imprisonment. Despite issuing the fatwa which sanctioned the assassination of Anwar Sadat, President Morsi committed his government to bringing Abdul Rahman back to Egypt.

The Mainstream Brotherhood

The Muslim Brotherhood is a peculiar NGO (non-governmental organisation). It enjoys political and financial backing from foreign interests whilst often working to undermine the governments in the countries in which it operates. Its writings are widely distributed, often free of charge. Within Egypt, the Brotherhood continues to build new mosques subsidised by the Gulf States, which double as places of political congregation. Dar-us-Salam Publications, the multi-million dollar publishing powerhouse, based in Riyadh but with branches in Pakistan, the UK and the USA, serves as the main distributor of texts by Brotherhood preachers.

The Brothers began to arrive in Saudi Arabia from the 1950s, under King Saud. There, Brothers and their relatives enjoyed well paid jobs and state support. The policy was continued by Saud's younger brother Faisal, who ruled Saudi Arabia after forcing Saud into exile in 1964. Funding and supporting the Brotherhood was a useful counterbalance to Nasser and his secular ideology of pan-Arabism. To further irk the Saudis, Nasser was also hosting the exiled King Saud, allowing him to make speeches broadcast to the region on Radio Cairo, undermining his ruling brother.

At the time, Nasser was winning the media war, broadcasting anti-monarchy and anti-Western propaganda from the huge Egyptian broadcasting centre on the banks of the Nile. Back in the 1960s, the Egyptian Voice of the Arabs radio station was hugely popular and influential, in much the same way the Al Jazeera satellite channel dominates Arab television news today.

However, the Arab defeat in the Six Day War of 1967, and the death of Nasser in 1970, effectively ended pan-Arab nationalism as a potent political force in the Middle East. Nasser's successor, Sadat, busily tried to remove the remnants of Nasserism from the state. However, Arab politics abhors a vacuum, and in the wake of Arab nationalism arose the Islamic awakening. At the forefront was the Muslim Brotherhood, who found an eager audience for their ideology.

The Arab oil embargo of 1973 was instrumental in enabling the revival in Islamist political thought. From that point, after the massive increase in the price of oil, the petroleum-exporting Gulf monarchies suddenly found themselves amongst the wealthiest nations in the world. These monarchies, Saudi Arabia in particular, had built much of their internal legitimacy upon Islam in lieu of any popular mandate to rule. The conservative Islamic theology had arisen in the desert, centuries ago, and had little in common with the more cosmopolitan attitudes of the Mediterranean countries. With billions of petro-dollars at their disposal, the Saudis began to spread their influence right across the Muslim world, funding books, schools, mosques, pilgrimages, social programmes, newspapers and preachers. It was once estimated that 90% of all the world's Islam-linked expenses were covered by Saudi Arabia. With this level of funding, it was natural that conservative Islamic ideas became more prevalent.

Inside Egypt, there was an almost total absence of foreign and domestic NGOs, as Nasser's Egypt simply did not permit such organisations to operate. Any that tried faced interference, harassment, or even imprisonment by the secret police. In spite of this, the Brotherhood survived and provided a ready-made network via which conservative reactionary Islam was able to spread. The ideology emphasised books such as *The Protocols of the Elders of Zion* which is still quoted by senior Brothers to this day. The Brothers also campaigned against what they saw as the four major enemies of Islam: Communism, Zionism, Capitalism and Secularism.

The Brotherhood operated like its smaller sister Hamas in Gaza, using superior funding and organisation to work with the masses that live in chronic deprivation to win their support. During the Mubarak decades, the Muslim Brotherhood collected millions and paid no tax. Nor was it legally regulated as a registered charity.

Today, the global spread of satellite television, the internet and printed media has provided Islamists with a worldwide platform on which to spread their views, often facilitated by Gulf funding. The use of the media in this way is not a recent phenomenon. Such methods have been employed by Islamists for many years; only the formats have evolved. Before satellite television, one of the most famous Muslims in Egypt was "the cassette evangelist," Sheikh Sharawi.

Mohammed Metwali Sharawi

Born in 1911, Mohammed Metwali Sharawi, the cassette evangelist, had been a founding member of the Muslim Brotherhood in 1937, and taught at the prestigious Al-Azhar Mosque, though he did not achieve notoriety until 1970, the last year of Colonel Nasser's rule. At the age of 59, Sharawi shot to fame when he took part in the country's first religious discussion TV programme, Nour ala Nour (Light upon Light). Sharawi quickly became the star of the show, upstaging the host Ahmed Farrag. Before long, the preacher had a television audience of an estimated 70 million.

Sharawi's message spread onto other television programmes, and through the then nascent technology of the cassette tape. Cheap, readily available and easy to reproduce, the cassette tape was immediately popular as a format for spreading Islamist ideas. The Sheikh was also subsidised by the oil sheikhs of the Arabian Gulf, in addition to Islamic fundamentalists across the world, who flocked to finance the new television star.

Sharawi adhered to a rigid, fundamentalist interpretation of the Quran. His earliest schooling mainly consisted of reciting the Quran by rote. Back then, the children were not encouraged to analyse or interpret the religious text, simply to memorise it and then apply the verses to their lives.

Though he did not achieve stardom until the 1970s, there is a suggestion that he had been seeking it for much of his adult life. In the 1940s, he wrote poetry glorifying King Farouk, comparing the monarch to the prophet Muhammad. He would do the same in the 1950s for Nasser. The Sheikh even defended his patron Sadat, who had bestowed upon him a ministry, quoting a verse from the Quran in parliament, "you are accountable to him but he is accountable to no one." The verse was meant to refer to Allah.

Sharawi was instrumental in creating a more socially conservative Egyptian society, warning the public away from the dangers of liberalism. The Egyptian writer, Ibrahim Issa, referred to his tactics as "terrorising the collective mind."

His influence was so profound that, by 1976, he was appointed the Minister of Endowments in the Egyptian cabinet, where he laid the foundations of Egypt's first Islamic bank. Even when he was not in government, his opinions on social affairs had the power to shape government policy. For example, until 2010, organ transplants were illegal in Egypt, mostly because Sharawi thought the practice to be against Islam.

Unlike Sayyid Qutb, he was not an intellectual. In fact, he was known to boast that he had not read any book except the Quran since 1943. In the media, he would attack Egypt's intelligentsia, such as the novelist and playwright Yousef Idress, the great philosophers Tawfiq el Hakim and Abdel Rahman Badawi, as well as the Nobel Prize laureate Naguib Mahfouz. The men had been critical of Sharawi's dogmatic opinions, and were deeply concerned that the Sheikh, seen as infallible by many Egyptians, would ultimately damage the nation's intellectual wellbeing. However, Sharawi had ensconced himself firmly within the regime; the state media leapt to his defence.

One of the Mubarak regime's tactics in the fight against terrorism was to undermine terror groups by appearing more Islamic than the terrorists. One of the ways in which it did this was to give the popular Sharawi a prime slot on state television for his "interpretation of the Quran" sermon-programmes. Sharawi's programmes (and others like them) squeezed the airtime available for secular political programming, which had flourished in the 1950s, 60s and 70s. It was yet another example of the way in which Egyptian political debate was dictated by the Islamists, and the secularists, leftists and liberals deprived of the oxygen of publicity.

In the early 1990s Sharawi achieved something of a publicity coup by apparently persuading several of Egypt's top belly dancers and female film stars to announce on television chat shows that they were going to give up their frivolous ways and don the veil, inspired by the Sheikh's teachings. Reports later appeared in the press, denied by Sharawi, that they had been given large sums of money from Saudi Arabia and abandoned the veil after discovering that the money that had been agreed was not forthcoming.

When the Sheikh travelled to London in 1987, he was funded by the Saudis who chartered an aeroplane for him and paid all his expenses. He returned the favour, sharply criticising the Iranian calls at the time to have the holy sites in Saudi Arabia, Mecca and Medina, put under the jurisdiction of an International Islamic State. It was a major issue at the time; clashes between Saudi police and Iranian pilgrims had left scores dead. When pressed by a British journalist, Sharawi refused to condemn Islamic terrorism outright, merely criticising its timing. Instead, he suggested that radical groups should work closely with the leadership of the Muslim Brotherhood and "avoid confrontation with the ruler's police", advising them to wait until the time is right, when society is ready to accept fundamentalist rule.

When Sharawi died in 1998, gushing tributes were paid by all the Islamic regimes and committed Islamists in the region. Saudi Arabia, where Sharawi had taught for a time at the King Abdul-Aziz University, lamented "the great loss of the Islamic nations." Moustafa Mashhour, then leader of the Muslim Brotherhood, declared, "Sharawi's fingerprints on Islamic teaching were matchless." Sharawi had in fact criticised the Brotherhood's "impatience" and the eagerness of some of the members to use violence.

His passing was marked rather differently by Egypt's liberals and intellectuals. The nation's feminists recalled the fatwas he issued supporting female genital mutilation (FGM) and his ruling that women should not be appointed to top government positions or become judges, due to their "incomplete minds."

Sharawi referred to the Christians as Dhimmis, a Quranic word meant to describe other faiths under the protection of an Islamic state, essentially second-class citizens who, until the 19th century in Egypt, had had to pay the Gizya poll tax to their Muslim protectors.

Dr Yusuf al Qaradawi

Dr. Yusuf al Qaradawi is probably the most popular mainstream Islamic preacher in the world today. He is, without doubt, Sharawi's heir who had now become the foremost Muslim ideologue of the digital age. He is widely known as the spiritual leader of the Muslim Brotherhood, and recently helped them draft Egypt's new constitution. Qaradawi's most important recent benefactor has been the Al Jazeera satellite broadcaster, which has provided Qaradawi with a global platform from which to preach. He first rose to prominence on the channel by way of twice weekly programme, *al Sharia wa al Haya* (Sharia and Life), broadcast globally by Al Jazeera, with regular viewing figures of up to 60 million.

Qaradawi is the self-appointed global Mufti, and regularly issues fatwas without regard to any established or recognised religious bodies. Some of his viewpoints, such as his assertions legitimising violence, have been very damaging to the image of mainstream Islam internationally.

During the 2011 uprising in Libya he issued a fatwa, "To the officers and the soldiers who are able to kill Muammar Gaddafi, to whoever among them is able to shoot him with a bullet and to free the country and [God's] servants from him, I issue this fatwa." Calling on his fellow Muslims to kill, even a hated tyrant, is very unusual for a mainstream Islamic cleric.

In his youth, he was arrested on a number of occasions in Egypt between 1949 and 1961, due to his association with the Muslim Brotherhood. In 1961, Qaradawi was posted to a teaching position in Qatar, though he continued to help develop the education and cultural structure of the Brotherhood and published essays and books that were absorbed into the Qatari educational curriculum. His essays relating to the *Thaqafat al Da'iya* (The Culture of the Preacher) were printed in the Brotherhood's magazine Da'wa, in the 1970s.

Like Sharawi before him, Qaradawi holds some extremely obscurantist views. Whilst stating it is not obligatory, he personally supports the practice of female genital mutilation. He believes it is sometimes "permissible" for a husband to beat his wife. He believes women who are immodest in their behaviour or dress are at fault if they are raped. He asserts that homosexuality is a "perverted act, a corruption, a shameless depravity and an aberration", deserving of the death penalty.

His supporters, of which he has many in the West too, denounce his critics as driven by Islamophobia. He was once invited to be the keynote speaker in London on the subject of A Woman's Right to Choose, with reference to the hijab. Qaradawi does not actually believe the matter to be one of choice, having stated, "the hijab is obligatory and a husband has the right to force his wife to wear it".

Qaradawi has also uttered anti-Semitic remarks that would not be tolerated on any Western mainstream platform. He has also openly praised Hitler for teaching the Jews "a divine lesson." He also accused the Jewish people of "exaggerating" the Holocaust. During a televised broadcast in 2009, Qaradawi declared that the Holocaust was "divine punishment for them. Allah willing, the next time will be at the hand of the believers." Qaradawi is an advocate of martyrdom in religious conflict and has advocated the killing of civilians. He justifies this in the case of Israel by simply declaring that there are no civilians in Israel.

His supporters also defend his statements by declaring them to be scholarly opinions and contextual interpretations. However, in a region in which literacy rates remain low in some areas and, having based his popularity on mass appeal, it is highly unlikely that his statements are being taken at anything but face value.

****

Many factors contributed to the social shift in Egyptian society that occurred during the years of Sadat and Mubarak. One of them was undoubtedly the preaching of Sheikh Sharawi and Yusuf al Qaradawi. Egypt, though under repressive dictatorship for much of the 20th century, was avowedly secular, and had adopted socially, if not politically, liberal values. It was known for its culture of intellectual debate, producing many towering figures of Arab intellectual life.

Egypt has become a deeply conservative, closed, and often xenophobic society. One example of this is the increasing hatred shown by Islamists towards the country's indigenous Coptic Christian minority whose faith predates Islam in Egypt by centuries. Anti-Semitism is now an accepted aspect of political discourse. Veils have become the default dress for the women of Egypt's cities, where once they were difficult to spot. The very language of politics has changed with Egyptian politicians warning of foreign plots and conspiracies, rather than promoting progress and reform. Famous writers and comedians are arrested for "insulting" Islam, the prohibition of which is judged to be a higher priority than economic development, regional stability or sexual violence. It is in this atmosphere that the Muslim Brotherhood thrived and was swept to power in Egypt.

CHAPTER 3

POLITICAL ISLAM IN POWER

The uprising in Egypt that ousted Mubarak was about freedom and prosperity, not about how to implement arcane aspects of politico-religious ideology, nor about the introduction Islam-compliant banking as a means of improving the country's economy. However, it is with these issues that the Islamists in power seemed most concerned. The new constitution was the first means whereby Islamists could impose their beliefs on the fabric of government in post-Mubarak Egypt. Many Egyptians feared it signalled stealthy Islamisation.

The Muslim Brotherhood have worked diligently for decades to ensure that one day a tipping point would be reached when its support among the population would be too great for it to be opposed. When that time came, an Islamic state would be established. For much of its lifetime, the Brotherhood had not had a popular mandate for such a radical change and they freely admitted it. In 2005, the Brotherhood's deputy chairman, Khairat al-Shater, declared, "Egyptians are not yet ready for the Muslim Brotherhood," because the population had not reached the prerequisite "state of proper Islamic belief". After 2011 however, the political landscape was different.

Initially, the Muslim Brotherhood established a political party as it did not actually have one, being more of a social and religious group, although it had been fielding independent candidates to parliament for years. Consequently, the Freedom and Justice Party was formed, the branding bearing more than a passing resemblance to the Islamist-leaning

Justice and Development party in Turkey. In the newly democratised countries of the Middle East the Turkish party has become the model newly enfranchised Islamist movements are keen to follow.

In April 2011, the Brotherhood declared it would only field candidates for half the parliamentary seats. In the parliamentary elections, held from November 2011 to January 2012, the FJP fielded candidates in every constituency. It then embarked on an organised public relations campaign which sought to persuade the public that it was a credible alternative to the regime of Hosni Mubarak. Indeed, one of its most skilful tactics was to lump together the secular political parties and movements with ex-regime opportunists. The Salafists were also successful, taking a third of parliamentary seats in the form of the Islamist Bloc, led by Al Nour, and helping to draft the new constitution.

The Brotherhood also promised that they would not field any candidates for the presidency. In the end, they fielded several. The first presidential candidate for the FJP, Khairat al-Shater, was disqualified due to money-laundering and terrorism convictions for which he was imprisoned. The Brotherhood subsequently fielded another candidate under the banner of the FJP, Mohammed Morsi. Another senior Brother, Dr Abdel Moneim Abu Fotouh, left the Brotherhood in 2011 to run as an independent. The Salafists, who represent a more zealous form of Islamism, formed their own Al Nour the Light Party and fielded the wildly bearded Dr Salah Abu Ismail who was later disqualified for concealing his mother's US citizenship.

The presidential election was divided into two stages, with only the top two candidates going through to the second round. After the first round, the highest placed candidates were Morsi and the former head of the air force and final Mubarak prime minister, Ahmed Shafik. Just under 25% of voters chose Morsi in the first round of the presidential election, and just under 24% voted for Shafik. However, as they were the top two candidates to garner the most votes, only they went through to the second round.

Morsi's campaign slogan against the Mubarak-era General Ahmed Shafik proclaimed "voting Shafik is voting for Mubarak Mark II and the army." Throughout the campaign, Morsi stipulated that new laws would have to be vetted by religious scholars. He also upheld the Brotherhood's declaration that women and Copts (Egyptian Christians who make up 10% of the population) must be barred from running for president.

According to official results, Morsi took 51.7 % of votes in the second round and General Shafik managed 48.3%. The Shafik campaign was disorganised, underfunded and ultimately tainted by association with Hosni Mubarak. The military had assumed, incorrectly, that the Islamists would lose the vote by fielding an unknown candidate. When counting both rounds, non-Islamist candidates received more than half of all votes in the presidential election. Many non-Islamists voted for Morsi simply because they could not bear to elect a Mubarak man as President. Turnout was low. In the second round, just under 52% of eligible voters cast their vote, somewhat undermining claims that the Brotherhood had a popular mandate to impose an Islamist regime.

The Muslim Brotherhood had a decisive weapon in its multiple electoral campaigns: the thousands of mosques across Egypt. Most Egyptians attend prayers every Friday, providing a captive audience for imams and preachers campaigning from the pulpit.

During President Morsi's open-air swearing-in ceremony in Tahrir Square – incidentally, not a legal requirement – the guests included the family of the blind Sheikh Omar Abdel Rahman. Rahman was a spiritual leader of the terror group Al Gamaa Al Islamiyya (the Islamic Group), and is currently in prison in the United States for his involvement in the 1993 World Trade Centre bombing. During the 1997 Luxor massacre carried out by Al Gama'a Al Islamiyya leaflets were left around the bodies of the victims (one of which was a five-year-old British child) demanding the release of Rahman. During the ceremony in Tahrir Square, Morsi also promised to try to secure Rahman's release.

Morsi seems an unlikely politician. He lacks personal charisma and senior political experience. His speeches are like those of a preacher in a village mosque. He is an engineer by trade, and was virtually unknown inside Egypt or even, for that matter, within the broader Brotherhood movement itself. He was first elected to public office in 2000 as an independent MP running under a quota system for non-regime MPs introduced by the Mubarak government, essentially a form of window-dressing to mitigate criticism of a lack of democracy by the West. Morsi's ideological mindset lies somewhere between that of the more radical Salafists and the moderate wing of Muslim Brotherhood. He spent some of his younger years studying and working in the United States in much the same way as Sayyid Qutb, the ideological father of modern Islamism, had decades before. Morsi's ultra-conservative past would no doubt damage his ability to conduct international relations, particularly with the West and Israel. A speech in which he made a call "to nurse our children and our grandchildren on hatred for them: for Zionists, for Jews," will haunt him.

The mistrust between the President and the military was readily apparent. To put it simply, the military were unconvinced that Morsi could deliver and maintain national unity, a touchstone issue that has defined Egyptian politics for decades. The economy was in freefall. Forty-five million Egyptians lived on less than $2 a day and unemployment was soaring. There was no new investment and the living standards of millions were much lower than those in Gaza. Most fundamentally, corruption – one of the main driving forces of the 2011 uprising – remained as rampant as ever, if not more so. Throughout his brief presidency civil unrest continued, much of it in response to Morsi's moves to consolidate power. Though the military's later actions against Morsi came as a surprise in the West, the military had in fact tacitly warned that they would take power from Morsi should he be unable to halt the decline in law and order. When General El Sisi took over from Field Marshal Tantawi as head of the armed forces (Tantawi had been forced to retire by Morsi), he warned in a speech at the Egyptian Military Academy, "The continuation of the struggle among political powers to run the country will lead to the collapse of the state, threatening the future generations." He went on, "The political, social and security challenges and the milestones facing Egypt right now constitute a genuine threat to Egypt's security and the cohesion of the state." The subtext of such remarks was obvious: the military was not yet ready to cede control of the country.

Liberal opposition to the Brotherhood began to peak after the appointment of the 100-member Constitutional Assembly in March 2012. Charged with drafting the new constitution, it was overwhelmingly composed of Islamists. Predictably, the constitution stipulated that the Sharia be the source of legislation in Egypt. As a result, women, minorities, secularists and liberals feared that the new law of the land would allow the Brotherhood to introduce a raft of retrograde legislation, and assist in the establishment of the Islamic state they had long sought.

The constitution was hastily passed by the Islamist-dominated parliament. The victory was sealed when the commission chairman,

Judge Samir Abou Al-Maaty, told a news conference in Cairo that 63.8% of voters, with a 33% turnout from an electorate of 52 million, had backed the constitution. When the Egyptian Supreme Constitutional Court sought to rule on the legitimacy of the constitution in late 2012 supporters of President Morsi, which included both Muslim Brothers and the more extreme Salafists surrounded the court and prevented the judges from entering. Parallel protests erupted across Egypt, mirroring the deep divisions that had plagued the country in the wake of Mubarak's departure. Many Islamist protesters held aloft the Quran, waving pictures of Morsi and the blind Sheikh Omar Abdel Rahman

The liberal and secular opposition remained largely disjointed. Many of the younger liberal activists who were very much the driving force behind the 2011 uprising refused outright to partake in the new political process, leaving them absent from the new political scene. Some liberal leaders, aware of the consequence of splitting the liberal vote, amalgamated to form the National Salvation Front. The Nobel laureate Mohamed ElBaradei coordinated the group and it included such well-known figues as former Secretary General of the Arab League, Amr Moussa, and Nasserist politician Hamdin Sabahi. Traditionally, many of these people and their parties, had been opposed to one another. However, they were forced to unite in their opposition to the Islamists. In order to counter the liberal protests against Morsi, the Brotherhood frequently used chain text messaging to summon pro-Morsi demonstrations in front of the presidential palace in Heliopolis, Cairo's mostly affluent suburb, in order to teach the enemies of democracy "a lesson."

Within the space of 18 months, the Brotherhood had won the presidential election, the parliamentary election, and the referendum on the constitution which they drafted. Their victory was complete. In parliament, the second-placed group were the Salafists, who advocated an even more austere form of Islamism than the Brothers. The secular parties and movements were left in disarray. However, despite the appearance of dominance, such a state of affairs would not last and though unorganised politically, the Brotherhood's opponents could muster real power on the streets of Cairo and Alexandria, not to mention Egypt's other great cities.

****

The Brotherhood felt they had the political credibility to implement its Islamist mandate. For the first time in their history they not only wielded power but could imprint the Egyptian state with the ideals of Hassan al-Banna.

Morsi officially declared that since the start of the presidential election, he was no longer a member of the Muslim Brotherhood, but he appointed many Brothers as his aides and advisors. His chief of staff came straight from Brotherhood headquarters to the presidential office, and many of his non-Brotherhood appointees complained that they had no influence and received their positions in a charade of pluralism.

It was abundantly clear to the Egyptian public that despite Morsi's independent façade, the Brotherhood was manipulating government from behind the scenes, and it had no scruples about pushing the country to the brink of collapse in the furtherance of its aims. As to the question of who was really behind Morsi and, where the real power lay, one must look to his advisers. One of his closest was Saad el Husseini, a hardliner who is also close to Khairat al-Shater, the real power behind the Muslim Brotherhood and its main financier. Shater is one of the two senior Brothers who controlled Morsi, the other being Mohammed Badie, the Supreme Guide of the Muslim Brotherhood.

When Morsi met with Badie, as he did in public on many occasions, he bowed before him and kissed his hand. It was a gesture of subservience, for Badie was Morsi's spiritual master. As a young man Morsi swore an oath of allegiance to the Brotherhood and its leader, as have all the other Brothers. Badie, born in 1943, has led the Brotherhood since 2010. He heads the executive command of the Brotherhood, the Guidance Office which is made up of 21 senior Brothers, almost all of whom had been imprisoned for their activities within the organisation at one time or another. The Guidance Office is effectively an Islamist politburo, though most of its members lack any real political experience.

Prior to the 2011 uprising, Badie openly supported President Hosni Mubarak, which no Supreme Guide had done before, and Mubarak responded in kind by releasing several hundred jailed Brothers. By the time Mubarak fell there were comparatively few (several hundred) Brothers still in prison. Many Egyptians, particularly liberals, were suspicious of the relationship. It was further believed that the secret co-operation between the Mubarak regime and the Brotherhood continued with the military after the fall of Mubarak. Indeed, many intelligence officers had formed close working and personal ties with Egyptian Islamists.

Khairat al-Shater, an engineer by training, is a multi-millionaire and chief strategist for the Muslim Brotherhood. Once Morsi's direct superior, he is ultimately responsible for the Brotherhood's political planning. It was al-Shater who brokered the deal with the Supreme Council of the Armed Forces which enabled both sides to save face, relieving the top generals, including Field Marshal Tantawi, of their power while simultaneously preserving all their privileges and offering them the highest medals of honour for serving the country.

Al-Shater, born in 1950, had been active in the Brotherhood since his teens. Exiled after the assassination of Sadat, he spent several years in the United Kingdom before returning to Egypt in the mid 1980s. He has been a particularly active organiser for the Brotherhood, whilst amassing a considerable fortune through his various businesses, most notably his own chain of furniture stores and supermarkets. By 1995 he was running the Brotherhood's greater Cairo branch. In 2006, he was arrested and charged with paramilitary activity. He was imprisoned in 2007. However, he was released in March 2011, a month after the fall of Mubarak. As he had only recently been incarcerated, he was in contravention of electoral rules and had to step down as the Brotherhood's first choice as candidate for the presidency. Not actually being allowed to be president did not prove a major obstacle for al-Shater since Morsi more than adequately served as his puppet. In a newspaper interview, one anonymous former Brother described Morsi as al-Shater's "errand boy," within the movement. A raft of presidential advisers resigned from the Morsi administration complaining that all the orders for the President's decrees and policies came straight from the Brotherhood's Guidance Office and were only given a cursory glance by the President before being passed as law.

When the President appointed new regional governors the list of candidates came from the Brotherhood's office. When the heads of the state-controlled media were replaced the new executives and directors were also suggested by the Brotherhood. The appointments were made without consulting any of the cabinet and the President's non-Brother advisers were likewise ignored.

Though technically Badie's deputy, al-Shater is increasingly seen as the real leader of the movement. He is a big man, a father of ten children and has an undeniable force of personality. He even has his own (self-designated) nickname, *El Muhandis* (The Engineer). Ideologically, he is deeply conservative and has been trying to realign the Brotherhood more towards the fundamentalist Salafist current of political Islam.

Morsi's statements in international relations were incredibly simplistic and belie a lack of understanding of foreign affairs in general. Though he has not mentioned the issue since becoming President, Morsi is an advocate of 9/11 conspiracy theories, writing about his suspicions regarding Al Qaeda's involvement in the event back in 2007. His mistrust of the United States continued; in 2010, he criticised President Obama's "empty words on the land of Egypt." Morsi, like many Egyptians and Muslims is convinced that the United States seeks to weaken Islam and the Muslim world through its Jewish-controlled media and has made statements to that effect in the past. Such anti-West stances have been a fundamental tenet of the Muslim Brotherhood's ideology since the days of Hassan al-Banna. The ideological hatred is the product of the fusion between religion and politics relentlessly propagated through Brotherhood propaganda. In the mosques, Imams are encouraged to preach hatred of Israel and the West to serve political purposes.

Morsi has also overseen a thaw in relations with Iran, which were broken after President Sadat's offer of asylum to the deposed Shah of Iran in 1980. Though there have been minor instances of the warming of relations between the two countries, it was not until Morsi became President that bilateral relations were restored. In 2012 Morsi attended a Non-Aligned Movement conference in Tehran, and Iran's President Ahmadinejad returned the gesture, visiting Cairo in 2013 for a meeting of the Organisation of Islamic Cooperation Conference. These were the first visits between Egyptian and Iranian heads of state since the 1970s.

The thaw in relations has been of deep concern in the West, especially to the United States. In part, aside from the fiery rhetoric coming from Tehran since 2005, there is a concern that the close relations between the two might mark a realignment of Egyptian foreign policy. Egypt and Iran's diplomatic schism over the previous 30 years was largely based around Egypt's positive relationship with the West, the United States in particular, and their treaty with Israel. Morsi has avoided as much as possible referring to Israel by name because the Brotherhood does not recognise the Israeli state. He has however, signalled his intentions to alter the Peace Treaty with Israel.

The United States policy on Morsi has been decidedly muted. They could not afford to alienate Egypt totally as Egypt remains a key American prospect for stability in the region, particularly with regard to the treaty with Israel. President Obama clarified the relationship with Egypt by stating that the United States "does not consider it an ally, or an enemy." The annual UN world leaders gathering in September 2012 offered a potential meeting between President Obama and President Morsi, although such a meeting never took place.

One of the early tests for US-Egyptian relations was the fallout from "The Innocence of Muslims," a low-budget American film, footage from which was released over the internet. The film, funded by American Copts, largely consisted of scenes mocking the prophet Muhammad and the origins of Islam. The Brotherhood initially planned massive anti-American protests in response. However, after a last-minute phone call from President Obama, Morsi promised to protect American installations in Egypt. In spite of Morsi's offer of protection, protesters did manage to break into the American embassy in Cairo, scale its roof and replace the American flag with the black flag of political Islam.

Mohamed ElBaradei has been particularly critical of the Muslim Brotherhood's stance towards Israel, accusing them of anti-Semitism. However, within Egypt, ElBaradei was ridiculed for his stance. The Morsi-appointed prosecutor general also referred for investigation the accusation that ElBaradei, along with several other prominent secular politicians (including former head of the Arab League Amr Moussa), was engaged in espionage on behalf of Israel in order to implement a "Zionist plot."

The Brothers have been less successful in their attempts to dominate the judiciary. President Morsi failed in his attempt to remove Egypt's attorney general, Abdel Meguid Mahmoud, of whom he disapproved because of his acquittal of certain former members of the Mubarak regime. It was a difficult problem for Morsi as the law forbade the President from removing the Attorney General. In order to remove

Mahmoud without overtly sacking him Morsi ordered him to accept the position of ambassador to the Vatican, a ceremonial and totally powerless appointment. Mahmoud refused to move and Morsi was forced to let him remain. Though Morsi backed down, it destroyed the little trust he had with the judiciary who stood by their beleaguered attorney general.

Once in power, the Brotherhood has repeatedly tried to use any legal means to intimidate its critics, particularly in the newspapers and on television. In January 2013, the Arab Network for Human Rights Information reported that, since Morsi had come to power in June 2012, more lawsuits had been filed on the grounds of "insulting the President," than those filed under all of Egypt's previous rulers going back to 1892. In April 2013, under increasing international and domestic pressure, Morsi ordered all the lawsuits dropped. Nevertheless, the Brotherhood had by that stage diligently worked to secure control of the Egyptian media.

In September 2012 Morsi ordered the reorganisation of the Supreme Press Council. The Supreme Press Council controls all matters relating to the press in Egypt and has the power to remove and appoint editors of state owned newspapers. Its reorganisation was significant because in January 2012 it attempted to draft legislation to protect press freedom in Egypt. In July 2012 it resisted an attempt by the Shura Council (the Islamist dominated Upper House in the Egyptian Parliament) to create its own committee for the appointment of the editors and chairmen of newspapers and publications. Even though the new appointments were of varying political and intellectual persuasions ultimate power resided with the Brotherhood. The new head of the Press Council was Ahmed Fahmi, Speaker of the Shura Council and member of the Brothers' FJP. With a senior Brother firmly in charge of the Press Council, it became a further implement of control of the Brotherhood and would no longer challenge the Brotherhood's decisions, as it had been doing thus far.

Another powerful new member of the Supreme Press Council was Fathi Shehab Eldin. Eldin, another FJP member, was appointed Chairman of the Culture, Tourism and Information committee, despite having previously worked on the Brotherhood's labour policy, having little experience in culture or the media. Eldin defended the new appointments to the Supreme Press Council, which included himself, by accusing critics of ignoring the diversity of opinion among the new members who did include a smattering of journalists, as well as leftist and liberal politicians. That defence was frequently used by the Brotherhood, who made non-Brother appointments throughout government, whilst retaining decision-making power for themselves.

Eldin quickly became one of the most powerful men in control of the Egyptian media. In early 2013 it was revealed that he had declared that, "the myth of the Holocaust is an industry that America invented," in one of his articles on the Brotherhood's website. In the same article he claimed this had been done to justify the war against the Axis powers by tarnishing their image, and that the six million Jews were in fact moved to the United States. In other articles he asserts that the attacks of September 11 2001 and the defeat of Al Gore in the election of 2000 were both Jewish conspiracies.

Though these viewpoints and theories may sound bizarre to the Western ear, they are in fact consistent with the Muslim Brotherhood's political ideology, the cornerstones of which are anti-West and anti-Semitic positions and a general belief in conspiracies designed to hold Muslim people back. Many of the specific charges mentioned – referring to, for instance, Jews moving to the United States during the Holocaust, have been levelled before by Islamist ideologues, such as Youssef Al Qaradawi.

In power, the Brotherhood has also continued its stance of sidelining and criticising traditional Muslim, non-political, leaders. For instance, the Freedom and Justice Party leapt to attack the Grand Mufti of Egypt, Ali Gomaa, after his visit to Jerusalem, rejecting him "whatever the reasons." The Grand Mufti is the top Islamic jurist, elected by fellow Islamic scholars after a career of studying Islam and the Quran. Gomaa is a moderate, and as such has found himself out of step with the Muslim Brotherhood on many occasions. He declared *The Protocols of the Elders of Zion* a forgery, called for calm during the Danish Cartoons protests of 2006 and decreed female circumcision to be both forbidden and un-Islamic. He declared that men and women should have equal rights, including the right to become President. All of these positions run counter to Brotherhood orthodoxy.

The new government in Egypt has also been largely ineffective in reversing the downward trend in Egypt's economy. It would turn out to be a fatal mistake for the Brotherhood. One of the economy's strongest sectors, tourism, has struggled to recover since the uprising began in 2011 and the election of the Muslim Brotherhood to government has not helped make the country attractive to Western tourists. Practically, the Brotherhood failed to restore the stability required for the country to attract tourists. Many within the country also feared that once the Brotherhood became entrenched, they would enforce gender-segregated beaches, and prohibit the sale of alcohol. The fears were not unfounded; such ideas were openly talked about by the Brotherhood in their election campaigns.

Since October 2012, the Brotherhood has been trying to legitimise itself by registering as an official organisation. When that happens, it will be obliged to open its books for inspection. The funding of the Brotherhood is a thorny issue for its leadership as it may expose an extensive network of corruption and potentially dubious sources of finance. It is often difficult to run free and open institutions in a region of authoritarian tradition. Within Egyptian political culture, religion and ethics are more concerned with duties than with rights, and obedience to legitimate authority is a religious obligation.

Though the street movement to remove them from power ultimately succeeded, the Brotherhood cannot be removed from the Egyptian political scene, at least not for the next few generations. The Brothers are held together by an ideology and a fanatical devotion to the imposition of an Islamic state in their country. The Brotherhood could, however, be sidelined by the emergence of a credible liberal class. Since it has come into power, however, the Brotherhood has effectively worked to sideline the few liberals that remain in Egyptian politics.

CHAPTER 4

THE LIBERAL MOVEMENT
AND ITS LOST VOICE

The 1923 constitution ushered in a liberal phase in Egyptian political thought, which had been developing during Egypt's 19th century political and cultural renaissance. In the early 20th century, Egypt's political elite did not believe that Islam could serve as a basis for national unity, nor a source of legislation and sought to build a modern state, modelled on those of Europe.

At the time, Egypt was very much in the heat of nationalist fervour, having risen up in the revolution of 1919 which forced the British to grant Egypt its independence in 1922. One of the dominant modes of political thought came to be known as Pharaonism, an ideology which stressed Egypt's pre-Islamic history and asserted that Egypt's ethnic and cultural identity was distinct from that of the Arabs.

Islam was associated with the Arab colonisation of the seventh century, and Egypt was also home to a significant minority of indigenous Christians who, at the time, were heavily represented in the higher political circles. As such, national identity and Egyptian nationalism in general became a secular phenomenon. Adli Yakan Pasha, the leader of the Liberal Constitutional Party, and prime minister three times in the 1920s, declared, "The constitutional regime, is the only form of government worthy of a nation such as ours which is steeped in civilisation."

The 1923 constitution cemented the concept of popular sovereignty in Egyptian political culture. The constitution took many practices and traditions that had arisen in Europe and implanted them in the Egyptian political system. Indeed, it was actually based on the Belgian constitution, selected as a model of constitutional monarchy. The constitution included provisions for freedom and thought and theoretically enshrined the balance of powers between legislature and executive, making the cabinet accountable to parliament. However, ultimate sovereignty lay with the King, who still had the power to dissolve parliament. The constitution also contained a curious provision for two-stage parliamentary elections, whereby the electorate would vote for electors, who would then vote for parliamentary candidates.

Egypt had been either subject to foreign colonial rule or domestic autocracy for many centuries and the constitution moved the country in the direction of popular democracy. It also provided the space in which the new political class could operate and gave political representation to those who had never had it before, even though the constitution has been criticised for producing a succession of weak governments and permitting periods of reduced democratic freedom.

The period from the 1920s was also notable for the significant economic development which occurred during that time. Certain industries, many of which were new to Egypt, began to thrive in the liberalised atmosphere. Banking, textiles, sugar, tobacco, aviation and tourism all helped to accelerate economic development. Industrial labour increased eightfold in the three decades from 1920 to 1952. Such economic development did not benefit everyone however. From the 1930s, the Muslim Brotherhood attracted hundreds of thousands of followers amongst the dispossessed urban masses and rural peasantry.

During the 1930s, many Arab countries, with some exceptions such as Egypt, still based their political culture on rudimentary tribal systems, often centuries old. Unlike her neighbours in the region, Egypt sought to be a Mediterranean, Arab and African nation, all at the same time. It had a new working class, labour unions; it had middle class with European sensibilities, and a neo-aristocracy of industrialists and landowners.

Concepts of personal liberty, equality and European-style social justice were appealing to many Egyptians, in particular the middle class and the families of the neo-aristocrats. At the same time, Europe was undergoing a period of incredible political turbulence which would ultimately lead to the Second World War. The explosion in political thought in the 1930s and 1940s spilled out of Europe and many of these new ideas were finding their way into the newspapers and publications being sold on the streets of Cairo.

The political parties were often eager to involve religious institutions in their political quarrels, which further weakened the liberal movement in Egypt. Egypt's political elites became bitterly divided, and the parliament often ended up in political deadlock. These elites had also become dangerously complacent, convinced that they would remain in their exalted position for the foreseeable future.

The Free Officers coup of 1952 was not a particularly surprising development, given the political inertia of the time. The resultant abolition of the flawed but workable 1923 constitution proved to be a step backwards for the Egyptian liberal movement. Politically, the events of 1952 could be described as the displacement of a liberal elite by a military elite. Despite having the term commonly attached to it, the change of government did not constitute a revolution. Though the coup was popular there was no public uprising or any general involvement of the population at large.

Many of Colonel Nasser's populist reforms to the structure and functions of Egypt's social, economic and political institutions were well received by the public but, in the long term, they caused enormous damage to the prospects for liberal democracy. The decades of military rule that followed led to an institutionalised concentration of power in a single personality, which continued from Nasser, to Sadat, to Mubarak.

Despite the often repeated generalisation that the Nasser era was one of 'mass participation' in politics, in reality the public had no active involvement in the making or implementation of policy. Later Arab dictators such as Saddam Hussein and Colonel Gaddafi propagated the same myth of mass participation, justifying their absolute power in the process.

Within the space of two generations, the autocratic regimes of the Arab world destroyed the liberal opposition class. The spread of alternative political concepts and liberal ideas generally was hampered by a culture of censorship and religious restriction. The situation was not helped by the mass Arab brain-drain of the 1970s and 1980s, when around half of

Arabs with PhDs, mostly scientists and engineers, emigrated to the West, unwilling to tolerate the social and economic pressure of life in an Arab dictatorship.

Though often outlawed or officially discouraged, the Muslim Brotherhood, as well as other Islamist groups, became the only potent political counterbalance in many Arab countries. However, despite the popularity of the Islamists in the Arab world, the entrenched Arab regimes never believed that they could be a credible threat, or that they could eventually form a government.

****

The Napoleonic expedition to Egypt of 1798 preceded the introduction of European philosophy and science which radically altered Egypt's understanding of itself in relation to the wider world. It came after Egypt had endured centuries of stagnation as a backwater province in the Ottoman Empire. Napoleon did not only bring soldiers, he also brought engineers, artists, scholars and scientists. Napoleon founded the famous Institut d'Egypt, dedicated to furthering the understanding of the arts and sciences within Egypt. Though initially staffed by European scholars, Egyptian scholars eventually became members. The expedition also sparked widespread interest in Europe in Egypt's ancient history, giving birth to the discipline of Egyptology. This fascination, though initially a pastime for wealthy Europeans, would also reinvigorate Egyptian fascination with their own past.

During the 19th century, several other major developments took place in Egypt, one of the most important of which was the development of secular education. In later years, Egyptians would start sending their children to be educated abroad, with France the most popular destination. These children would bring back new ideas and political concepts, and allow the country to participate in an ongoing cultural exchange. Qasim Amin, a renowned jurist and philosopher born in 1863, epitomised the drive for social engineering in a traditional Muslim society. During his years of study in France, he was inspired by the political and social freedom which the state guarantees to the French citizen. He became one of the first leading figures in Egypt's earliest reformist movement, the *Nahda*, Awakening.

In 1899, Amin published one of the most controversial books of its time, "The Liberation of the Woman." In it, he forthrightly addressed the status of women in Muslim lands and challenged centuries of tradition relating to divorce, the veil, relations between men and women and a woman's right to participate in society. He concluded that it was a restriction of liberty for Egyptian women that had allowed a country with such a proud history as Egypt to fall behind the European colonial powers. He also believed the inferior position of women was the result of a patriarchal cultural tradition, rather than Islam itself. Indeed, he was critical of Egyptian culture for denying women their Quranic rights.

Predictably, his daring writings triggered tremendous controversy and were rejected outright by intellectuals and common Egyptians alike. Amin was not deterred however, and published a further book on the same topic in 1901. Aside from being an eloquent writer, Amin was an active social reformer. He actively participated in the early call for the foundation of the first secular university in the Arab world, Cairo University, opened in the year of his sudden death in 1908. Amin left a legacy that saw him named, not without some subsequent controversy, as the "father of Egyptian feminism."

The cause of emancipation of Egyptian women was advanced by women as well, one of the most notable of whom was Huda Shaarawi. Shaarawi was born to an aristocratic family in 1879 and later married a prominent nationalist politician. As a young aristocratic woman, she spent her early years in a harem, secluded from the outside world. She had been politically aware from a young age, in part due to the time afforded her to educate herself, having been married to her cousin at the age of 13. When she was a young woman, she founded the first institute for female education in 1910. This was at a time when most Egyptian women were mostly confined to the home and veiled whenever they appeared in public. Female education was very rare indeed, and tended to be restricted to teaching traditional "feminine" disciplines such as midwifery.

One of the turning points for women in Egypt was the 1919 revolution against British rule, when women turned out on the streets to protest. Shaawari organised demonstrations specifically for women; in the most famous, women stayed out in the burning sun for three hours, after being ordered to disperse by the British. In 1923 Shaarawi established the

Feminist Union in Egypt, the first of its kind, and set about challenging the traditional conditions of marriage, divorce and education. She was also famous for rejecting the veil after her husband's death, ceremoniously removing it in public at a railway station in 1923. Though she campaigned for women's rights and suffrage, many of her demands were not met in her lifetime. She resigned from the Wafd Party after it repeatedly ignored her and her feminist cause. After leaving nationalist politics, she dedicated herself to the Feminist Union, leading it until her death in 1947.

Another unlikely feminist champion was a young actress named Fatima al Yusuf. In 1925, still in her mid-twenties, she published a magazine, named *Rose al Yusuf*, borrowing the title from her own nickname. Whilst the magazine initially discussed acting and stage technique, it became an overtly political publication, advocating social reform and women's rights. The magazine carried caricatures of political personalities, and her outspoken opinions once landed her in prison for a short period. Nevertheless she continued to put all her energies into the magazine, which continued to sell.

Imam Mohammed Abdu, a close friend of Qasim Amin during their years in Paris, was another pioneer and social reformer. His progressive ideas came very much from an Islamic perspective, as he was the first Mufti to call for the evolution of interpretation of Islam, a viewpoint known as Islamic modernism. Abdu felt that Islamic jurists and thinkers relied far too much on archaic interpretations of Islam, prescribed by clerics centuries before. In order to keep up with modern times, he argued, it was essential that Islamic study evolve in tandem with current events.

He believed that the principles of the Enlightenment which had contributed so much to the growth and dominance of Western civilisation were principles just as applicable to the Islamic tradition. He travelled widely throughout the Middle East and Europe, meeting with academics, religious leaders and politicians. Through his travels and his studies he came to view freedom of thought as an essential facet of civilisation, a freedom which had been diminished in Egypt. To that end, he expended a great deal of effort towards education and interfaith understanding. He also condemned many early Islamic practices, such as polygamy, as no longer relevant in the modern world.

His progressive views led to accusations of blasphemy by his detractors. Despite his appointment as Grand Mufti, the highest Islamic position in Egypt, he was often attacked by the other Ulema both at Al-Azhar University and in print, accused of, among other things, favouring visits to Europe over pilgrimage to Mecca.

Mohammed Abdu died in 1905. Like Qasim Amin, he was also instrumental in setting up Cairo University. The University was meant from the outset to be a secular institution, where mosques, churches or synagogues would not be permitted.

The spread of secular education allowed social mobility for the first time in Egypt. The liberal class of the late 19th and early 20th century was predominantly made up of the children of aristocratic families who, for all their reforming zeal, were disassociated from the poor of the country. Members of the next generation of liberal elite could now come from much poorer backgrounds though many, of course, still came from wealthy or middle class families. This new liberal class was peopled by university-educated professionals, many of whom would hold considerable cultural power through the media and academia.

Egyptian liberals were among the first in the region to address the issue of hatred of the Jews. Sheikh Ali Yousif, a nationalist, and editor of Cairo's *Al-Mu'ayyad* wrote in 1912, "it is not for us to look askance at them with jealousy, and vengeance because of their enlightenment, and progress…then we will lose a highly industrious element, so needed by us always, especially at this critical moment."

Throughout the 1920s, Egypt produced some of its brightest stars in science, literature and art. By then, many ministers and prime ministers were graduates of leading universities in Britain and France. Many of the men, and women, who made up this new liberal elite were centred around the Wafd Party, formed out of the political fervour of the 1919 revolution against British rule.

The Wafd, which literally means *delegation* was formed by the Egyptian nationalist Saad Zaghloul, with the ultimate goal of ending the British occupation of Egypt. Their name came, in part, from their attempt to be Egypt's delegation to the 1919 Paris Peace Conference, in addition to travelling to London to present their case for independence. They were denied both opportunities. Nevertheless the party, not the first Egyptian nationalist movement, came to dominate Egyptian politics, and came to control Egypt, under successive governments after the departure of the British in 1922. Although the party was staffed at its highest levels by upper class nationalists, it incorporated many working people from both industry and agriculture.

For the most part, Egypt's liberal movement came out of and thrived in Egypt's cosmopolitan cities. In the more affluent urban areas, European dress codes and mannerisms were adopted. There were thriving Greek, Jewish, Armenian, Italian and French communities, particularly on the Mediterranean coast. Cities and towns were bustling with trams and connected by railways. Fashion, the theatre, and cinema flourished. Even brothels were legalised.

Though its numbers were small, the new liberal class was able to use its immense cultural capital to gain influence in politics. As a result, the movement was open to criticism that it was simply serving the interests of the higher social classes in the country, as well as those of foreigners, to the detriment of the majority of Egyptian people.

****

After the first wave of liberal reformers like Amin and Abdu came a second wave, many of whom had directly benefited from the changes their predecessors had brought to Egyptian society.

Taha Hussein was of this second generation of modern Egyptian reformers. The man was an intellectual phenomenon. Born to a large family in a small village in Upper Egypt, the young Taha was blinded as a child by an inept village doctor. Despite his humble origins, Hussein would become a behemoth of Arab literature, and epitomised the whole Arab liberal movement.

Educated in a local Quranic school, or *Kuttab*, Hussein won a place at Al-Azhar University. However, he soon lost interest in Islamic scholarship. When the University of Cairo opened in 1908, he was eager to apply so he could experience secular academic education and was duly accepted. In 1914, he became the first student to be awarded a doctorate from the university. Later, he would further his education in France, attending the University of Montpellier and the Sorbonne. Back in Egypt, he continued an academic career that would mire him in controversy, simply for his pursuit of academic veracity.

One of his most controversial books was *On Pre-Islamic Poetry* in which he asserted that a great deal of what purported to be pre-Islamic verse had been forged by Muslim scholars of later eras for various reasons, one being to give credence to Quranic myths. He went on to infer that the narrative of the Quran was not necessarily undiluted historical fact. For this, he was accused of apostasy.

The enraged clerics of Al-Azhar University sought to prosecute him for insulting Islam. However the prosecutor threw the case out as Taha was merely expressing academic opinion. Despite such legal protection, he was removed from his position at Cairo University and the book was banned.

In another audacious book, The Future of Culture in Egypt, he argued that Egypt belonged to a wider Mediterranean civilisation and, in order to free itself of European control, would have to adopt European institutions and attitudes. Later in his career Hussein was able to implement some of the very policies he had been advocating for decades. In 1950, he was appointed minister of education, bringing in free state education which he believed to be the birthright of all Egyptians.

Perhaps the most famous Egyptian writer of the 20th century was Naguib Mahfouz. Of all the towering figures of the Arab renaissance, perhaps none occupied so large a space in the literary heart of Egypt. However, he was amongst the last great voices of his kind and thinkers like him can no longer flourish in such a restrictive and conservative environment. Born in 1911, he was privileged to see the dramatic changes Egypt underwent in the 20th century and gifted enough to write about them with a wit, clarity and imagination admired across the world.

Besides his literary output, his opinions would often anger the conservative religious forces of the Middle East. His outspoken support for the Camp David Peace Accords with Israel in 1978 led to his books being banned in many Arab countries. Just over a decade later, he condemned the death sentence placed on Salman Rushdie's head by the Ayatollah Khomeini, declaring that though he did not agree with the work either, any such concern was trumped by the prerogative of free expression. He would then label the Iranian theocrat a terrorist and find himself on an Islamic fundamentalist death list.

His defence of *The Satanic Verses* reignited the furore surrounding one of his earlier novels, *Children of Gebelawi*. The story retold the history of the Abrahamic faiths, through the allegory of children living in a Cairene neighbourhood. Accused of blasphemy, Mahfouz received a raft of death threats, including from Omar Abdul Rahman, the terror leader imprisoned in the United States, a man that Mohammed Morsi pledged to work to release.

One of his earliest domestic champions was Sayyid Qutb, during his days as a literary critic in the 1940s. The two came to know each other socially, and remained in touch until Qutb's death. In his semi autobiographical novel, *Mirrors*, one of the characters was a thinly veiled portrait of Qutb. Mahfouz wrote kindly of the man's human generosity and intellect, although also about how uncomfortable he felt looking into his eyes, hinting at a fanatical spirit within.

In 1988, he was awarded the highest accolade for writing in the world, the Nobel Prize for literature. He is the only Arabic-language writer to have won the prize.

In 1994, despite his police protection, an Islamic radical stabbed Mahfouz in the neck outside his home in Cairo. Mahfouz survived the attack, but the consequent nerve damage left his hand crippled, which severely impeded his ability to write. Despite going almost totally blind, he continued writing into his nineties, even if only for a few minutes a day. He died in 2006.

Egypt's liberal class began to steadily decline in 1953 as its cultural influence diminished. It was supplanted by the left-leaning segment of intelligentsia, co-opted by the new military autocracy. The liberal class was further damaged by the Islamist awakening that began in the late 1960s which was somewhat encouraged by Sadat in the 1970s as a means of undermining domestic opposition. Hosni Mubarak attempted to steer a middle course, marked by pseudo-liberal policies, such as regular, if predictable, elections and a tentative freeing up of the media.

During the 1980s, religious attitudes in Egypt retreated to pre Napoleonic times. The Wahhabi interpretation of Islam had spread from the deserts of Saudi Arabia and found its way into Egyptian towns and villages, imported by thousands of Egyptians returning home after working in the Gulf States. The hijab, which so many Egyptian women had cast off decades before, returned in force. Egyptian men had grown tired of the cosmopolitan attitudes that had dominated Egyptian cultural life, and grew suspicious of women.

Modernity had become indelibly associated with the West, and was seen as damaging to Islam.

Mubarak tolerated smaller opposition parties. However, the only party with any real power was his own National Democratic Party. Liberals never had a real chance of organising on a national level. Many Egyptians, by no means supporters of Mubarak, opted to join his party as the only means of engaging in public life.

In 2011, a new generation of young liberals braved the security apparatus to lead the uprising which toppled Mubarak. However, this group soon lost the momentum. More than any other group, they sorely needed funding and time to organise themselves into new political parties.

The Muslim Brotherhood was able to rely on sympathisers abroad and predominantly, though not only, on the wealthy Gulf States for material and political support. Perhaps the natural foreign allies of the liberal class in the post-Mubarak Egypt would be liberal organisations in the West. To a certain extent, there has been such support from overseas. However, the liberal movement in Egypt is hesitant to accept too much support from the West, lest it be accused of pandering to foreign interests. Prominent liberals, such as Mohamed ElBaradei have suffered greatly in Egypt due to their association with Western culture. Furthermore, there is no platform in the West that can provide anything like the financial and political sustenance provided for Egyptian Islamists by the wealthy Gulf Arabs. Billions of dollars have been spent on Islamist groups throughout the world, through building centres, mosques, 'humanitarian' organisations, and social programmes. The ultimate purpose of which is the spread of political and radical Islam.

The liberal movement remains broadly divided, though it has at least sought to consolidate, with many of the disparate parties uniting in the form of the National Salvation Front. Many of the young liberals who drove forward the uprising of 2011 remained conspicuously absent from the political system as it developed in the months and years following the fall of Mubarak. One reason for this was the lack of any central leaders or leadership committees in the 2011 uprising. Many of the movements which organised the street protests were not hierarchical political parties in the traditional sense. The power of street protest proved itself again in 2013 with the ousting of President Morsi. The movement to remove him from power was as much driven by those with vested interests in the old Mubarak regime as the new liberals, an unlikely alliance. However, the tipping point which saw Morsi removed from power was precipitated by the Brotherhood government's poor handling of the economy which was exacerbated by structural problems dating back decades. Though it succeeded in allying with the military in forcing political change, it is unlikely that the liberal movement will be able to organise itself into a cogent political unit, or at least one powerful enough to contest the leadership of the country.

Often the young men and women who took to the streets during the protests against Mubarak and subsequently turned out against the ruling military council, and then against Morsi, boycotted the elections and the political process, arguing that elections could not possibly be fair, unless the entirety of the state apparatus was brought down. The Islamists, however, had no such qualms. Their political pragmatism, honed after decades of repression, was apparent as they systematically positioned themselves to gain the most from the parliamentary and presidential elections, as well as the constitutional drafting process and subsequent referendum. The liberals left a vacuum in the political system, which the Islamists naturally exploited.

In modern Egyptian political culture the Islamists were able to argue that freedom and democracy were not as important to Muslims as respect for Islam and, though they did not outrightly deny the need for human rights and social justice, these needs would be subservient to the Sharia. Egypt's constitution, ratified in 2012, is testament to this attitude. According to the vague terms of this constitution, it would seem that only conservative male Muslims qualified as full citizens. Women, followers of non-Abrahamic faiths or atheists, were not provided with full protection or equal rights under the law. After the military removed President Morsi from power and dissolved parliament, the Islamists were able to claim that they were the true democrats, having had that democratic right to representation voided by the military. It was a bizarre state of affairs, where the country's least democratic elements could claim the most democratic sovereignty. The liberals were left having to catch up again.

Most of the new generation of liberals has not served the regimes of 1952 to 2011. They were marginalised, replaced by civilians and intellectuals who worked against the long term interests of their society to further the short term ambitions of the military regimes in which they served. After the initial excitement of populism faded, their interests tended to revolve around either survival or individual financial gain.

It is incumbent upon the liberal movement to mobilise itself across the country and make itself an appealing choice for the newly enfranchised Egyptian electorate. It will be a difficult task, as it will have to change the very heart of Egypt's political culture in the process. As the events of 2013 proved, liberals are still forced to rely on the military to provide them with a space in modern Egypt. Such an alliance did not look durable.

CHAPTER 5

WHAT WENT WRONG WITH MUBARAK

I n an interview with an Italian newspaper in 2004, Hosni Mubarak declared, "instant freedom and democracy can cause earthquake in a country: for instance, what would happen if a majority of extremists were to win parliament? You can put your money on it." Such sentiments were common amongst the pseudo-secular Arab regimes. The vehement resistance against having democracy thrust upon them from the outside made them impervious to the urgent needs of a struggling and restless public. Admittedly, Mubarak did yield to public pressure, making some concessions to democratic freedom, though his personal domination of the matters of state never receded, and it was that above all else that caused his downfall.

By the time Nasser died the military was involved in governing Egypt in its entirety, from the presidency down to the borough council, a trend that continued until Mubarak came to power. Under Mubarak there was a blend of autocracy and democracy, a laissez-faire liberalism. It seemed there was a continual ad hoc process of reform taking place, quietly observed by the country's conservative and reactionary Islamists. However, the process had no clear direction. In any case, the events of 2011 illustrate just how unsuccessful Mubarak's attempts at modernisation were. They were too little, too late, and they failed to serve their purpose, i.e. to alleviate the dissatisfaction of the people.

Although this tactic seemed to work well, there was no way that the government could hope to co-opt everyone. History has largely forgotten that there were uprisings against the Egyptian regime before 2011. In 1986, thousands of poorly paid conscripts rioted for three days. They belonged to the Central Security Force, a paramilitary force designed to assist the police. The government depended on them for riot control and general suppression of unrest. In response to rumours that they would be conscripted for four years, rather than three, they tore through the parts of Cairo frequented by tourists, burning down hotels and shops. The riots only ended when the army was brought in to suppress them, at a cost of 107 lives.

Another major revolt, often ignored by many Middle East analysts and historians, was the anti-Nasser uprising of March 1968, in which the police fled Helwan city and the army entered and occupied the campus of Cairo University, firing tear gas and shooting at demonstrators. Universities were closed for a month; the army took up strategic positions in Cairo; the state enforced a media blackout, blaming foreign forces and internal subversives for the civil strife.

The protesters also attempted an arson attack against the headquarters of *Al Ahram*, the semi official newspaper, and a symbol of Nasser's propaganda machine. Indeed, the editor in chief, Mohamed Hassanein Heikal, was a long time confidante of Nasser and served as his minister of propaganda.

Perhaps the best known Egyptian uprising of the last few decades, aside from 2011, arose spontaneously in 1977, tearing across the country from Aswan to Alexandria. The "Bread Riots" were a revolt against President Sadat's austere economic measures, imposed upon him by the International Monetary Fund. They included ending subsidies on basic foodstuffs such as bread. Eighty were killed and 800 wounded.

Although Anwar Sadat's peace with Israel and his economic reforms had severely damaged his popularity, the regime never imagined that Sadat might be assassinated. The layers of security surrounding him, and the considerable intelligence resources deployed domestically to uncover conspiracies against the state attest to that. Nevertheless, Sadat was assassinated on October 6, 1981, as he saluted passing soldiers in a military parade. The assassination was carried out by some of the very soldiers to whom he stood to attention, the army having been infiltrated by Egyptian Islamic Jihad. State-controlled media enforced a total blackout after the assassination to protect the regime at all costs, as it dutifully did 30 years later during the initial phase of Egypt's Arab Spring. The internet and modern mobile communication have made such a response much harder in the 21st century, though that did not stop the regime cutting the nation's Internet service as the protests heated up in 2011.

Hosni Mubarak assumed the presidency after Sadat's death. He was a trusted Vice President, appointed in a nod to the armed forces, an important aspect of Egypt's autocracy. He was never destined for the presidency. His rise was accidental. After his contribution to the war of 1973, he hoped he would be made ambassador to London. Sadat had surprised everyone, including Mubarak himself, by offering him the vice presidency.

Mubarak, a career military man, was no demagogue. He did not bother with the grand populist schemes and projects that so occupied his predecessors. Under Nasser, Egypt had undergone a profound ideological revolution. Egypt had become the political centre of the Middle East and Nasser's doctrine of Arab nationalism and non-alignment profoundly influenced regional politics. In some respects Sadat's presidency was equally monumental. Sadat's ideological shift towards the United States and his peace with Israel represented one of the most significant political realignments of the Arab world. Under Mubarak on the other hand, there was no profound change or ideological guiding principle. In effect, Mubarak's regime existed solely to perpetuate itself, its main concern being its own survival. Mubarak essentially continued Sadat's policies and saw Egypt lose its position at the political and economic heart of the Middle East. Like Sadat before him, Mubarak was not convinced that 'Arab nationalism' was a credible political force. This rejection undermined his prestige among the nationalist left, who still had influence over the politics and media of the Arab world in the 1980s and 1990s. Some of the old Arab nationalists, who flourished under Nasser, were co-opted by Saddam Hussein and Gaddafi, whilst satellite TV networks like Al Jazeera found time to give platforms to old Nasserists.

Mubarak's moderate reforms attracted toothless functionaries and older leftists whose interests lay in the privileges and special positions afforded by their association with the regime. Vitally, he maintained the regional status quo, pleasing the United States by overseeing regional military and economic co-operation whilst upholding peace with Israel.

He was also keenly aware that the presidency had only come to him after the murder of his patron. He knew that when leading a state like Egypt complacency was a death sentence. As such, the regime's security infrastructure was of paramount importance, while human rights were never a priority. The Mubarak regime used its monopoly of the media to employ a small segment of intelligentsia to defend the status quo. Such a technique was common during the years of Sadat and Nasser, and many of those pseudo-intellectuals old enough defended Mubarak with the same vigour as they had Nasser all those years before. These people were basically ideological mercenaries, specialised in the manipulation and distortion of public opinion, rather than military prowess. They acted to articulate and justify the major ideological and organisational attitudes of those in power.

The luxuries of travel abroad and salaries commensurate to those of their Western counterparts were not readily available to the Egyptian middle classes. Joining the regime was a straightforward method of improving one's career trajectory. The middle classes filled influential positions in the government and its institutions, as well as those in the state-controlled media.

The regime attempted to pre-empt any political activity both inside and outside Egypt, considering any political enterprise as a threat. Embassies in certain key capitals had detachments of secret police posing as diplomats. In expanding their domestic operation abroad, the government could gather intelligence on and undermine any Egyptian social or political organisation which chose to organise on foreign territory. Egypt was not alone in employing this tactic; almost all Arab regimes followed the same method of subverting dissident activity abroad.

The tipping point for Mubarak was when he relinquished the state monopoly on the media. He did so for many reasons, some of which were beyond his control. International satellite television and the internet allowed information to flow into Egyptian households. The old tools of information management that had protected his predecessors were rapidly becoming obsolete with the onslaught of portable, easy to use and readily available digital media.

The new 'independent' media fomented agitation as much as confusion. The satellite broadcasters were not necessarily guided by journalistic integrity, rather they served the interests of their various paymasters, whether Iran, the Gulf, Gaddafi or Saddam Hussein. Many journalists were bought on a free Arab media market, ready to defend or attack in print or on television, switching sides with ease. Some became multi-millionaires. Saddam Hussein was famous for paying cash to pliant journalists to promote himself in the region.

Within Egypt, the privileges bestowed upon those who worked as intermediaries and apologists for the regime created a network of mutual self interest. As the regime became dependent on its intellectual supporters, they, in turn, became dependent on the regime.

Traditional Egyptian intellectuals, who had flourished in the early to mid-20th century, were denied their predestined central position in Egyptian society. At the same time, society at large began to reject 'intellectualism.' That attitude became the norm throughout the Arab world; cerebral pursuits were regarded as alien Western concepts. Intellectuals themselves were considered pro-imperialist, pro-West or pro-Zionist. That point of view persists amongst the Muslim Brotherhood, the men at the helm of the first post-Mubarak Egyptian government.

By the end of his rule, Mubarak had let many Islamists out of prison and eased media censorship. Islamist political prisoners numbered in the hundreds. Nasser had 20,000 of them in concentration camps at the time of his death. Even the Supreme Guide of the Muslim Brotherhood praised Mubarak as 'the father for all the Egyptians,' not without some controversy within the ranks of political Islam.

The regime encouraged rivalry between the army and police by separately offering them patronage and subdividing them into competing services. Those who served in the elite presidential guard received the greatest perks. It was these perks that made senior military service worthwhile. A general's annual salary was typically low by Western standards. However, when the perks of housing, subsidised travel, subsidised schooling and holidays were included, the job became attractive.

Mubarak did not brutalise his people, nor instigate a personality cult, to the same extent as some of his fellow Arab dictators. However, he was the last figurehead of a regime that had perpetuated itself over six decades, and as a consequence he bore the weight of the anger of desperate masses. Just as his predecessor was assassinated by radical Islamists, Mubarak's life was put in danger repeatedly by radical Islamists who sought to kill him. In total, he suffered six assassination attempts, the closest of which was in 1995 in Addis Ababa, Ethiopia, when he miraculously survived an ambush on his motorcade by a team of gunmen lying in wait.

Mubarak's democratic concessions were also badly thought out. Initially he followed the lead of many Middle Eastern dictators by having simple yes/no referenda on his presidency, holding them in 1987, 1993 and 1999. Each of these dubious ballots produced overwhelming majorities in favour of his presidency. In 2003, the United States fought a major war in Iraq on the pretext of bringing democracy to the region, while Egypt, one of their strongest allies in the Middle East, had virtually no democratic credentials at all. The United States pressurised Mubarak to rectify this imbalance.

In February 2002, President Bush produced his "Greater Middle East Initiative" calling for democratic and economic reform in the Middle East. It was widely attacked by the press within the Arab world, as an example of American imperialism that lacked understanding of the cultural nuances of the Arab states. That reaction was encouraged by the political leadership of the Arab states as the initiative posed a threat to the regimes in the region. The initiative called for the emergence of a civil society in the Arab world and included the caveat that reform should come from within, which was also ignored.

On 2 June 2005, the Arabic media reported that President Bush had spoken on the telephone to President Mubarak for ten minutes. Bush had demanded that there must be free elections in Egypt, with multiple candidates. Bush had also criticised the violence with which pro-democracy protesters had been met during the previous week's constitutional referendum.

The multi-candidate presidential election of 2005 was one of the first major democratic initiatives, followed that year by multi-party parliamentary elections. The presidential elections were a landmark in the Arab world as they actually resembled modern democratic elections, rather then simply being a referendum on the presidency which had been the case since the 1950s. In any case, the electoral institutions, state security apparatus and the media remained under the firm control of the

President. After the election, Mubarak's nearest competitor, Ayman Noor, who won 7% of the vote, was imprisoned. The parliamentary elections were still heavily weighted in favour of the ruling National Democratic Party, though the Muslim Brotherhood, running as independents, won nearly a fifth of the seats, becoming the largest opposition bloc. In the 2010 election the government sought to eradicate the Muslim Brotherhood from parliament and the NDP 'won' 94% of the seats. It was reminiscent of Nasser's 99.95% election 'win' in 1956.

Such implausible results proved that democracy in Egypt was a charade. According to the Democracy Index 2010, Egypt was ranked 138 internationally and 12th among Arab states on the list of democratic regimes. Egypt had poor showings in other international rankings as well. According to Transparency International's 2010 corruption index, Egypt was ranked 98 in the international corruption table. Egypt came below Qatar (19), Oman (41), Bahrain (48), Jordan and Saudi Arabia (50), Kuwait (54), Tunisia (59) and Morocco (85).

Mubarak's predecessors died in office and were given send-offs befitting the national heroes they never were. When Mubarak stepped down, he was put on trial, wheeled in and out of court on a hospital bed. During the uprising itself, some protesters even held aloft pictures of Nasser, seeing him as a national saviour rather than the instigator of the very regime they were trying to bring down. In the Cairo Metro, opened during the Mubarak era, the station that bore his name was renamed, and all traces of the word 'Mubarak' were erased from the network, but the Nasser and Sadat stations were left untouched.

In the last decade of his rule, he succumbed to political and economic strategies devised by the businessmen who gravitated towards his son Gamal, widely thought of as the next President of Egypt. Initially, Mubarak was wary of his son's scheme to assume leadership of the country. Mubarak, his son and the wealthy cliques surrounding them were the subject of constant gossip and mockery among Egyptians. However, Bashar Assad's smooth succession following the death of his father in the summer of 2000, encouraged Arab dictators to plan on keeping power in the family.

Suzanne Mubarak, though an educated and cultured woman of some political weight, allowed herself to be tempted by cronyism and nepotism. She became obsessed with the prospect of Gamal taking over the reigns of power from his father and was instrumental in appointing key ministers and ambassadors. Suzanne would become a hate figure, epitomising the corruption and entitlement of the ruling elite. Rumours abounded that she was not a Muslim and social conservatives resented the fact that a woman had such a prominent place in political life.

Under Nasser, Egypt's economy was totally dominated by the state. Sadat, faced with crippling debts and declining revenues, could not maintain the policy so he opened Egypt up to foreign capital and the forces of the global free market. Mubarak could not handle a state-controlled economy, nor was he able to competently manage a free market economy. Instead, he presided over a muddled middle ground of economic management which, in practice, amounted to a kleptocracy. Towards the end many of the beneficiaries of this corruption were associates of his younger son Gamal.

The economy Mubarak inherited suffered badly due to endemic distortions in the system which allowed insiders to manipulate the system for personal gain. The state banks lent billions on the basis of political connections rather than credit rating or feasibility of return. Macro-economic stabilisation produced some success, as the state's hard currency reserves rose from virtually nothing to about $30 billion, at the expense of public services.

National economic projects were selected on the basis of which could yield the greatest personal wealth for ministers or officials, rather than for the good of the economy. As the primary responsibilities of government were neglected, corruption led to economic stagnation which manifested itself as poverty, poor healthcare, food shortages and a famously dangerous transport network.

Consequently, much of the state's liquid assets were appropriated by private individuals and a substantial portion of Egypt's wealth found its way abroad. Egypt's economy was never strong; the future was uncertain and individuals who stood to gain from access to the regime were guided by insecurity and greed. As is often the case with corrupt governments, there was a rush to accumulate as much wealth as possible with the result that respected families began to resemble mafiosi.

The traditional middle classes were in decline and educated graduates struggled to provide for their families. Many would take on two jobs to make ends meet. The arrivistes who replaced the traditional middle classes during the Mubarak years tended to be much more sympathetic towards Islamism. They often came back from working in the Gulf with money to spend on property and mosque-building. They imposed their recently acquired social conservatism on their families, friends and employees.

Any improvements in Egypt's economy did not manifest themselves in the alleviation of the destitution of the masses. In spite of heavy state subsidies on basic goods and fuel, almost 22% of the population lived below the World Bank defined poverty line of less than $2 a day. In rural areas the figure was just under 44%, rising every year since 2000.

In contrast, the new cash-rich class began to adopt the habits of the rich in the Gulf States; they imported Filipino maids in uniforms and employed Russian dancers at their extravagant weddings. Prostitution also increased, with foreign sex workers being the preferred choice of the wealthy.

The professional and working classes, unable to find work at home often chose to work in the Gulf, if only to make ends meet and have a chance of saving some money. In the process, Egypt became the largest exporter of labour in the Middle East, with a million Egyptians living and working in the Gulf States. Although they were earning relatively good money many of these workers had to put up with the formal indignity of labouring in the Gulf. They would often have their passports taken from them at the airport, have to pay a commission for a native 'guarantor' who would reap a high percentage of their salary, and run the risk of expulsion on the slightest pretext, or if there was political disagreement between their respective governments. During the 2011 uprising, many expatriate Egyptians staged solidarity demonstrations in front of their embassies in Western capitals. In Saudi Arabia and Dubai brief protests were swiftly dispersed by the police. In Kuwait, Egyptians were warned that any protesting would result in immediate deportation.

Many Egyptian workers also headed to neighbouring Libya, North Africa's major oil exporter. There, Egyptians were repeatedly expelled by Colonel Gaddafi, after he accused Egypt of doing too much to promote relations between Israel and the Arab states, or not enough to revoke international sanctions levied against Libya.

For much of Mubarak's time in power, inflation was in double figures, even above 30% for periods in the 1980s. Though inflation was brought under control in the late 1990s and early 2000s, it began to rise again in 2004, wildly fluctuating and soaring to over 20% in 2008. The turbulent inflation made living conditions uncertain for the vast majority of the public and was compounded by wholesale corruption amongst the wealthy. In 2005, the Minister of Finance, Dr Youssef Boutros Ghali, nephew of the former Secretary General of the UN (and since 2011, a fugitive in London) complained that only 2,000 companies in Egypt paid some form of tax while only 300 companies paid their taxes in full.

The roots of corruption in Egyptian society predate Mubarak. Indeed, corruption had been apparent in Egyptian society since Ottoman times. However, the modern culture of corruption was first manifest in the years following Sadat's policy of Infetah or Opening. In order to stimulate private investment, a ten-year tax and customs relief on investments was established and a blind eye turned to unscrupulous business practices. Such a policy invited abuse as companies would make full use of the concessions by borrowing hundreds of millions of dollars for paper projects that vanished after a decade.

The corrupt entrepreneur was able to reap incredible wealth with little effort by bribing all those he did business with, or were supposed to be regulating said business. Mubarak was said to have told such people in a friendly reception that he "knew how they made their money and how corrupt they were, so they better stop moaning."

The question of Mubarak's personal wealth and presumed embezzlement has never been satisfactorily answered. His opponents put the figure at tens of billions of dollars, mostly quietly stashed in foreign bank accounts, without producing any proof or likely locations as to its whereabouts. The Muslim Brotherhood promised during the presidential election of 2012 that if it won the election it would bring $200 billion of Mubarak's money back into the country. No money has so far been forthcoming.

Egyptian banks are still reticent about giving details of their transactions with those in power. The media blames Western governments for the disappearance of funds, though they do not question the complicity of Egyptian and Arab businesses and institutions that aided and abetted decades of corruption.

Despite Mubarak's supposed personal wealth, and the perception that a select few businessmen had grown very rich, free enterprise was hampered by a bureaucracy that was deliberately tortuous to navigate. Any kind of economic activity required a huge outlay of bribes from the start. For example, to open a petrol station permission would have to be sought from the army, the ministry of tourism, the ministry for oil, the ministry of agriculture, the ministry of interior and the local municipality. Each level of bureaucracy was another obstacle and the relevant civil servants knew they could be as intransigent as they liked and demand bribes. The black market thrived and shady business arrangements were so common that it was not unusual to purchase a flat in Cairo worth a million pounds by simply handing over a suitcase of banknotes.

Within Egypt the state took little responsibility for education, transport, health and other public services. According to the Human Development Index, Egypt ranks 111th out of 177 countries, still some way from the top 100. Some 23% of Egyptians use the poorly funded Egyptian state health providers, and 57% opt to go private, in spite of the cost. Mubarak's government had a particularly poor record on public health. For example, due to a badly managed vaccination campaign against the parasite Bilharzia from the 1950s to 1980s, Hepatitis C infection rates in Egypt are the highest in the world. Fifteen to twenty per cent of the population is infected.

In spite of the provision of universal state education, the standard is generally recognised to be fairly low. Literacy in Egypt is only at 73% (63.5% for women and girls). Thirty per cent of Egyptians go to university, but only around half of them actually graduate; teaching standards are notoriously bad. With poor standards of state education, 58% of Egyptian families invest in private tutoring. With Egyptian families unable to depend on the state to provide an adequate education for their children, society has become more stratified as the rich have been able to hire the more expensive tutors to give their child the advantage over their peers.

There were some positive points. Infant mortality fell from 120 per 1000 in 1980 to 24 per 1000 in 2011. However, such benefits were not evenly distributed across the country, with the southern governorates remaining consistently poorer than their northern counterparts, and rural areas still incredibly poor by comparison with the cities.

The state monopoly of print and broadcast media seldom gave platforms to constructive voices in matters of development, politics and economics. Commentators preferred to wax lyrical about regional problems rather than about the actual interests of the population. The regime was reluctant to open up the media but, in the end, Mubarak did so. Likewise, the elections of 2005 were Mubarak's doing. Though by no means free and democratic by Western standards, other political parties were at least permitted to take part and did make some modest electoral gains.

While the regime did respond to public and international pressure, among the higher echelons of power there was a widespread reluctance to engage with any new talent or to instigate meaningful reform. Consequently, the Egyptian street, like so much of the Arab world, simmered with an anger that failed to interest the men at the top.

Mubarak and the United States

In the aftermath of the September 11, 2001 attacks the media and the US administration repeatedly discussed the fraught relationship between the United States and the Muslim world. The most potent question was how some Arabs had become so lethally radicalised as to commit such an act in a faraway place. In truth, the West had been under threat of Islamic terror for a decade previously and there had been attacks against Western interests in the region in the 1980s.

One of Mubarak's most significant acts during the Cold War was to allow thousands of Islamists (many of whom were in prison) to leave Egypt for Afghanistan, which, with the benefit of hindsight, now seems unwise. However, at the time, the United States saw these Islamist radicals as useful in the fight against communism.

Mubarak also eagerly supported the United States throughout the crisis of the Iraqi occupation of Kuwait. Egyptian participation in the coalition to evict Saddam Hussein from Kuwait was a crucial element of the American plan to raise Arab opposition to Iraq. Mubarak's participation reaped handsome rewards for Egypt; the net result was $20 billion in international debt relief, as well as considerable financial reimbursement.

Over the years, the United States contributed more than $60 billion to Egypt in the form of military aid and direct financial support. As its strongest ally in the Middle East, there was frequent co-operation in matters of intelligence (unthinkable with most other Middle Eastern countries) and American training of Egyptian military officers. Domestically, the United States had to answer why so much money went to such an undemocratic country. US policy-makers were actively trying to promote democratic reform inside many other Arab states by both incentive and sanction.

One of the solutions the United States hit upon was the Direct Public Diplomacy programme, where funding would be allocated directly to NGOs and Egyptian charities, rather than having to pass through the government. It was also intended that this money should help develop civil society in Egypt, and in the process lead to democratic transformation. The regime hated the programme, seeing it as interference, but they were forced to accept it because it was a precondition for the rest of the attractive aid package that went straight to them.

Grooming Gamal

Probably the biggest single factor leading to the demise of Mubarak was his son and heir apparent, Gamal. As Hosni Mubarak entered his eighties, it was clear that he would not dominate government the way he once had. As the father retreated from public life, the son began to take a more active role and, in doing so, surrounded himself with some of the most detested individuals in Egypt.

Gamal appeared unimaginative and arrogant, and had an unfortunate ability to make enemies easily. He was rumoured to have appointed the entire cabinet, as well as key ambassadors. His disagreeable attitude was even clear to his own father who, at the height of the 2011 uprising, was reported to have snapped at his son, "you brought down my honourable military career, you have ruined my name!"

Mubarak never actually named his son as successor. Gamal's most vocal advocate for presidency was probably his mother, Suzanne. Mubarak evidently did not trust anybody to be named his successor; though tacitly he supported his son's claim, it was never publicly admitted. This allowed other contenders to stake a claim for the presidency. Aside from Gamal, the two most plausible candidates to succeed Mubarak were Amr Moussa, Secretary General of the Arab League, and Omar Suleiman, the Head of the Intelligence Service. In any case, the question of succession turned out to be irrelevant.

Mubarak stepped down on 11 February 2011 after 18 days of protests across Egypt. Even though he voluntarily stepped down, on 24 May 2011, he was ordered to stand trial for the premeditated murder of protesters. The trial of Hosni Mubarak was a farce from the beginning, a political drama replete with literally dozens of lawyers jostling for prestige in court. The Islamists predictably called for his hanging in Tahrir Square, seeking the redemptive power of retributive violence to cleanse the political system.

However, the largest flaw in the trials of Mubarak and his ministers was their selective nature. The indictments were largely restricted to those who had been in power in the last decade, regardless of their actual role. For example, Youssef Boutros Ghali, the finance minister, was sentenced to 30 years in prison in absentia for redistributing impounded cars among civil servants, and using ministry printers for his election campaign. His trial lasted six minutes. There had been many more characters intimately involved with the rule of the country since 1952, many of whom committed human rights atrocities, who evaded public scrutiny.

In some ways, Hosni Mubarak is a tragic figure. Publically, he rarely seemed happy, his smile often tinged with sadness. He never smiled at all after the death of his 12 year old grandson in 2009. He was rumoured to be especially close to his grandson, the child of his elder, favoured son Alaa. His health deteriorated significantly in the late 2000s. He was repeatedly incapacitated by stomach cancer, which he hid from the public. He began to lose weight and his skin looked waxed and ashen, as the toxic effects of the cancer and the inexorable effects of age began to show. He routinely used make up for interviews and dyed his hair in a vain attempt to present the illusion of youth. Mubarak sometimes appeared to be suffering from the early stages of dementia.

Mubarak's survival as President indicated a pragmatism unseen in his successors. Unlike Nasser or Sadat, he never was politically active in his youth. He spent most of his career in the air force and did not even go into politics until the age of 46.

He studiously avoided anti-Semitic rhetoric. However, he was also stubborn and proud, and unlike Ben Ali of Tunisia, he flatly refused to leave Egypt when he was offered the opportunity by the generals, announcing, "I will die in Egypt, I am not leaving my country."

CHAPTER 6

SCAF AND THE TURBULENT TRANSITION

E gypt was essentially a military dictatorship after 1952. All of her leaders had risen out of the military and most Egyptian men served in the conscript army. Serving in the military confers considerable benefits in Egyptian society. Large areas of central Cairo are given over to military bases and social clubs.

However, since 1952, those generals who demonstrated any curious political inclinations were pensioned off or offered a senior civilian position. By the year of Nasser's death, the army had ceased to be a centre of political decision-making, though it did retain its social and economic privileges. The grand Soviet-style military parades through Cairo were brought to an end. Around the same time, defeat in the 1967 war was a crushing blow to the military's prestige, though it did recover somewhat with early gains in the 1973 war.

The Mubarak presidency hampered the autocratic rule of the military. He was an outsider, an Air Force general, rather than an army man. Mubarak, like Sadat and Nasser before him, was well aware that since he had come to power through the military, a younger and more dynamic competitor could also rise through the ranks, threatening his position. He preferred a hybrid quasi-democracy mixed with autocracy that increased police power at the expense of the army. He presented himself as a statesman, wearing a well-cut suit and did not bother with the elaborate military uniforms Sadat donned for state occasions.

There were some officers who were indeed trusted by the regime, and whose opinions would be considered in matters of policy. However, their influence lay in ties of family or friendship. Cronyism and nepotism could often outweigh ability or experience when an officer was considered for promotion. As a result, Egypt's military became something of an inert organisation, inflexible and resistant to change.

The Supreme Council of the Armed Forces, almost always abbreviated within Egypt to SCAF, commanded the country's military, which included each branch of the armed forces, and its general intelligence service. It assumed power on 11 February 2011. Though often accused of being a military junta, it was not one in the traditional sense, nor did it make major political decisions domestically or internationally. The management of the country was largely left untouched. Aside from Mubarak's cabinet, key ambassadors and bureaucrats remained in place, and in any case, the SCAF lacked the resolve to impose its authority. Throughout the transition, the SCAF remained opaque, presenting the outward impression that it sought to maintain the status quo, regardless of any reformist intentions it may have had.

In power, the Generals engaged with the Islamists, but less so with high profile liberals such as Dr Mohamed ElBaradei. The army believed that it understood the Islamists but its judgment was guided by old intelligence reports rather than by a dynamic assessment of the country's needs. As such, the military misjudged Islamist intent. With no clear road map for transition, it became very difficult to maintain objectivity, and act as a neutral arbiter between Egypt's political factions. As the transition wore on, the military leadership played political games of bewildering complexity.

The SCAF are basically professional soldiers, highly trained and well-disciplined. In the wake of Mubarak's departure, they kept the army, and the country, in one piece. When most of the police disappeared from the streets, they took on the responsibility of maintaining law and order. Their ability to do so commanded respect among the public. They were not political in any wider sense. There was a mutual distrust between them and other political groups. Many believed that the SCAF were spying on them. There was also a generational imbalance, since the SCAF were much older than many of the liberals and protesters. Field Marshal Tantawi and his deputy, General Sami Anan, were particularly reluctant to be open with the public about their governance of the country.

It was the Generals who succeeded in easing Mubarak out of the presidency. However, they did not grasp the complexities of the transitional process. Like Mubarak before them, the SCAF ignored or underestimated the underlying causes behind the uprising. They were merely aware of the structural aspects of the crisis, rather than broader problems, such as the loss of the moral authority of the state and its anachronistic institutions.

As rumours and counter-rumours proliferated, the public believed the SCAF were only interested in limited reform, fearing their ultimate aim was to control Egypt's politics. The Brotherhood monitored every announcement, proclamation and development. The Brotherhood's strength lay in their lack of action, as they quietly bided their time, waiting for providential opportunities. However, when an opportunity arose, they moved to take full advantage. For instance, they remained quiet about their electoral intentions, however when the time came for elections, they used their local networks to campaign extensively, seeing them sweep into power. Meanwhile, the old politicians, once quiescent to the old regime, infiltrated the broad coalition of secular forces. These secular forces, however, were still divided, and many did not trust each other. Often, the younger protesters, who had been out on the street campaigning for Mubarak's departure, preferred to boycott the political process, depriving the secular coalition of younger and more dynamic members.

Just as the Wafd Party had done before 1952, the liberals simply waited for power to fall into their laps, rather than working towards it by mobilising the masses in their favour.

The Muslim Brotherhood gained the initiative by isolating the various factions that made up Egypt's new civil society, and helped turn the SCAF against the liberals. The Brotherhood repeatedly claimed to support the SCAF during the transition, while at the same time led protests demanding retributive action against members of the former regime, which they knew the liberals would support and continue, even after the Islamists had retreated from the streets. The SCAF responded to the perceived threat by arresting some leading activists and confiscating the NGO assets which in turn created a rift with the US, as many of those organisations received US funding. If the SCAF believed that such a move would help its popularity by appealing to some kind of street xenophobia, then it was a miscalculation. It simply further damaged their reputation.

The SCAF were thus isolated, attacked by all the liberal factions. Their only international benefactor, the United States, was losing patience. The issue of foreign funding of Egyptian political groups led to a curious double standard on the part of the SCAF. They consistently ignored the serious implication of funding from Gulf oil states to Egypt's Islamist groups, but were willing to humiliate the NGOs as a front for US interests, despite the fact that their foreign funding was far more meagre.

This three-way conflict, between the SCAF, the United States and liberal Egyptian civil society, ultimately benefited the Muslim Brotherhood. The Brothers also received huge funds and in tandem with their nationwide network of followers, were able to dramatically raise their profile on the Egyptian street. The more liberally inclined NGOs and groups, with some guidance, could have asserted themselves on the street far more effectively than they actually did.

Meanwhile, the suspicion of a deal between Muslim Brothers and SCAF gained some traction in the months before President Morsi's victory in the election. The 'devil you know' attitude was taking root. The state had large files about virtually every prominent or even semi-prominent Islamist. After all, many of them had served prison sentences, including Morsi himself. This wealth of intelligence misled the Generals into thinking they knew who they were dealing with. There were numerous rumours of secret arrangements between Brotherhood and military. These rumours could easily have been started by the Brotherhood themselves, since it could easily benefit them to alienate the liberals further from the SCAF.

Both the secular liberals and the SCAF also made a fatal tactical blunder; wrongly assuming time to be on their side. Any government would have had difficulty managing the transition after Mubarak stepped down. Even so, the SCAF made a number of poor decisions, which damaged their reputation with the public. Nor did they make the best use of events and situations which turned out in their favour, often taking them for granted. They also wasted month after month in futile discussions.

They were over-cautious. The unity of the SCAF itself began to break down as the generals found it harder and harder to trust one another. Reluctant to voice their opinions to one another, consensus became ever more difficult to reach. The Generals were also reactive, rather than active. They were often influenced by a few hundred or thousand activists in Tahrir Square, forcing them to make knee-jerk policy decisions. At the same time, scenes of soldiers suppressing demonstrations, sometimes with violence, began to play out in the local and international media, further damaging the SCAF's reputation and hastening calls for their departure.

Their handling of the Mubarak trial was less than graceful. They wheeled the bedridden former President, their commander only a few weeks previously, out into a cage within the courtroom. It was another miscalculation; they had thought that humiliating the President would placate the protesting masses. The author of this book spoke to the doctor responsible for Mubarak's health during his incarceration. He reiterated that in his professional opinion Mubarak was in poor physical and mental health, and unfit to stand trial. However, the physician did not dare report to that effect, fearing the furious public backlash.

However, the trial of Mubarak was a mere diversion. The public was looking for genuine socio-political change, rather than courtroom drama.

The Revolution is Not Over Yet

The SCAF is made up of only 19 generals. When power was thrust upon them, they actually had little idea of what to do with it, aside from the inevitable moves for self preservation, such as attempting to make their budget immune from government oversight. They almost became confined to Cairo itself and did not interact directly with the public. These men were not politicians and, throughout their careers in military service, public interaction had never been required of them. Inevitably, they failed to manage increasingly volatile public opinion.

Throughout the transition, the SCAF acted in a manner that recalled how Lord Lloyd, a British High Commissioner in Egypt during the 1920s, described Britain's role in Egypt at the beginning of the last century, "power without authority; responsibility without control." Freedom House, the American pro-democracy NGO, noted little improvement in political freedom in Egypt after Mubarak. The harassment of NGOs, restrictions on the media and poor treatment of women protesters such as the notorious 'virginity tests,' discredited the SCAF as arbiters of democratic transition. With such chaos and uncertainty, the uprising in Egypt was dubbed "half a revolution," and there were numerous slogans at protests proclaiming, "The revolution is not over yet!"

The SCAF lacked buoyancy and their judgment was questionable. They were often forced to back down after making controversial decisions, which further undermined their standing in the eyes of the public and the world at large. Their poor communication skills were also a handicap. Their poor English and absence of diplomatic experience led to their weak understanding of the subtleties of American and European policy with regard to the Middle East. Often reading documents and communiqués in translation, there was ample room for clumsy misinterpretation. Many of the generals rarely travelled abroad or even had experience in dealing with Western policymakers. At the same time, the West was continually frustrated by their lack of urgency and the opacity of their planning.

There is something in the Arab psyche that applies here and is apparent in generals and grocers alike: an innate desire "to make believe what you are not," which gives way to self-delusion and, ultimately, failure. Modesty has no place and is considered a weakness in much of the Arab world. Even those living in abject poverty are inclined to believe that the American government has in some way conspired to bring about their situation. Likewise, one or two generals deluded themselves into believing that their position was approved by the US administration. Mere small talk between a SCAF general and the US ambassador would then be subject to public gossip for weeks.

The responsibility of government was a huge workload for the SCAF. Their actual job description was to run the military, not a country. On top of that, it was a country which seemed on the verge of tearing itself apart. All the generals had bedrooms attached to their offices, which they were forced to use as the strain of work occupied all of their time. As they spent long hours away from their families, they began to irritate each other and their family lives suffered. When Ramadan arrived the transition slowed down even further. The generals grew lazy and helped to paralyse each other. Field Marshal Tantawi was terrified that if he left Cairo he would not be allowed back. Every general suspected the others of secret dealings, especially with the US or Muslim Brotherhood. Some, like General Anan, rather enjoyed his colleagues' suspicion that he might be America's man in Egypt.

The SCAF voted on major decisions through buttons labelled yes or no. In this manner, decision-making was reduced to binary outcomes, rather than multiple possible courses of action. Thus, they became something of a political nonentity, deciding without interacting with the public or without proper political discussion among themselves.

Had they realised the providence of their position, they could have followed the example of Turkey, the only minimally functioning democracy in the Arab Middle East. However, they were slow, careless of the fact that time was running against them. The SCAF also missed the opportunity to put in place a temporary political administration drawn from within Egypt and its expatriate community in order to get the state running efficiently and act as a nucleus of a new Egypt.

Former Prime Minister, Abdel Aziz Hejazi, who was co-opted as a member of the SCAF consultative committee, was unclear about the direction of the SCAF and what was expected from him in his advisory capacity. The SCAF did not seem to care about politics or economics. When the author of this book raised the issue of Egypt's dismal living standards with two SCAF generals, they smiled and made light of it.

Conduct of foreign policy was shambolic, as the case of the Field Marshall refusing to take a call from President Obama illustrates. The same attitude was apparent in their unproductive discussions with visiting politicians and the perception, on the part of those who dealt with them, that they were extremely arrogant. They also appeared to be conducting foreign policy individually; they would not inform one another when they visited foreign countries. However, they were all aware of the single most important aspect of foreign policy as far as the West was concerned, their relationship with Israel. In a visit to the British House of Lords organised by the author together with Lord Clive Soley, the Head of General Intelligence, General Mowafi, asserted that the Peace Treaty with Israel would be a red line for any forthcoming government.

A general's pay is a modest US$40-60,000. Very few of the generals, in spite of the paraphernalia that came with their job, could afford to visit foreign countries. Unlike their political counterparts, they had not studied in the West. They were unfamiliar with Western culture. They did not trust their interpreters, which made political interaction difficult, even unproductive.

The Military's Business Empire

For almost 60 years, the military's business empire has been protected by the state and completely hidden from public scrutiny. The political scientist Amr Hamzawy, formerly of the Carnegie Middle East Center, believes things have changed post-Mubarak and that the parliament elected in 2011 was a big part of that change. He estimates that the military may control up to $60 billion, or 30 percent of Egypt's total $180 billion economy. He elaborated in GlobalPost, speculating that the military "are keen on securing their economic assets" by trying to preserve the remnants of the old regime that will allow them to continue to avoid transparency and accountability to parliament.

Professor Khaled Fahmy, of AUC, reached a similar conclusion, claiming that the military "are not subject to any Parliamentary scrutiny, the Egyptian government auditing office has no control or knowledge of them".

There was a glimpse of the military's economic might during the recent currency crisis, when the military intervened to prop up the Egyptian central bank with $1 billion cash to stabilise the faltering currency. The military propping up the state rather than the state propping up the military? This was a hard pill to swallow.

WikiLeaks released a secret cable to Washington from US Ambassador to Egypt Margaret Scobey which claimed that the Egyptian military was "becoming a 'quasi-commercial' enterprise itself". The cable, dated September 2008, went on to say that "military-owned companies, often run by retired generals, are particularly active in the water, olive oil, cement, construction, hotel and gasoline industries... We see the military's role in the economy as a force that generally stifles free market reform."

The Egyptian military, some 400,000 strong, is structured into three distinct categories: the commissioned officer rank on top, then the non-commissioned grade and, at the very bottom of the pyramid, the vast army of conscripts who serve in the army. Surplus conscripts are passed on to the police force. Conscripts are paid $20 a month, below the average Egyptian wage.

Commissioned officers salaries and perks are astronomical by Egyptian standards. Above all, they pay a peppercorn rent, and everything, from cars to schooling, is generously subsidised. They are furthermore encouraged into building a portfolio of real estate through a multitude of loopholes.

The size of the military exceeds Egypt's needs, as conscription rules are arcane and outdated. It enrolls a significant number of illiterates and misfits, which impedes its purpose. Egypt's military needs a much smaller, highly-mobile force.

Robert Springborg, a professor in the department of national security affairs at the Naval Postgraduate School in Monterey, California, and authority on the Egyptian military, believes that the generals "will try to massage the new order so that it does not seek to impose civilian control on the armed forces". He says, "It's not just a question of preserving the institution of the army. It's a question of preserving the financial base of its members."

Professor Springborg believes that Egypt's top military ranks have enjoyed a pampered existence in sprawling developments such as Cairo's Nasr City, where officers are housed in spacious, subsidised condominiums and that officers in the Egyptian military are making "billions and billions and billions" of dollars.

Extraordinary, the military controls bakeries, farmland and factories that make everything from tanks to toasters, as well as hospitals and the toll roads to the highly profitable port of Suez. Their "economic empire" extends into just about every corner of the country, including petrol stations, hotels, shopping complexes and even their own chain of supermarkets.

The latest constitution committee, headed by former Mubarak Minster Amr Moussa, exempted the military from public oversight, retained the military's right to try civilians in military courts and allowed the military to appoint its own minister to control Intelligence agencies. What chance is there for democracy when a huge chunk of the country's economy and policy making are outside the jurisprudence of the state? Such exploitation encourages a huge amount of corruption and ultimately undermines any constructive drive for modernity and rule of law.

The oversensitive subject of the military acquiring an "extra territorial status" in its budget and financial activities has been a no go area for almost sixty years. Hamzawy has been the target of media ridicule for talking about this "state within a state" that the military has become. He has been called a fifth columnist and "closet Islamist" and criminal charges have recently been levelled against him for "insulting the judiciary" a crime that could land him in jail.

The sovereignty of the state and a genuine democracy will only be possible once the military's business and land acquisition empire are brought under the jurisdiction of the legal system and parliament.

The United States and the Generals

The US administration was placed in a difficult position after Mubarak's departure. The two major powers in Egypt, the SCAF and the Muslim Brotherhood, were not natural allies of the United States. The problem was compounded by the fact that within the United States, Egypt is not a foreign policy priority, even in the context of the wider Middle East: Iran and Israel are of far greater concern to American public and policymakers alike. The United States has also seen its influence wane in the region in the last few years and so finds it increasingly difficult to apply pressure to Middle Eastern governments. According to an article by former US Middle East negotiator Aaron Miller, "The Obama administration believes that the military – not the Brotherhood – has been mainly responsible for subverting the democratic process, and yet is really hard-pressed to do much about it."

Throughout the transition, the sense of US frustration with the SCAF was more than apparent. Although the CIA had a long history of co-operation with Egyptian intelligence, it still failed to read the generals' political motivations and planning. On the diplomatic side, the United States was used to dealing with the cosmopolitan statesmen of the Egyptian foreign ministry and government elite, rather than with these elderly generals. In September 2011, when the Israeli embassy in Cairo was attacked, it emerged that the SCAF had been ignoring phone calls from Washington concerning the securing of Israeli interests in Egypt. Field Marshall Tantawi personally ignored attempts by American

Defence Secretary Leon Panetta to contact him at the time. The revelation demonstrated exceptional political ineptitude and arrogance. The SCAF's ambivalent attitude towards the American administration was ultimately to their detriment. It did not win them support on the street and forfeited the confidence of their most powerful ally.

One of the early problems in the relationship between the SCAF and the USA was the matter of USAID, the American international development department, placing advertisements in Egyptian newspapers inviting grant proposals for funds of $100 and $65 million, for both economic and "democratic" development. The SCAF took this as a direct insult by the United States at the very least, and at worst, an attempt at subterfuge. The American advertisements also amounted to a re-allocation of economic aid which Egypt was already receiving, and the SCAF were likewise insulted that the US should try to bypass their input in the distribution of money meant for Egypt. The Egyptian government insisted that they should have a say in the recipients of aid.

The petulant response of the SCAF on the issue of American funding of NGOs in Egypt led to a damaging confrontation with the US. The generals overreacted, identifying foreign conspiracies in their poorly analysed intelligence reports. In an effort to demonstrate their patriotism, they completely alienated themselves from the secular opposition. They also damaged their ability to reach a political solution to the continued unrest on Egypt's streets.

The government, through its state owned newspapers, announced that American economic assistance was in fact humiliating Egypt, and called upon Egyptians to boycott American aid. The minister of planning and "international co-operation," Fayza Aboul Naga, a Mubarak-era appointee who had been kept on by the SCAF, told an American newspaper, "I am not sure at this stage we still need somebody to tell us what is or is not good for us – or worse, to force it on us."

American support for NGOs within Egypt was never a secret. After Mubarak stepped down, American Secretary of State Hillary Clinton allocated $250 million in economic aid, specifically to "support the transition." The SCAF continued the policy line of the Mubarak regime, that economic aid for the funding of Egyptian civil society constituted a violation of their sovereignty. While none of the money actually directly funds any political parties, American democratic development is designed to expand the civil society of target countries. This kind of support is known as Direct Public Diplomacy and has been a key strategy in American foreign relations for over a decade. The programme includes workshops and seminars designed to teach civilians how to set up political organisations and actively campaign within their countries.

The Americans knew that this would be a problem. In April 2011 America's ambassador to Egypt, Margaret Scobey, warned Egyptians that too often in the days of Mubarak American funding of civil society in Egypt was described as "interference," and she expressed a hope that after Mubarak this would no longer be the case. It was a warning to the SCAF. SCAF's response was to treat American DPD aid with more suspicion than even the Mubarak regime had done.

In December 2011, Egyptian security forces raided the offices of 17 foreign NGOs. In February 2012, the Egyptian authorities arrested 43 people, at least 17 of whom were Americans. The United States was furious. Hillary Clinton warned that America would withdraw all aid to Egypt if the dispute was not resolved. In April 2012, shortly after the United States renewed its $1.3 billion aid package to Egypt, Egypt put pressure on Interpol to issue international arrest warrants for 15 NGO workers who were no longer in Egypt, one of which was for an American diplomat who had served on the National Security Council under George W Bush. Interpol refused the request.

The issue of American funding for civil society was also heavily criticised by the Muslim Brotherhood and Islamists in general. Islamist groups who, in any case, have never been the recipients of Western aid money, routinely condemn American pro-democracy funding as a further tentacle of Western imperialism designed to impose secular rule on Egypt. Such groups have long condemned USAID's pro-democracy projects as aimed at strengthening their secular, pro-West opponents. This position is somewhat hypocritical given the fact that the Muslim Brotherhood receives considerable funds from foreign sources.

"We tell America and its allies lurking in Egypt: end your evil interference in Egypt's internal affairs, interference that we condemn as a conspiracy against the future of Egypt," announced Hafez Salama, one of Egypt's most popular Islamist ideologues.

Western funding of NGOs in Egypt did actually constitute a threat to the country's Islamist groups. Western funding would inevitably flow towards the organisations with a more liberal outlook and would also help non-Islamist charities in the provision of social services, which in many ways is the bedrock of the Islamist strategy to gain popular support.

Aside from the matter of aid, the United States repeatedly declared that it was unsure about the SCAF's commitment to democratic freedom. When these concerns were expressed directly to the generals, they were largely ignored. By appearing so resistant to transition, the Muslim Brotherhood were able to present themselves as the champions of democratic freedom in the new Egypt and use the mistrust of the generals as a means of developing their own popular support. This played well abroad. Even left-leaning media outlets, such as the *Guardian* in the UK, came out in support of the Muslim Brotherhood as the legitimate government in Egypt, in spite of the fact that the Brotherhood's social conservatism is at odds with liberal Western ideals.

The SCAF have largely blamed outside influences for their own failings. The controversy following American funding of civil society was consistent with a policy followed in Egypt for several decades, that any domestic unrest is the result of actions by "external agitators." Publicly, the SCAF criticised the United States; Egyptians are used to blaming the United States and Israel for a variety of domestic problems. Privately, however, the SCAF were more inclined to blame the Gulf States, especially Qatar. Though they are not specific, the common view in Egypt is that Qatar funds Islamist organisations as a means of increasing its own regional influence.

The implication that the United States was somehow responsible for the uprising affecting Egypt led the United States to assume that the Egyptian government had not changed in either orientation or outlook since the days of Mubarak. The United States began to make public declarations to that effect.

****

Ultimately, the singular achievement of the SCAF was to facilitate a Muslim Brotherhood takeover of government in Egypt. Unlike the secular and liberal factions in the country, the Brotherhood were able to benefit from the SCAF's mistakes. Fundamentally, the Generals were not suited to power and, in many ways, it would have been too much to expect more competence. It cannot be forgotten that the street protesters who brought down Mubarak also sought to bring down the SCAF, and they would therefore never be co-operative. In an Egypt where the SCAF faced hostility from within their own ranks, and in every other major political grouping, the SCAF's first tenure in charge of Egypt ended in a whimper, ushering the Muslim Brotherhood into power.

When the military took power again in 2013, General El Sisi was more than aware of the criticism levelled at his predecessor. Civilian interim politicians were appointed instead, to ensure that the SCAF could not be accused of acting as a military junta. Despite massive popular support for their actions in removing Morsi, the Brotherhood and many in the Western media still labelled it a coup. Though the military decided not to run the transitional government, few in Egypt will be under any illusion as to where real power lies.

CHAPTER 7

THE BROTHERHOOD'S CONSTITUTION OF 2012

Since Mubarak's downfall in early 2011, what constitutes Egypt's national identity has been the subject of bitter debate. The 2012 constitution was meant to settle that dispute. However, it raises serious concerns in a country previously known for its secularism and tolerance. Fears began as soon as the 100-member committee was tasked with drawing it up. The Constituent Assembly was appointed in March 2012 and was overwhelmingly composed of Islamists. Many non-Islamist members resigned in protest at Islamist domination, to the disadvantage of the other groups which make up Egyptian society.

The Constituent Assembly was first suspended in April 2012, after a court ruled it to be unconstitutional. Undeterred, the Islamist-dominated parliament elected a new Constituent Assembly which produced a 234 article draft constitution, to be put to the public by the end of the year.

The new draft constitution was deeply divisive and further tore at the fabric of Egyptian society. It was supported by the major Islamist powers in Egypt; preachers such as Yusef al Qaradawi tried to shame their followers into supporting it, warning that if the constitution was rejected by the voters, Egypt could lose $20 billion of Qatari investment. Liberals and secularists were terrified that the constitution would be a first step on the path towards theocracy, stamping Islamic authority on the Egyptian state.

Back in 1923, a constitution was drafted by a commission presided over by a former prime minister, its members recruited from various political circles. They represented the old legislative assembly of 1913: notables, the intelligentsia, merchants, lawyers, judges and religious leaders, including Christians and Jews. Hussein Rushdi Pasha, who oversaw the process, was an eminent jurist, and a man of vast administrative experience. Abdel Aziz Fahmi, the man tasked with the wording of the constitution, was similarly steeped in the law and eager to draft a modern liberal constitution that would measure up to the European models. Questions as to what would be the sources of legislation and whether religious law should remain the standard of political conduct were answered by stating that Islam was the religion of the state and legislation must be in accordance with principles of freedom and morality. At the same time, the constitution called into question any need to consult traditional religious institutions in the modern world by simply leaving them out of the legislative process.

Ninety years later a constitution which totally refutes the thinking and ethos of 1923 was written. It was the structure which the controversy of Brotherhood rule in Egypt revolved around. The economy was in a state of crisis for over two years and unemployment remained high. The public were angry that the general breakdown of law and order had not been resolved. As such, the constitution acted as a lightning rod at which furious Egyptians could vent their anger, a symbol of the misplaced priorities of the Brotherhood government.

The final draft of the constitution was hastily completed in a non-stop 19 hour session by a committee desperate to get a draft out before the Supreme Constitutional Court could annul the document by claiming the assembly was not representative of the Egyptian people. It was put to the public in a referendum held in two stages, on December 15 and 16, 2012 and approved by 63.8% of voters, though with a turnout of only 30%. Sensing the underhanded approach of the new regime, the judiciary refused to supervise the referendum.

Only 10 million Egyptians approved the constitution, out of just under 52 million eligible voters. Such a retrograde document, with its various legal ambiguities and its provision for religious domination, could only complicate Egypt's transition towards democracy. For the Brotherhood, the passing of the constitution was not about power to the people but a means of exerting further control over Egypt's institutions.

According to the constitution, only conservative male Muslims will be afforded the full rights of a citizen. Women, followers of non-Abrahamic faiths and atheists will not be afforded these same rights. At face value, the constitution seems to protect the rights of women and religious minorities, while also declaring Egypt to be governed by democratic principles. Article 1 announced that Egypt is to be governed by a "democratic regime" which, according to article 6, is founded on "consultation, equal citizenship." However, these guarantees are consistently impaired by caveats which declare that these rights can only be in adherence to religious law.

For instance, article 68 declares that "the state will do everything to promote equality between women and men," though "without abandoning the judgments of Islamic law." These judgments may often be arbitrary and made by jurists who have no democratic right, or even the necessary religious training, to make sweeping judgments pertaining to Islamic law. Many of these judgments stipulate an inferior status in inheritance, no say in divorce or rights to custody of children. The constitution makes one appallingly patronising reference to women, declaring the state will help them "strike a balance between their family duties and their work in society." As a result, gender equality only exists by favour of the man. Women will only have it if they obey their husbands or fathers and accept their secondary status, as prescribed by religion.

According to the constitution, Islam is not the sole source of legislation. However, enshrined within the document is a stipulation that it is the "primary" source of legislation. For a document meant to decree the manner in which a country is governed, this is a frustrating and ambiguous clause. It could mean that Egypt's legislation will emanate from traditional secular sources. However, these sources will be subservient to the Quran or, more specifically, to a clerical judgment on what the Quran has to say about a given issue. Considering that many of the world's billion-plus Muslims live vastly different lives, and hold countless multitudes of different opinions, such a decree is meaningless and ultimately means that legislation will be written to suit the opinions and prejudices of those drafting it.

Regardless of how progressive an interpretation of the Sharia may be, the sheer fact that it must ultimately defer back to a centuries-old religious text means that it can never be considered secular or liberal. Articles 43 and 44 demonstrate this inherent tension. Article 43 declares that "freedom of belief is inviolable, whilst 44 forbids insult of "the prophets." This is a direct contradiction, and it is not difficult to imagine which article the government should favour if a case or issue brings the two into conflict.

The constitution also claims to safeguard freedom of thought and expression. Journalists are free to set up media outlets provided they notify the authorities. However, such a clause is totally redundant. The idea that an Egyptian could, under Brotherhood rule, set up a publication and dedicate it to questioning the veracity of the *hadith* or the *sunna*, is absurd.

Freedom of belief is guaranteed, as long as that belief is restricted to the Abrahamic religions. Specifically, article 3 of the constitution grants Christians and Jews the principles of their religious law as the main source of regulation for their personal status. All the while, the constitution asserts that the Sharia is the main source of legislation. Such stipulations ignore the rights of those who have other faiths, those who do not believe and those who may have faith, but perhaps not want their religion, or their religious masters, to dictate their rights. Under Brotherhood rule, these people were marginalised, though if the Islamists grew more confident or began to accommodate radical Islamists, this marginalisation would develop into open persecution.

The constitution takes a distinctly paternalistic attitude to its citizens. Article 10 asserts that the family, not the citizen, is the foundation of society, granting the state the power to "preserve the inherent character of the Egyptian family, its cohesion, stability and moral character." It then claims that "the family's foundations are religion, morality and patriotism." Since the family unit in Islamic society is usually dominated by the male patriarch, it seems that women will have to surrender authority over their own lives to their male relatives. Fundamentally, the constitution presents complex, evolving notions (such as morality) as simplistic solutions to questions of national identity. Ultimately the idea that the state can uphold a superior morality is nonsense. The constitution appears to say that polygamy (at least up to four wives) is morally acceptable, whereas having a girlfriend or boyfriend is immoral. Presumably the state now has the power to make those decisions on behalf of its citizens, imposing its judgments on the people.

The ambiguous language of the constitution also raises a pertinent question mark over what the state would do to those individuals who did not abide by the moral values it had laid down. Prohibition, fines, imprisonment, punishment and re-education would necessarily have to be employed to enforce its religious laws: a dismal prospect for 91 million Egyptians.

The Islamic prescriptions in the constitution posed the threat that Egyptians may be watched over by some kind of Muslim Big Brother, watching their every move to ensure they are compliant with Islamic codes of conduct. Article 11 declares that "the state promotes morality, decency and public order," and empowers the government to "safeguard and protect morality and public decency" and "religious and nationalist values." It is unclear what this actually means; it could easily signify a move to bring in religious police of the Saudi sort. Indeed, many within the Muslim Brotherhood have been calling for such an institution for years.

Schoolchildren will likewise learn to adhere to these values as article 60 decrees that religious education be mandatory for all levels of education up to university. Likewise article 71 ensures that children develop "spiritually" and "morally," among other things. The inevitable question is what is the Islamic definition of morality? Some medieval Islamic practices which were largely abandoned in the 20th century may be considered to be moral by certain Islamist jurists, though not by modern society.

Since the constitution is so open to interpretation, the onus is on the liberal and progressive elements of Egyptian society to assert and argue for their modern moral judgments so as to deny the Islamists a monopoly on morality. This will be hard as arguments based on religious prerogatives are notoriously difficult to debate.

In an apparent bid to pacify the military, the constitution has retained the provision that the SCAF commands the armed forces. However, it also decrees the formation of a new National Defence Council, which although retaining the top Generals and Admirals, would include the President and some of his cabinet ministers. This new council would ultimately run the armed forces and determine the military budget, a privilege the SCAF had tried to reserve for itself.

The constitution left many Egyptians furious. The young street protesters who forced Mubarak's departure feel that they were not protesting so that this document could be written. Those liberals who wanted a constitution to guarantee human rights and personal freedom did not get it. The military, who sought to protect their independence from the government, have seen control of the armed forces taken away from them. The judiciary, which at times threatened to derail the constitution, warned of a legal and legislative nightmare because various vague Islamic prescriptions would somehow need to be distilled into workable legislation.

Egypt is known for having one of the earliest administrative and legislative systems in history. The pyramidal (no pun intended) system of government can only work if it has the requisite checks and balances. Throughout the beginning of the 20th century Egyptian governments had too many checks and balances, as government after government crumbled, to be replaced time and again by ineffective bureaucrats. During 60 years of dictatorship, Egypt had too few checks and balances; a mere three men dominated political life for all that time, until the situation finally became unsustainable in 2011.

Shortly after Morsi ratified the constitution, the Egyptian pound fell to a record low. Protests on the street continued. Given the intensity of opposition, it was always unlikely that such a constitution could bring about economic progress and political stability. When the army took power from Morsi in 2013, the constitution was immediately suspended, not to be reinstated until it had been substantially amended.

CHAPTER 8

THE SHARIA

S haria law has been at the heart of heated and sometimes violent clashes between traditionalists and modernisers throughout the Arab and Muslim world for many centuries. The question of its application is neither religious nor legal, it is political. Even the term Sharia law is something of a misnomer. Sharia is simply the Arabic word for law, and Sharia law effectively means "law law." However, in the Islamic context, the Sharia refers to a legal system exclusively derived from the sacred texts of Islam.

The legal systemisation of Islam as a political tool began more than a century after the death of the Prophet Muhammad and was completed by the end of the 9th century. Its creation was spurred by the conquests of Byzantine and Persian territories by the first Muslim Empire. These lands had their own long established legal systems; however, the Muslim Caliphate did not. Legal questions were asked of the Muslim leaders who developed their own law as they began to construct their own administrations. The Sharia was based on the interpretations of the Quran which were then in vogue, and an ad-hoc reconstruction of sayings attributed to the prophet (the Sunnah) and his four righteous Caliphs. The reliance on the Sunnah was necessary as the Quran does not contain within it a comprehensive legal framework, a point conceded by most Islamic authorities. The Sunnah refers to all the biographical information relating to Muhammad and is often regarded as synonymous with the Hadith, which literally means "the statements" of the Prophet. Thus, the

Hadith is required to lend legitimacy to many Islamic rules, and provide a precedent to determine the Prophet's opinion on various matters relating to family, relationships, crime and punishment.

The adherents and preachers of political Islam, particularly the Muslim Brotherhood, who have been the most vocal advocates of the reintroduction of the Sharia, believe that the Quran and the Hadith, which were compiled over a thousand years ago, provide the requisite basis for a complete system of jurisprudence and legislation in the 21st century.

Attempts to codify the Sharia in a modern context are not new. The Ottoman Empire introduced its own codified version of the Sharia in 1877, known as Mecelle. This system introduced the codes and practises of the Sharia into a civil code applicable to believers and non-believers alike, throughout the Empire and its vassal states. The civil code was actually heavily influenced by contemporary European law, though it exempted family matters, which remained the dominion of the religious courts. Mustafa Kamal Ataturk abolished the Caliphate in 1924, and Mecelle was abandoned two years later, though Mecelle would continue to be used as the basis for the legal systems of many of the Ottoman Empire's successor states in the Middle East for some decades.

Prior to the dissolution of the Ottoman Empire, the Caliphate, a system of rule nominally based on the Islamic Empire in its very earliest years, existed as a way for the Sultan to assert religious authority. In 1923, the eminent Egyptian religio-political leader, Ali Abdel Raziq argued that "Caliphate was neither a basic principle, nor a necessary institution in Islam," and explained that the "Prophet Muhammad had not established polity, or state, and the Sharia was a mere spiritual-moral law, having no connection with political authority or the earthly government of men."

Unlike most of the states that rose out of the ashes of the Ottoman Empire, Egypt never actually adopted the Mecelle system. Egypt introduced constitutional reforms in 1922, and adopted a system broadly similar to that which Turkey would follow over the same period. It updated conventions on family law, determining the minimum age of marriage to be 16 for girls and 18 for boys, and also introduced a written requirement of consent from women for marriage in order to abolish the tradition of child marriages.

Such an opinion illustrated the liberal ideas and opinions shared by many of those Egyptian religious scholars, initially trained at Al-Azhar but also educated in Europe. Many of these men questioned the traditional religious teachings, being more interested in applying European legal systems and modernising Islamic teaching to make it relevant to contemporary life.

Traditionalists and proto-Islamists were under attack in the liberal constitutional Egypt of the 1920s and 1930s. The cosmopolitan intelligentsia saw them as backward and reactionary. At the same time, the feminist movement was gaining traction and inspired a series of reforms in areas like child marriage and polygamy. Women's rights have long been a contentious issue for Islamists. Throughout the 20th century, the secular Arab states often made feminist social reforms a means of undermining the power of their recalcitrant Islamist factions.

Sharia first returned to Egyptian politics during 1980. In that year, the Egyptian constitution of 1971 was amended to make Sharia the main source of legislation. Sadat made the concession in a tense political climate of Islamist appeasement. At the time, Sadat was desperately trying to co-opt the Muslim Brotherhood and the Islamic "street," who were furious with him for his alliance with the United States and peace treaty with Israel. Ever since, the nature of the Islamic constitution has been a source of intense controversy. Many Egyptians are desperate to retain the secular nature of the state, while the Muslim Brotherhood has continually sought to impose the Sharia on the legal system.

The Egyptian constitution of 2012 stipulated that the Sharia be the source of legislation and prepared the legal system for the introduction of Sharia-based laws. Egypt's secular legal codes began to unravel. Within and without the country, progressive Egyptians are deeply concerned that the imposition of the Sharia will be an obstacle to the development of a civil state and push Egypt back from the brink of modernity.

****

There is no evidence that Sharia law was ever applied throughout the Islamic Caliphate. The Sharia did not apply to non-believers, who were permitted to retain their own legal systems. Neither was it properly codified, but determined by judges (*qadis*) appointed by the Caliph. The rule of the Caliph was centred around their person and his tribe. It was a kind of medieval tribal feudalism clothed in religious authority. Today some Islamists believe that in order to properly implement the Sharia, the Caliphate must be restored, i.e. Muslim states should coalesce into a single Muslim empire, the ruler of which combines absolute political and religious authority.

The Sharia evolved from a set of practices laid down in the Quran and subsequently the Hadith. The legal system envisaged total and unqualified submission to Islamic jurisprudence, its verdicts were considered expressions of divine will. The jurisprudence of the Sharia was not moulded by public consensus but determined by Allah himself and is therefore perfect and supersedes any other state or common law.

Over the centuries, Islamic jurisprudence was guided by various, often contradictory, schools of thought, all of which were influenced by the prevailing political environment at the time. There are four main doctrines of Islamic religious jurisprudence, or *fiqh*, the Hanafi, the Hanbali, the Zahiri and the Shafi'i. Each employs different interpretations, but all developed mainly out of the 9th century Abbasid Caliphate. These approaches remain central to Islamic legal scholarship to this day.

No new schools of religious law have been established for more than a millennium, although there have been various attempts by Islamic modernisers and progressives to introduce reformist approaches from time to time. Each of these schools of thought, or *Madhhab*, was developed by an early Islamic scholar, who lent his name to their respective Madhhab. All of these schools of thought are dependent on reasoning or analogy derived from the Quran and Sunnah, and so each requires intense study of the Hadith.

Bukhari

Muhammad al Bukhari, who lived from 810 to 870 CE compiled what many Muslims see as the definitive version of the Hadith. Bukhari was not an Arab, having been born in the city of Bukhara in what is now Uzbekistan. At the age of 16 he accompanied his widowed mother and brother on pilgrimage to Mecca and began to devote himself to a life of studying the Hadith. Bukhari, having learned Arabic and about Arab culture, sifted through the plethora of names, tribes, lineages and stories from remote places, not recorded in the historical record but derived solely from oral tradition. During that time, he is said to have spoken to a thousand people and accumulated hundreds of thousand of traditions.

After a further 16 years of travel and study, Bukhari returned to the Caucasus where he distilled his massive collection of muddled sayings and half-remembered stories into a volume containing 7,275 traditions. Each was neatly compartmentalised into relevant chapters, so as to provide an easily navigable system on which to base religious jurisprudence and daily life.

Sunni Islamic authorities are extremely protective of Bukhari. They refuse to allow scholarly examination of how a teenager from the Caucasus could travel through such a vast empire, collect, verify and authenticate the true sayings of the Prophet and separate them from numerous fictitious attributions, nearly two centuries after the Prophet's death. Indeed, the very fact that Bukhari disregarded tens of thousands of traditions deemed unreliable is regarded as evidence of his academic tenacity. A task of this magnitude seems physically and mentally impossible for one person to take on. Even with a huge body of scholars, a thorough knowledge of the Arabic language and access to written historical records, none of which Bukhari had, such a body of work would be a subject of tremendous debate as to its veracity. It must also be remembered that Bukhari would have been writing at a time when royal courts employed poets to praise the Caliph and oral traditions were subject to the political whims of their storytellers. However, to this day, a scholarly critique of Bukhari's work is considered blasphemous.

There are even conflicting accounts of his life. Some traditions claim he accumulated 600,000 sayings of the Prophet, some put the number at half that. The date at which he published his Hadith varies according to different sources. The length of time he spent studying is also disputed.

Shortly after Bukhari completed his work, political upheaval rocked the Muslim world, particularly the Abbasid civil war and the Zanj revolt of the 860s which are beyond the scope of this book. The environment was certainly not conducive to freedom of thought and enquiry. The Shiite rivalry was at its peak and as a result, the reconstruction of the Hadith was biased against Ali, the fourth Caliph, son-in-law of the Prophet and the man to whom the Shiite owe their allegiance. In such a heated political environment, one must question the motivation of those who compiled the Hadith and asserted certain sayings to be true above others. Control of the Hadith was a useful political tool, since ascribing the views of later scholars and jurists to the Prophet Muhammad gives them greater power among the faithful.

The wild accusations of blasphemy levelled at anyone who ventures to re-examine that period of history are counter-productive and indicative of a lack of confidence in their teachings. Islam will only evolve as a religion if it engages in a process of self-examination. This has happened before in the Islamic Empire. Spain under Muslim rule was renowned as a centre of theological study and Islamic reform. During the Islamic Golden Age, the Muslim tradition produced innumerable scientists and philosophers who left their mark on history. However, since that time Islamic scholarship has stagnated and Islamic reformers have been marginalised by those who remain rigidly committed to the teachings of past centuries.

The studies of the Hadith which have been undertaken by non-Muslims attest that many of the sayings are derived from a variety of pre-Islamic sources. The Hadith are often inconsistent; for example, the Hungarian Orientalist Ignac Goldziher showed how early Islam was often willing to borrow from Christian sources, how even derivatives of the Lord's Prayer appear in the Hadith. However, at other points Islam is remarkably hostile to non-believers, denying the right of Muslims to marry non-Muslims. The Sahih Muslim Hadith, one of the six major books of Hadith, declares that with his last breath the Prophet decreed that there be a curse on Jews and Christians. These are just two examples, but the Hadith are littered with utterances, supposedly from Muhammad, that are hostile to non-believers.

Nevertheless, modern political Islam insists on affording the Hadith the potency of the Quran itself.

What Does Sharia Law Entail?

Penal law within the Sharia is heavily dependent on *qesas* or the retribution of the victim; an eye for an eye, an ear for an ear and so on. These acts of retaliatory justice are conducted at a local level by the families concerned and it is the prerogative of the victim or his family to either prosecute the perpetrator or opt instead for compensation in the form of blood money. Essentially, the family of the victim, rather than the state, has the ultimate discretion to decide whether the offence is a crime or not. Such an arrangement is basically a modification of the old tribal management of disputes reinforced by divine oversight. Though it is easy to see how such a system could evolve in nomadic tribal societies living in sparsely populated deserts centuries ago, it is totally unsuited to modern contemporary society.

Whilst violent crime and assault is supposed to be policed by vigilantes in the victim's family, Sharia mandates that the state maintain discipline in crimes relating to free expression. These crimes are regarded as much more serious than those of violence, as evidenced by the extreme punishments prescribed for them. Apostasy or defiling the name of the Prophet warrant beheading while adultery results in stoning to death or beheading. The preference in the Sharia is to have these painful and humiliating executions take place in public. Robbery and theft are resolved by amputating the offending hand. Such brutal practices have been documented this century in Afghanistan, Saudi Arabia, Sudan and other parts of Africa and Asia where the Sharia has been implemented.

Family law within the Sharia is a contentious issue and open to abuse, especially by males who reserve the right to choose husbands for their daughters and take more than one wife for themselves. According to the Sharia, a wife cannot file for divorce on account of her husband's infidelity, nor does she have a right to object to polygamy.

Wives have a fixed dowry, agreed before the marriage with her family, irrespective of any acquired wealth. As a result, a millionaire can leave his estranged wife penniless. In fact, husbands have the absolute power of instant divorce without any judicial process. Paternal rights always supersede maternal rights. The guardianship of children is the responsibility of the husband or nearest male relative in the husband's family.

Children from a wife's previous marriage have no inheritance rights from their stepfather. In practice, the compulsory rule of inheritance means that 90% of a dead man's estate goes to the wife with children (with preference given to male children) and the rest divided between the other wife or wives. A daughter inherits half the share owed to her brother and brothers inherit equal shares irrespective of age difference – in other words, an infant gets the same share as a wage-earning adult brother.

Application of the Sharia is determined by Islamic courts. These courts are centred around the judge and neither plaintiff nor defendant is granted legal representation. Judgment is final and there is no organised system of appeal. The testimony of two male witnesses is required to establish guilt, though this number may rise depending on the severity or type of crime. Often, again depending on the subject, the testimony of two women is required to match that of one man, though two male testimonies outweigh that of four females.

Naturally, these practices vary according to the different parts of the world in which the Sharia courts have jurisdiction. In fact, the Sharia may vary greatly between courts in the same region. The variations are dependent on which *fiqh* the court adheres to, and are subject to the innumerable local inflections and interpretations of the Quran. The irony is that a justice system based on the immutable and final word of God actually results in multitudes of different judgments and precedents, indeed, far more than any codified system of civil law.

Since the application of the Sharia is taken so seriously by its adherents, regional variations in the Sharia may lead to conflict and even civil war, as has happened in the Sudan, Somalia, northern Nigeria and Pakistan.

Shiite Muslims, who number around 200 million, do not believe the validity of most of the Hadith narratives, nor accept Sunni-dominated Sharia law. The advocacy of Sharia law further deepens the schism between the two major communities of the Islamic world.

The Napoleonic conquest of Egypt and Muhammed Ali's subsequent state-building project radically altered the administration of justice by introducing general common law and a European-style judicial system. By the 1930s, the Sharia courts had been abolished in Egypt.

Much of the Arab and broader Islamic world abandoned the Sharia in the 20th century. However, reform was generally piecemeal and in many Islamic countries there have been growing calls for the reintroduction of the Sharia for decades, with proponents arguing that it is a religious duty for Muslims to submit to the Sharia. As a result, aspects of the Sharia have gradually returned. For example, Tunisia banned polygamy back in

1956 but increasingly powerful voices are now calling for its re-introduction.

The rise of Islamist politics over the past 30 years in the Arab world, which has accelerated in the wake of the Arab Spring, will inevitably lead to confrontation over the Sharia. The Sharia is a symbolic battleground between secularism and Islamism. Within Egypt, millions of Christians are deeply concerned that the Sharia will further marginalise them politically, further restricting their freedom of religion and forcing them to be subject to a legal system organised around a religion which is not theirs. The idea of a non-Muslim judge presiding over a Muslim dispute has never been fully accepted. Likewise, there is a real danger than the testimony of a Christian in a Sharia court will be discounted.

The application of the Sharia to the trials of modern life will always be problematic because the notion that every aspect of a Muslim life can be dictated by the Quran and Sunnah is absurd. Consequently, millions of pious Muslims are paralysed by the fear they may be committing a mortal sin because they are unaware of the Quran's take on digital media, modern sports, advanced medicine, modern technology, Western interaction etc. Predictably, the Quran and the Hadith have very little to say on these matters, though the Hadith contains more than enough passages instructing Muslims on the correct way to eat dates or how a woman should deal with menstruation.

Taliban rule in Afghanistan entailed a nationwide application of the Sharia, supported morally and financially by individuals in certain conservative Muslim states, in spite of the religiously sanctioned brutality which it inflicted on the country. Sudan applied the Sharia for more than 20 years. So divisive was it, that it led to the partition of the country between the Muslim North and the non-Muslim South.

The Muslim Brotherhood are the current major advocates of the Sharia as a workable legal system. When in power, they enshrined the Sharia in Egypt's constitution, though they did little to explain the actual details of what their Sharia law would entail. Though they do allow senior preachers or politicians to publically pontificate on potential Sharia-compliant laws, they distance themselves from any statements that provoke public outcry.

Ultimately the rudimentary application of the Sharia in countries such as Tunisia and Egypt will prove unpopular. Given the choice, the public will always favour codified common law and due process. With the notable exception of Saudi Arabia and the Gulf, where the government is wealthy enough to buy the compliance of its citizens, Sharia courts only flourish in rural developing countries, or at least in countries with few urban centres. There is a disturbing trend where such courts are the only legal body, in remote places such as Yemen or Somalia for example, where instant justice such as beheading or amputation of limbs is carried out. For a variety of reasons, the media in the Muslim world is often reluctant to report on such gross abuses of human rights.

The imposition of the Sharia by the Islamists who controlled Egypt was a very real and very frightening possibility. It was what brought hundreds of thousands of Egyptians out onto the streets in protest against the government of Mohammed Morsi.

The wedding of Queen Fawzia (centre, with flowers) to Iran's Crown Prince, Muhammad Reza Pahlavi, later the Shah of Persia (to her right), in March 1938. On the far right is her sister, and her brother, King Farouq stands left with his wife, the Queen.

Members of Ali Maher Pasha's second government surround King Farouk I.

Emir Faisal (right), who later became King of Syria and then King of Iraq, with Chaim Weizmann, President of the Zionist Organization and later First President of Israel, in 1919.

Gamal Abdel Nasser with King Saud and Shukry El Kuwatly, 1956.

Hassan Al-Banna

Sayyid Qutb

Sheikh Sharawi

Dr Yusuf al Qaradawi

Hosni Mubarak and Anwar Sadat, just moments before Sadat was assassinated.

Ali Abdullah Saleh, Muammar Gaddafi and Hosni Mubarak, October 2010, with Amr Moussa (laughing) in the second row.

General El Sisi salutes Mohammed Morsi during his swearing in as Minister of Defence and Head of Armed Forces in August 2012.

Mubarak and sons in court, 2013 at the police academy special court.

Dr Mohamed ElBaradie

Bassem Youssef

A protester holds a sign depicting General El Sisi and Abdel Nasser.

*Mohammed Morsi and other senior figures of the Muslim Brotherhood on trial,
November 2013. A soundproof glass box was added for subsequent appearances.*

*A delegation of British MPs visit Egypt in 2011 (organised by the author), seen here
outside the Muslim Brotherhood headquarters in Muqattam, since raised. Left to
right: Ahmed Al-Sheikh, Cathy Frisina, the author, Christina Dykes, Lord Muhamed
Sheikh, Lord McNair, Tobias Ellwood MP, Dr Essam Al-Irian, deputy leader of the
Muslim Brotherhood, Lady Fiona Hodgson, a spokesman for Muslim Brotherhood
and Bob Stewart MP.*

The author speaks to protesters in Tahrir Square, Cairo.

Young pro-Morsi protestors in court in November 2013, wearing prison-issue white uniforms and scarves.

The author (second right) takes part in a round table discussion at the House of Commons in London, chaired by Liam Fox (second left), then Minister of Defence, and including: Abdulaziz bin Abdullah Al Hinai, Ambassador of Oman (far left) Abdulla Al-Radhi, Ambassador of Yemen (third left), Julian Lewis MP (centre), Daniel Ronen (fourth right), Ashraf Elkholy, Ambassador of Egypt (third right), and the political scientist Mamoun Fandy (far right).

The author (third right) addresses a conference as part of a panel shared with, to his left, Lord David Howell, Minister of State for the Foreign and Commonwealth Office and Sir David Blatherwick, former British Ambassador to Egypt.

CHAPTER 9

THE UNITED STATES, EGYPT
AND THE ARAB WORLD

The relationship between the United States and the Arab world is still dominated by the events of 11 September 2001, which was preceded by decades of American involvement in the Middle East. The United States has crucial interests in the region, namely continued access to oil supplies and support for the state of Israel. However, the quest for stability in the Middle East has perplexed American policymakers for decades. In 2004, the American political scientist Joseph Nye wrote:

> "The Middle East presents a particular challenge for American soft power and public diplomacy. Not only was it the home of the terrorists who attacked the United States on September 11th, 2001, but the region has not adjusted well to modernisation"
>
> Joseph S, Nye Jr, *Soft Power.*

Over the years, the United States has spent more than $200 billion in military and economic aid on this region, mostly to Israel, Turkey and Egypt. The United States also maintains a significant military presence in the oil-producing Arab states, which is costly, and it has engaged in multiple foreign military interventions in order to protect its Middle Eastern oil supplies.

Egypt is the second largest recipient of economic aid from the USA after Israel. However, many Egyptians regard Japan more favourably because it built the prestigious Opera House by the Nile in Cairo. The USA on the other hand funded the renovation of Cairo's sewers, drinking water plants and the electricity grid, but these projects are rarely mentioned in the state-run media.

Many of the countries in the region are dominated by political dynasties that have monopolised power for decades, stifling all democratic opposition. Such an environment, together with economic stagnation and occasional periods of intense political turbulence, makes the region an ideal incubator of radical jihadism, an ideology diametrically opposed to American ideals and activities in Muslim lands.

Many Arabs have grown up on a steady diet of anti-American and anti-Israeli propaganda, fed them by the government or other religious authorities.

Colonel Nasser harnessed the power of the mass media as far back as the early 1950s, using it as a means of bending public opinion to his will. One of Nasser's most trusted propagandists was Johann Von Leer. Von Leer worked for Joseph Goebbels in the Nazi propaganda ministry and found work in Nasser's Egypt following the war. Having specialised in anti-Semitic propaganda for the Nazis, von Leer eased into his new position as manager of anti-Israel propaganda in Egypt. As a result, nearly all the information provided for Egyptians on Judaism and Israel was filtered through a Nazi.

When many citizens of the Arab world learn about the United States they do so within a particular narrative of repression and conspiracy in which the USA is engaged in a scheme to undermine and attack the Muslim world. Consequently, many Arabs are unaware of the US intervention to protect Muslims in Bosnia and Kosovo, nor its considerable economic aid to Palestine. While these regimes fed their people on anti-American and anti-Israeli propaganda, they would simultaneously present themselves to the US as the only guarantor of American interests in their country, being as it was, racked by anti-Americanism.

The Arab world is a mass of contradictions. Its oil-producing states are blessed with enormous wealth but it remains one of the least industrial regions in the world. Some of its states are on the cutting edge of modernity, others among the world's poorest. It is the spiritual home of Islam, the religion to which the vast majority of Arabs adhere, but also of Christianity and Judaism. Fossil fuels and tourism are its main commodities but their revenues are not evenly distributed; social tensions are rife, aggravated by endemic human rights abuses. In the public imagination, the entire region is hostile to the United States, yet most Middle Eastern governments are firmly allied with America.

The Gulf War of 1991 was a major cause of Arab resentment towards the US. Even though the war was waged on behalf of an Arab state, it was seen as yet more interference by the USA. The United States was seen as siding with the wealthy Gulf monarchies rather than with the poorer Arab republics. The subsequent break-up of Iraq, blamed on the USA, and American support of other regional dictators was seen as evidence of American hypocrisy.

The complexity of the regional political landscape is often simplified by the Arab regimes for the benefit of their people. For example, the Iran-Iraq war which devastated the two nations that fought it, was barely reported in the Arab media, whereas Iraq's invasion of Kuwait was discussed without implicating Iraq as an aggressor. In that manner, the United States was seen as responsible for all the problems of the Islamic world, rather than the dictators themselves.

In the wake of September 11 2001, the George W Bush administration outwardly committed itself to a long-term democratic transformation of the Middle East. The project employed both the hard and soft power reserves of the United States although, at the end of a decade, results were mixed.

The commitment brought about a new doctrine which decreed that positive change in the Middle East could only come about through the intervention of the Western powers, namely the USA. However, it very soon became apparent that this would be a long-term project. In November 2003, George W Bush declared that America was engaged in a 'generational struggle for the democratisation of the Middle East.' This doctrine was guided by the narrative of the United States' success in ending the Cold War. Like the War on Terror, the 'Democratisation of the Middle East' would be an ongoing foreign policy objective for the USA.

Condoleezza Rice, the National Security Advisor and Secretary of State under George W Bush, declared in a speech in Cairo, "for 60 years the USA has pursued stability at the expense of democracy in the Middle

East and has ended up with neither," adding, "from now on it will align with those who saw freedom as the indispensable platform for stability, prosperity and security and against the tyranny that bred despair, rage and terror." The speech was mocked in a satirical theatre show in Cairo for its overtones of American imperialism. Dictators such as Hosni Mubarak who had long benefited from US support, without criticism of their internal affairs, were vexed by the change in American rhetoric and commanded their media to relentlessly criticise the United States. Up until that point, the United States had openly backed what British journalist David Gardner termed the "local variant of Stalinism."

****

American involvement with Egypt and the Arabic-speaking world dates back to the first Barbary war of 1801 to 1805, when the navy of the young United States deployed to North Africa in an effort to stop American sailors being sold into slavery by the Barbary corsairs along the coasts of modern day Morocco, Algeria, Tunisia and Libya. In 1869, Khedive Ismail invited American officers, most of whom had served the Confederacy, to help command and train the Egyptian army. At the same time, the US Consul General provided an annual confidential report about the state of affairs in Egypt for Washington.

At the start of the 20th century, Egyptian leader Saad Zaghloul rushed to take advantage of President Woodrow Wilson's call for the self-determination of colonised nations in the aftermath of the First World War. Many Arab leaders, including Jews and Christians, attended the Peace Conference at Versailles, hoping to take advantage of President Wilson's commitments, as laid out in his famous 14-point plan. By the end of the conference, however, many of the Arab lands were divided between the colonial powers, namely Britain and France.

Two decades later, President Franklin D Roosevelt met with King Farouk of Egypt and King Abdul Aziz bin Saud aboard an American battleship anchored in the great Bitter Lake, midway down the Suez Canal, on his way back from the Yalta summit with Churchill and Stalin. This meeting with the Arab leaders signified a rise in the influence of the United States in a region, which until that point had been dominated by the traditional colonial nations. The Bitter Lake was a sensible choice of venue; beyond any existing territory, it respected the still considerable British interests in the region. However, in the years following the Second World War, a greatly weakened Britain would lose its status as an imperial power and be marginalised by the emerging superpower, the USA.

One of the earliest American interventions (some would say manipulations) in the Middle East was the support of General Al Zaim's Syrian coup d'état in March 1949. General Al Zaim, Chief of Staff of the Syrian Army, was encouraged and given instruction on how to carry out the coup by Major Meade, the US military attaché in Damascus and CIA agent Miles Copeland. The United States saw the intervention as a means of removing the difficult Shukri Al Quwatli, who was proving resistant to American interests in the region vis-à-vis an armistice with Israel, permitting a major oil pipeline to run through Syria and outlawing the popular Syrian Communist Party. After the bloodless coup brought Al Zaim to power, the US demanded that he bring about parliamentary democracy in Syria.

The General, however, had his own ideas, and promptly set about detaining those officials he believed to be corrupt, before setting up a military dictatorship. The Americans attempted to ply him with military aid. The General's regime, which included secular reforms and a peace offering to Israel, proved unpopular and looked liable to lead to a revolt. The CIA was forced to get rid of him.

At the CIA's prodding, he was overpowered by some middle-ranking officers led by Colonel Adlib al Shishakly and Sami al Hinnawi, who took control of army units, surrounded his house and arrested General Al Zaim and his Prime Minister Al Barazi. On 14 August 1949, the two men were put against a wall in the Mezze prison and shot. Hinnawi ended up as leader of the military junta, though Shishakly outmanoeuvred Hinnawi and overthrew him, resulting in a breathtaking three coups d'état in one year.

The Syrian debacle was a lesson for the USA. By attempting to replace a national leader with a military strongman with dubious political credentials, they actually made the country far more unstable. According to Miles Copeland, they needed "an elite, bound to a sub-elite, in alliance with some politicians, which in turn had roots in the populace." The US was determined that the Syrian incident not be repeated in Egypt, or throughout the Middle East.

Almost every US President and foreign policymaker has had an initiative or project for the Middle East over the past century. The plans either take place under the full gaze of diplomacy or via the clandestine world of intelligence and espionage. There was a particular buzz around the region in the years following the Second World War as decolonisation got underway and the international system clumsily aligned itself into the opposing camps of the Cold War, leaving the Middle East in a state of uncertainty. The CIA was active in the Middle East through its regional headquarters office in Cairo (which later moved to Beirut), shepherded by Kermit Roosevelt and Miles Copeland, who directed the political paths of various regimes in the Middle East in the years following the Second World War.

In 1952, Egypt was a priority for the United States which tasked Kermit Roosevelt with selecting the right individuals for the USA to work with. At the time, there was a real belief that Nasser had the force of personality to make decisions in USA interests, which they knew would be unpopular with the public. The Americans knew that hostility to Israel would be a key aspect of any Arab leader's popular mandate, and were under no illusion that they could force a dictator to make any peace overtures, having previously made that mistake in Syria. Unfortunately for the US, Nasser's force of personality was too strong, and his Arab nationalist ambitions had no need of the United States.

In the 1950s, the Eisenhower administration consistently favoured King Saud of Saudi Arabia over Nasser as a potential leader of the Arab world. President Eisenhower believed that King Saud would have more authority as Saudi Arabia was very much the centre of Islam, containing the two Holy Places, Mecca and Medina. In the process the United States could use Islam as a weapon against the "godless" communists. The British hated Nasser and repeatedly lobbied the USA to get rid of him. However, the USA decided that they would seek to undermine Nasser, partly through their alliance with Saudi Arabia. This was in contrast with their policy regarding Mossadeq of Iran whom the CIA ousted in an engineered military coup, at the behest of the British.

Eisenhower naïvely assumed Mecca and Saudi Arabia carried more weight than they actually did in the Middle East. Cairo was still very much the centre of Islamic thought and culture in the Islamic world. At the same time, the CIA hoped that they could find a "Muslim Billy

Graham" who would effectively mobilise the religious fervour of the Middle East against communism. They even believed at one point that the young King Faisal of Iraq, son of the Sharif of Mecca, could be such a holy man. In 1955, the USA chose Baghdad as the venue for the signing of an ambitious new treaty, meant to create a pro-West Muslim alliance in the heart of the Middle East. The Baghdad Pact, officially known as the Central Treaty Organisation (CENTO) was modelled on NATO and signed by Iran, Iraq, Pakistan, Turkey and the UK. The USA initially did not join, despite being instrumental in its formation. The Pact was somewhat undermined when the Iraqi monarchy was overthrown by a military coup in 1958 and Iraq promptly withdrew from the treaty. Despite initial promise, the pact did very little to fulfil its original purpose, to inhibit Soviet influence in the region.

During the Suez crisis of 1956, Eisenhower was furious with Britain, France and Israel for taking military action against Egypt without consulting the USA. Aware of the massive anti-Western backlash the act would cause and its undertones of colonialism, he compelled the foreign powers to withdraw, resulting in a humiliating backtrack for Britain and France. Nasser, however, claimed the victory for himself and used his new fame and credibility to undermine or even destroy other conservative regimes in the region.

Nasser caused a great deal of panic in the West when he decided to welcome the USSR into Egypt by accepting Soviet economic and military assistance. The Americans were terrified that communist influence would spread from Egypt to the rest of the region. Thus the Middle East entered the Cold War, and the states which rose from colonial control found themselves forced to align with either the West or the East. Meanwhile, Nasser used his considerable popular appeal in the Arab world to agitate anti-West feeling throughout the region. Radio Cairo was his favourite tool for broadcasting his political manifesto beyond Egypt's borders, though he was also willing to pay other Arab newspapers to ensure they did his bidding. According to Miles Copeland, the Americans were surprised to discover that Nasser's payments to Lebanese media were actually more than those of the CIA.

In Lebanon in 1958 the United States invoked the Eisenhower doctrine for the first time, in response to Nasser's threat to the balance of power in the region. The Eisenhower doctrine stipulated that the United States would respond militarily to protect regimes threatened by communism. At the time, Lebanese Muslims were calling for Lebanon to join the United Arab Republic, Nasser's Arab nationalist project which saw Egypt and Syria ruled as one state. The US sent its Sixth Fleet into action, landing 14,000 marines in Beirut to support the beleaguered President Camille Chamoun. Nasser was furious at Chamoun for not breaking diplomatic relations with the West in the wake of the Suez crisis, and for his inclination towards the pro-West Baghdad Pact. Chamoun was a Christian and, like most of the Lebanese Christian community, favoured close ties with the West. Iraq's pro-West monarchy had just been toppled by an Arab nationalist coup and Chamoun was terrified that Lebanon's Sunni Muslims would do the same to him.

Keeping an eye on the reward of economic aid, Arab leaders were more than willing to dabble in Cold War politics for reasons of domestic prestige. The Arab League was split into two factions. Egypt and Syria led the nationalist and pro-Soviet regimes, who dubbed themselves 'progressive forces'. Nasser called the pro-West Arab states that were led by Saudi Arabia 'reactionary forces'.

The first inter-Arab military confrontation which broke out in adherence to the new paradigm was the now largely forgotten North Yemen civil war which began in 1962 and raged until 1970. At its height, Nasser committed 60,000 Egyptian troops to the conflict, in support of the Yemeni Republican forces who had staged a coup d'etat against the ruling Iman al Badr, the last King of Yemen. Meanwhile, the royalists were backed by Saudi Arabia and Jordan. The war resulted in huge loss of life on all sides, and left 26,000 Egyptian soldiers dead. The North Yemen civil war was one of a succession of coups and counter coups which left the Arab world in tatters, each often backed by various foreign interests. The North Yemen civil war involved many of the same ingredients present in Middle Eastern conflicts today: the first use of chemical weapons, superpower funding, neighbouring countries sending foreign fighters and a resolution little different from the start of the war.

Meanwhile in Washington, Eisenhower made way for a young charismatic President named John F Kennedy. Like Wilson before him, President Kennedy was an idealist who sought to modernise the Middle East. He was instrumental in abolishing slavery in Saudi Arabia and

Yemen in 1962. He was also an opponent of Israeli development of nuclear weapons; he believed they would start a nuclear arms race in the Middle East.

During the Nixon years, Henry Kissinger famously engaged in 'shuttle diplomacy,' travelling throughout the region to bring about a resolution to the Yom Kippur War of 1973 between Israel and a coalition of Arab states led by Egypt. All the while, the United States provided military assistance to Israel while the Soviets were doing the same for Egypt and Syria. After the ceasefire, Kissinger persuaded Israel to return land it had seized back to Egypt. Although US assistance to Israel included the largest military airlift in history, Kissinger's efforts to mitigate Egyptian territorial losses helped warm American-Egyptian relations, which had been cool since the 1950s. They also paved the way for further co-operation throughout the 1970s and beyond.

President Carter continued along this line after Sadat opened Egypt to the USA. The long sought peace treaty between Israel and Egypt, the first Arab state to open relations with Israel, was brokered between Sadat and Israeli Prime Minister Menachem Begin by Carter in the Camp David Accords, in 1978. However, for Sadat, peace with the Jewish state would come at a high price and ultimately cost him his life.

Sadat was a victim of his own propaganda. Throughout the early part of his presidency and during the Nasser years, Israel and the United States were consistently depicted as the enemies of Egypt. When he made peace with Israel and opened Egypt up to the USA he faced a massive public backlash, particularly from the Muslim Brotherhood whom he had initially encouraged. When Arab dictators tried to subtly balance public opinion, letting their media stir anti-Israeli and anti-American sentiment, they often failed.

President Bill Clinton continued Carter's work, presenting the United States as the only mediator capable of bringing together Israel and the Arabs. Clinton oversaw the signing of the Oslo Accords in 1993 and, when Yitzak Rabin and Yasser Arafat shook hands on the White House lawn that year, they stood on either side of Clinton. However, Clinton saw his efforts to bring peace to the region as one of his greatest failures as President. He desperately tried to bring about a lasting agreement between Arafat and Ehud Barak at the 2000 Camp David Summit, but negotiations came to nothing.

However, the USA's recent interest in the Middle East was not limited to mediating conflict. At times they have instigated conflict. The CIA's support of Arab fighters in Afghanistan against the Soviet Union remains a source of continued debate. Though many of the Arab fighters were themselves well-funded and had no need of US funding, it is certainly true that the United States funnelled arms to Afghanistan in the 1980s and tacitly encouraged Arab fighters to go to Afghanistan, once again seeing paramilitary Islam as an ally against godless communists. Numerous Islamist ideologues declared a jihad against the Soviet Union, with the approval of the USA.[1] Later, the *Mujahedeen*, those engaged in jihad, claimed victory after the Soviets fled Afghanistan. Two of the most famous Arab fighters in Afghanistan were, of course, Saudi Arabian Osama Bin Laden and Egyptian Ayman al Zawahiri. At the time, Bin Laden was himself a fundraiser for Arab paramilitary activity against the Russians and Zawahiri was one of a number of Egyptians who gravitated towards Bin Laden, creating a network around him. Many of these Egyptians had been active in radical Islamism since the 1970s, and found in Bin Laden a willing sponsor and spiritual leader. It was out of these groups that the loosely associated global network of terror cells that would come to be known as Al Qaeda gestated.

The radical Arab Islamists found fertile soil for their beliefs in the mountains of Afghanistan, and later Pakistan, Sudan and Yemen. They set up training camps, were well-armed and were able to canvas volunteers for suicide missions. This approach marked a new phase in international terrorism. Whereas previous terror attacks were often against the peoples and states who were in direct conflict with the terror groups involved (eg. Palestinian terror attacks against Israel), these new terrorists had new enemies, mostly the United States, whose actions were not affecting them directly but whose foreign policy in general was some kind of unbearable affront to them as Muslims.

The cumulative effect of these groups was the attack on the United States on 11 September 2001. The hijackers came from Saudi Arabia, the UAE and Lebanon, all states considered allies of the USA. A raft of

---

1 Declaring jihad against a foreign enemy in order to secure Islamic support is actually a tactic often used by various regimes in the past. The Ottoman Sultan declared a jihad against the infidels in the First World War, encouraged by his German allies. On the opposing side, Sharif Hussein of Mecca declared his jihad on Germany, encouraged by the British and their promises to make him King of Arabia.

copycat attacks followed, such as the 7/7 bombings in London, the train bombings in Madrid and the nightclub bombing in Indonesia. Again, these attacks were committed by civilians against civilians and justified in terms of an abstract clash of civilisations between Islam and the West.

Facing a stateless and militant enemy, whose motives are generally irrational, the United States was forced to use new tools to combat the threat. Later on, the War on Terror was regarded as too costly, politically unpopular back home and the source of irreparable damage to America's reputation in the Arab world. Large-scale military interventions, such as the invasion of Iraq, were eschewed in favour of soft power initiatives and military options based on intensive intelligence operations, culminating in surgically targeted killings. The culmination of this policy was the US Direct Public Diplomacy initiative and the ongoing use of drone missile strikes against targets in remote areas such as the mountains of Yemen or Pakistan.

The most famous soft power initiative was of course President Obama's speech in Cairo in 2009. However, much of the Arab world has come to criticise the speech as a set of empty promises, thanks to the continued struggles of the Obama administration to make any headway in the Israel-Palestinian problem, and Obama's sanctioned use of drone attacks in Islamic states.

In 2012, anti-US sentiment was further stoked when a video poking fun at the origins of Islam appeared on YouTube. Tempers flared and, encouraged by the usual Islamist ideologues, reached a point where a mob attacked the American embassy in Cairo, attempting to set it alight while tearing down the American flag and replacing it with the black flag of Islam. In neighbouring Libya, a similar scene was enacted, though with far worse consequences (which later turned out to be premeditated), ending with the murder of the American ambassador in Libya, which somewhat dampened American enthusiasm for the Arab Spring.

The US Direct Public Diplomacy Initiative

A Gallop poll in 2004 cited that a mere 6% of Egyptians have a favourable opinion of the USA. In contrast, a similar poll found that 70% of Americans have a favourable opinion of Egypt. A 2012 poll found that

71% of Egyptians oppose American aid to Egypt, and 74% oppose American funding of Egyptian civil society. Many Egyptians believe that the ultimate American goal in the region is to weaken Islam and the Muslim world. Such a belief is the result of a fusion of religion and politics, which has created an ideology that seeks to blame the outside world for its ills.

One of the developments in post 9/11 US foreign policy has been the attempt to exert the direct political influence inside Islamic states as well as using traditional diplomatic channels. This has meant engagement with the public beyond the purview of the state, in an effort to dissipate anti-American sentiment and promote democratic reform. The plan was for the Arab public itself to help develop its own civil society, which would then exert a more powerful influence on the state than the many millions of dollars directed straight into Arab military budgets.

The move initially met fierce resistance from the Arab regimes that had previously kept tight control of their media and been very resistant to active NGOs in their territories. Nevertheless, the USA continued to fund NGOs in Egypt and in other Arab states, much to the annoyance of the governments in question. When the SCAF transitional government arrested Americans and NGO workers funded by the USA involved in Direct Public Diplomacy, relations between the United States and the post-Mubarak Egypt were severely damaged.

Since so much of the Arabic media gave a platform to anti-West orators, the West also decided to invest in the Arabic media. The BBC had been doing this for many decades, projecting British cultural influence through its famous World Service language services, paid for by the British government rather than the BBC itself, though not since 2010. The original core staff of the Al Jazeera satellite broadcaster actually came from the original short-lived BBC Arabic TV channel. The Americans invested in their own satellite channel with Al Hurra TV in 2004, formed after the American invasion of Iraq in 2003. Since that time, the channel has been accused by Arabs of being pro-American and by Americans of having an anti-US bias. These efforts have also encouraged journalistic exchanges and further English language teaching in the region.

Support of NGOs played an important role in redressing the lack of secular resources in the Middle East at a time when Islamist organisations received millions of dollars from individuals in the Gulf States. The initiative was also meant to develop lasting relationships with future leaders in the Middle East, help sponsor them and encourage their access to the media. Occasionally this resulted in working with individuals who manipulated their position in order to receive foreign funding.

Despite the more open approach, the CIA is still heavily involved in the Middle East. The CIA budget is larger than that of entire countries in the Middle East. It would be naïve to underestimate the role it plays in exerting soft and hard power in the region in defence of US interests.

The United States faces an uphill battle in attracting different shades of Muslim youth, many of whom are alienated from their own governments and those of the West. More than 50% of the Middle Eastern population is under the age of 25. Many of them face bleak economic prospects and blame the US and Israel for their misfortunes. Even if the architects of their misfortune are their own governments, the blame ultimately resides with the United States, who will have variously supported or undermined those regimes in the past. Their understanding of modern democratic politics is limited, as they have never experienced democracy themselves.

In many Muslim countries, politicians either permit or quietly support imams who indulge in hate speech against the United States on a weekly basis in their mosques. Likewise, university activism is directed against the United States and Israel rather than against their own corrupt and incompetent governments. Even Hosni Mubarak, one of America's staunchest allies in the region, allowed the rhetoric in the mosques to go on, as well as all the anti-American agitprop in the media. The laissez faire approach to anti-Americanism was all the more noticeable given the Egyptian state's dim view of freedom of expression. It was a calculated political move; Hosni Mubarak's predecessor had been assassinated because he was seen as too close to the United States. Mubarak believed he could straddle public opinion by co-operating with the United States diplomatically while distancing himself from the USA publicly. Considering Mubarak was the subject of six assassination attempts and was eventually ousted from power, it was not very effective.

The United States also established informal channels of communication with the Muslim Brotherhood for pragmatic reasons. Though their natural allies in the region are the secularists and the liberals, they know that the Muslim Brotherhood represents a powerful trend in Egyptian public opinion and that they need to have a working relationship with them in order to have any influence at all.

In spite of such public diplomacy, the image of the United States has continually suffered in the Middle East. Its unwavering support for Israel and its various military interventions have been seen as a continuation of an aggressive American foreign policy. It must also be remembered that Sayd Qutb's Islamist philosophy, still resonant today among the Arab world's Islamist ideologues, was shaped by the time he spent in the USA. In some ways, modern Islamism is a reaction against American culture and economic power, so the military escapades and support of dictators could be deemed irrelevant. It must also be remembered that Arab politics of the 20th century was forged in the crucible of the anti-colonial movement, and now that the USA has taken on the mantel of symbolic colonial villain that was once held by Britain, France and the Ottomans, it bears the brunt of nationalist anger.

In the modern Middle East, many Arabs are consequently far more receptive to countries like Russia and China, who are today attempting to invest in the region. The USSR, despite its "godless" nature, was a staunch ally of the Arab nationalist regimes, particularly Syria, and provided many Arab states with military assistance in their wars against Israel.

Today, Syria is facing civil war and a general political breakdown. The jihadists emerging from the conflict will be as hostile to the West and the USA as they always have been. The response of the USA to the Arab Spring protest was muted, which means that the USA cannot expect allies from among those movements or in the new governments which will ensue. Indeed, though the USA played a vital role in ousting Gaddafi in 2011, its ambassador in Benghazi was murdered by Islamist radicals in 2012.

The USA has a chequered history in the Middle East and cannot deny that it has repeatedly interfered with internal affairs in the region. As long as myths about American ambitions persist and, as long as Islamist politics remain popular, the USA will need to work hard to win support in the Arab world.

CHAPTER 10

THE ARAB LEAGUE

Throughout its 70-year existence, the Arab League has served no useful purpose. Each Arab state, whether large or small, pursues its purely self-interested policies. Despite protestations to the contrary, many states in the Arab League actually have very little in common with one another. The Arab League has also wasted billions that would have been better spent on alleviating starvation and poverty in some parts of the Arab world.

Arab legal systems range from almost medieval Islamic courts to Western-style judiciaries. Some countries, such as Morocco and Algeria, have implemented a moratorium on capital punishment, others regularly hang their criminals and some even retain stoning on their books. Though some have not had an execution for years, not one Arab state has actually abolished the death penalty, a measure that would be very much in step with modernity.

Their economies vary enormously. The oil-producing Gulf States count themselves among the wealthiest on the planet, while countries such as Yemen are some of the world's poorest. Some of these countries retain monarchies that have been in power for centuries, whilst others consider themselves nationalist republics, though sometimes retaining the idea of dynastic succession for their leaders. Other countries, such as Lebanon, claim to have parliamentary democracy, albeit one divided along sectarian lines. In terms of education, Kuwait has an adult literacy rate of 99% while, at the bottom of the table, Somalia can barely claim 55%.

The traditional vernacular of citizens of the Arab League states, irrespective of religion, is the Arabic language, or to be more accurate, their own regional dialect of Arabic. This regional organisation of Arabic-speaking states seems redundant in the modern age. During the Arab Spring, it did not make any meaningful resolutions or interventions and was merely used as a rubberstamp for the UN and Western powers to intervene in Libya.

The League is defective; citizens of its member states share their language, intermingled with bits of history and bits of religion, though they can claim no more cohesion than any group of neighbouring countries in any part of the world. On the contrary, there is more infighting and subversion between Arab states than most other regional blocs, such as the Hispanic nations or the countries of south-east Asia.

The Syrian civil war signalled the end of the Arab nationalist myth of a unified Arab people. The Arab League became irrelevant to the region's political calculations, while the regional players in the conflict turned out to be Iran, Qatar, Saudi Arabia, Turkey and Hezbollah in Lebanon.

Certainly, the Arab League has never been a unifying concept; on the contrary, it has proven time and again to be an obstacle impeding inter-Arab relations. The Arabic-speaking nations are wildly diverse in culture and outlook. The only area that can be considered truly "Arab" is the Arabian Peninsula. In fact, their main point of unity is their dictatorial character. Not a single Arab League state can be considered truly democratic, so they have struggled to deal effectively with major political issues and crises.

****

The Arab League is based in Cairo and its offices are staffed by mid level diplomats and bureaucrats who collect large government salaries. In order to justify its existence, the League holds periodic meetings, usually annually, though sometimes not for several years at a time. Since the year 2000, they have been fairly regular, taking place in late March every year, with the exception of 2011. These meetings have no clear political purpose. The summits are often blemished by petty regional rivalries, and attendance is often marred by a string of snubs and boycotts. Disagreements often break out over the matter of who will chair the summits. They seldom end with meaningful resolutions to alleviate poverty or present united political fronts on topical issues. During the initial phases of the Arab Spring, in 2011, the states did not even meet, preferring instead to handle their own internal uprisings.

For a long time, the Arab League has been dubbed a "club for Arab dictators." Despite the self-importance of the leaders, the organisation actually means very little to the typical 'Arab man in the street.' Issues pertaining to human rights are never discussed. When the Arab League came to deal with the Arab Spring, it did so purely in terms of the various states' foreign political agendas, rather than as a means of fulfilling public aspirations for political freedom.

When major events rock the Arab world, the League does little, and other international organisations, or states, take action. Throughout the Syrian conflict, the United Nations provided the response and the forum for potential discussion, rather than the Arab League. During the Iraqi invasion of Kuwait in 1990, the Arab League was paralysed as various states sided with Iraq or Kuwait, and others stayed neutral.

****

Perhaps unsurprisingly, the idea for an Arab League did not originate in any of the Arab states. From the early to mid-20th century, many Arab states had very little to do with one another and few seemed to have any appetite for a political commonwealth. The Arab League was a British invention, developed during the Second World War as a means of gaining Arab support against the Axis powers. Previously, the British had promised to help form a united Arab state during the First World War to gain Arab allies against the Ottoman Empire, a promise which came to nothing.

Historically, the great powers sub-divided Asia into different, often overlapping, geographical categories such as the Far East, the Near East, the Orient, the Subcontinent, etc. The concept of a single Middle East geopolitical unit originated in the British Foreign Office during the 19th century, and the term was first coined popularly in 1902, by the American strategist Alfred Mahan. In recent times, the term has become conflated with the "Arab world." With the discovery of oil in Arabia, the Arab world suddenly became of vital significance to world powers, whereas interest in the region had previously been reserved for the colonial nations, particularly Britain, as the Suez Canal and the Trucial states (today known as the United Arab Emirates) were vital stopovers on the passage to India.

The Victorian British Field Marshal Lord Kitchener saw the Arabic-speaking parts of the Ottoman Empire as a potential buffer zone to protect the imperial British interests in India and Asia, which have significant non-Arab Muslim populations. Kitchener also understood the sentimental influence that Arab peoples had on the non-Arabic speaking Muslims, due to the privilege afforded to Arabic-speakers within Islam.

The Ottomans encouraged pan-Islamism in order to keep their Empire together, granting the title of Caliph to their Sultan, Sharif Hussein of Mecca, who initiated the Arab revolt against the Ottomans in the First World War. King Faisal of Iraq harboured ambitions to become the King of the Arabs and even asked Britain to recognise him as Caliph of the Muslim world as a reward for supporting Britain against the Ottoman Empire (though it was the Ottomans who had appointed him to his post in Mecca in the first place).

The British, through Sir Henry McMahon, High Commissioner in Egypt, encouraged the pan-Arab movement in order to provoke sedition against the Turks throughout the Arabic-speaking Ottoman provinces. In 1915, McMahon and Sharif Hussein wrote a series of letters to each other in what came to be known as the McMahon-Hussein correspondence. In the exchange, the British would promise the Arabs a state of their own in return for an alliance against the Ottomans during the First World War. In the end, the British reneged on their promises and divided the Arab lands of the Fertile Crescent between themselves and the French.

By the Second World War the British were again making noises about an Arab political union. Sir Miles Lampson, a High Commissioner in Cairo at the time, suggested a form of "Federation between the Arab States," formed under British guidance, in order to preserve British interests in the region. At the start of the war, in May 1941, British Foreign Secretary Anthony Eden issued a statement proposing that the United Kingdom "approved strengthening the economic, cultural and political ties between the Arab countries."

Though the architecture of the Arab League was designed by the British, the idea of an Arab League was first adopted by Nouri al Said of

Iraq, who discussed the idea with Nahas Pasha, Prime Minister of Egypt in 1943, with a view to creating an Arab forum. In 1944, Nahas, the leader of the largest Arab state, invited the independent Arab states to Alexandria for a summit, where they formulated a protocol for co-operation and solidarity between the Arab nations. The Arab League was eventually formed in 1945, comprising Egypt, Iraq, Lebanon, Saudi Arabia, Syria and Transjordan. Yemen joined a few months later. Over the years, the Arab League would expand to 22 members, encompassing all the Arabic-speaking states, including Somalia, and the tiny sub-equatorial island of Comoros.

There was never a major tangible desire for pan-Arab self-determination among the former Ottoman Arabic-speaking provinces. Even the Greater Arab state foreseen by the likes of TE Lawrence and Emir Faisal ibn Hussein (of the Arab revolt) only encompassed Greater Syria – today's Jordan, Israel, Palestine, Lebanon and Syria – and what is now Iraq. Egypt had been seen as a distinct cultural territory for centuries, North Africa and the Maghreb were very much in the Francophone sphere of influence and Arabia was the domain of the House of Saud.

One example of an ill-judged political union from within the Arab League was the United Arab Republic of 1958 in which Egypt and Syria were merged and run as a single country. Nasser himself had never even visited Syria until 1958. Syrians and Egyptians had little interaction with one another. At that time tourism between Arab states was all but unheard of and social links between the nations tended to exist for the privileged few rather than for the masses.

At the height of the Cold War, many of the core Arab League states tilted towards the communist bloc, thus becoming a threat to the Islamic regimes as well as to the West. The Gulf States, however, have always been more open to the West. Such political disunity further impedes the Arab League's usefulness.

When political crises rock the Arabic-speaking world, as they do with alarming regularity, the Arab League has been ineffective at finding a solution. This is particularly apparent when one member state decides to invade another. Nasser's military interference in Yemen in 1962 left the League divided and ineffectual, just as when Iraq threatened to invade Kuwait in 1961, and when it actually did so in 1990.

****

After the Second World War, sovereign Arab states began to emerge from the ashes of colonial provinces and mandates. At the core of Arab state-building projects lay an ambiguity. Many of these states had until very recently been colonial vassal states, and for many of them the concept of citizenship had yet to be settled. Many Arab nations were at varying levels of development and were deemed incompatible on economic and demographic grounds. Some states still retained tribal systems as a foundation for political identity, and had no national allegiance based on the concept of a nation where citizens were equal under the law. In some Arab states, the remnants of these tribal systems still have influence to this day.

There has been no attempt at institutional harmonisation; their legal and monetary systems are fundamentally incompatible. The currency of each country is different and not easily interchangeable. Some use the Persian dinar, some use the local pound, while the West Bank and Gaza prefer the Israeli Shekel. There is no economic parity between many Arab countries. In Dubai, the police use Ferraris for patrol cars while, in Sudan just under half the population lives in poverty.

The ethnicity of the Arab League is similarly complex. The Arabic-speaking peoples contain a myriad of ethnic identities. The Sudanese are seen as closer to Africa (so much so that South Sudan seceded from the North in 2012 to become a Christian African state), while many Egyptians regard themselves as ethnically distinct from the Arabs of Arabia and the Levant. Meanwhile, many Lebanese Christians (Maronites) do not believe they share their ancestry with Muslim Arabs and many North Africans regard themselves as Berber. The variation in ethnicity is not necessarily as important as the vast cultural differences that result.

North Africa is culturally a very different place from Arabia. Their ethnicities and lifestyles are totally foreign, and historically, North Africans have been an intrinsic part of Mediterranean history for centuries, whereas the Gulf States developed from nomadic desert tribes, for example. Many of these states have also been shaped by decades, or in some cases centuries, of foreign colonialism. For instance, culturally and economically, Algeria has more in common with France than it does with Yemen.

It would be more accurate to rename the region 'the Arabic-speaking world,' rather than 'the Arab world.' Like Latin, standardised literary Arabic only exists in its written form. The spoken Arabic language itself is subject to numerous regional dialects and local inflections. Some of these dialects are so varied that they could almost be classed as different languages and rendering conversation between, say, a Tunisian and a Yemeni, for example, almost impossible.

The question of women's rights is difficult and controversial in many Arab countries. Saudi Arabia is the last country in the world not to grant women the vote, although King Abdullah has promised that women will be able to vote in municipal elections in 2015. Most of the Gulf countries did not grant the vote until the 21st century, with Qatar leading the way in 1997. However, women were granted the vote in the Arab republics by the 1960s. The question of the vote is moot however because in many of these countries women and men can vote but their vote will not influence the outcome and lead to a change of government. They are able to vote for local councils or semi-elected parliaments.

Freedom of movement, often a central tenet of many political unions, is frequently obstructed within the Arab League. Arab citizens often face complex barriers as they travel, live and work across the region and can occasionally be subject to deportation as a result of their government's foreign policy. Often, those who travel for work between the Arab states have their passports withheld, their movements controlled and many have no employment rights at all.

In December 2001, Freedom House concluded that "Islamic and Arab nations had diverged with the rest of the world on democracy.... Since the early 1970s when the third major wave of democratisation began, the Islamic world and, in particular, its Arab core has seen little evidence of improvement in political openness, respect for human rights or transparency." The report went on to rank Iraq, Libya, Saudi Arabia, Sudan and Syria as among the most restrictive nations in the world.

Just over a decade later, that same organisation reflected on the Arab Spring in September 2012 and declared "the gains made in the Arab world during Arab Spring are very fragile and in its chaotic aftermath leaders may slip back into authoritarian rule...Bahrain slipped backward, and Egypt edged up only slightly." The report concluded "it is unclear whether the popular dismissal of old models of authoritarianism will translate into enduring public support for novice representative government and contentious institutional reforms."

In Freedom House's Democracy Index of 2011, the Middle East and North Africa ranked as the least free region in the world, scoring 3.62 out of 10, after sub-Saharan Africa, scoring 4.32.

The fault lines within the organisation are deep, perhaps too deep for it to survive as a credible organisation. The failure of the organisation is all the more apparent given the comparative success of similar political institutions, such as the British Commonwealth (also set up by the British to retain global influence) and the African Union. The African Union member states overlap with those of the Arab League, and have been far more active in attempting to alleviate political problems in these states. For example, the African Union sent peacekeepers (albeit poorly funded and few in number) into Sudan during the ongoing Darfur crisis, while the Arab League, which includes member states of considerably larger wealth, did nothing, although Qatar took it upon itself to unilaterally attempt to mediate peace talks.

****

The Gulf Co-operation Council (GCC)

The GCC is the only successful regional union in the Arabic-speaking world. Its united foreign and security policies have been successful and were arrived at totally independently of the Arab League.

The GCC (officially the Co-operation Council for Arab States of the Gulf) was established in 1981 to boost economic co-operation between member states through collective security policy and economic union so as to form a meaningful and effective regional bloc. In many ways the GCC has sought to emulate the European Union; it has its common market and plans to adopt a single currency. In the Gulf States, large standing armies are out of the question because they either do not have the necessary numbers or are fearful of military takeover. Ultimately, the GCC depends on the United States for security, although it does tend to possess a small but hi-tech air force. The GCC has proved a successful Arab bloc that, in practical terms, has no need of the Arab League. In 1991, it presented a united front during the Iraqi invasion of Kuwait, successfully lobbying United States to help expel Iraqi troops from the country. In 2011, fearful of the spread of the Arab Spring into their undemocratic regimes, the GCC sent Saudi troops to suppress the unrest inside Bahrain.

In terms of foreign policy, the GCC has consistently presented a united position against Syria and recently agreed an $8 billion package for the reconstruction of Yemen. Regarding Syria, the Gulf monarchies have always mistrusted the Arab republics, and will be eager to ease Assad out of power. As for Yemen, the small country at the bottom of the Arabian Peninsula is a major security concern for the GCC, acting as a hotbed for jihadi terrorism which could easily be directed at GCC states. Yemen is also the major route by which drug and people smugglers find their way into Saudi Arabia.

The remaining Arab monarchies, Jordan and Morocco, have both been invited and provisionally accepted into the GCC, which would make the council less a regional council, more a union of kingdoms.

****

During a conversation with a former Secretary General of the Arab League, HE Ahmed Asmat Abdel Maguid, the author asked why none of the previous Secretary Generals ever leave a legacy. Maguid replied that none of them ever had any voice and each Arab state has power of veto, making meaningful decision-making impossible.

Arab League resolutions are rarely implemented fully and effectively, as each state has its own agenda and is unwilling to forgo its own national interests for some sort of greater Arab good. The major challenges facing the Arab League in recent years have been in Sudan, Bahrain and Syria. The uprising in Bahrain has proved immensely damaging for the tiny Gulf State. However, Bahrain has the staunch support of Saudi Arabia which will not allow the democratic/protest movement to unseat the Bahraini royal family. As a result, the Arab League has done little to address the matter, aside from criticising Iranian propaganda against the country.

The Syrian Uprising has developed into a civil war in which Qatar and Saudi Arabia are supporting the Islamist rebels with arms and money. In 2011 the Arab League sent a team into Syria to monitor possible human rights abuses by the Syrian government. The mission was somewhat undermined when it transpired that Sudan's previous Head of Military Intelligence, a man who has faced allegations of complicity in genocide and other war crimes, led the commission. This problem will arise time and again as the authoritarian and undemocratic nature of member states will continue to undermine its credibility as a body capable of upholding international law and bringing about conflict resolution. In 2012, the Arab League has awarded the Syrian National Coalition Syria's seat on the Arab League. Should the civil war continue without resolution, however, the Arab League will be forced into a humiliating re-recognition of Syria, particularly as the SNC actually carries little weight within Syria itself.

The largest human rights disaster in the Middle East in the last decade has been the conflict in Darfur, Sudan, between the Sudanese government, pro-Arab militia and non-Arab Sudanese separatists. As mentioned previously, despite the incredible losses of civilian life, in the hundreds of thousands, the Arab League has done very little to intervene. In 2012, Israel launched an air strike against Sudan, bombing a missile factory in the country. The attack was not reported in the Arab media, and the other Arab states made no protest, nor did Sudan call a meeting of the Arab League, realising it would be a waste of time. The attack was forgotten in official circles and media within a week.

The one issue on which the Arab League has presented a united front has been Israel. The Palestinian Liberation Organisation was actually established at the 1964 Arab League summit in Cairo. The Arab League dutifully condemns Israeli attacks against the Palestinians and one of the major upheavals of the Arab League was the expulsion of Egypt in 1978, in the wake of the Egyptian peace treaty with Israel.

However, in terms of actual tangible co-operation, aside from obligatory statements of solidarity, the Arab League states often refused to back each other against the state of Israel. For instance, during the 1948 Arab-Israeli war, Egypt planned an independent Palestinian state in Gaza but its efforts were undermined by King Abdullah of Transjordan. The King ordered his British military chief, General Glubb, not to help the Egyptians as he annexed the West Bank into his territory. Egypt effectively lost the war on 15 October 1948 as Israel increased its forces in the southern front, encircling the Egyptian army. Again Abdullah made it clear to General Glubb that he "had no desire to help the Egyptians."

From the moment of Israel's creation, the Arab League supposedly issued a blanket economic boycott of the new state. However, in reality the boycott has not been properly enforced, and is particularly ineffective now that Egypt and Jordan have made peace with Israel. The Arab League boycott did not prevent the Israeli economy from developing to a Western standard. Meanwhile, many Arab economies, excluding the Gulf States, have struggled to cope with their expanding populations and their provision of public services has been poor. Today both Jordan and Egypt have normalised relations with Israel and many Palestinians work within the Israeli economic system, rather than with neighbouring Arab states. In fact, the Palestinian territories are more integrated into the Israeli system than many Arab neighbours want to admit.

****

The importance of the Arab League has often been superseded by countries within the Arab world. Egypt was very much the powerhouse of the Middle East. It was home to the largest population, an economic hub for the region and very much a cultural and religious centre of the Islamic world. Nasser exerted his political will on other countries in the region, making Egypt the centre of political power. Cairo became a "collecting centre" for disaffected politicians, discontents and subversives in the Arab world, especially under Nasser. Many were used by his propaganda machine, including a young Saddam Hussein.

However, although once the granary of vast empires, and the pivot upon which they turned, Egypt has been overtaken by Qatar in terms of shaping of the Arab Spring. Such a state of affairs is ironic, considering Egypt actually had an uprising and Qatar, an undemocratic monarchy, did not. The Qataris seek to influence the politics in the rest of the region by using their vast fossil fuel income as leverage. That income is applied in various different ways, from direct government aid to influence via the media, specifically, the phenomenally popular Al Jazeera satellite network. The Qatari political mandate is not consistent however. Although they attempted to mediate a peace deal over the Darfur crisis in 2009, the Qataris were one of the major contributors to the violence in Syria, through the provision of weapons and funds to the Syrian rebels.

As things stand, several Arab states are facing disintegration along ethnic or religious lines, as happened in Sudan, Iraq and Lebanon. Syria, Libya and Yemen are the next most likely candidates for general political breakdown over the next decade.

Each Arab state adopts its own peculiar closed political systems, without a proper constitution, social policy or modern judicial system. Despite their large populations and low labour costs, they have no major agricultural or industrial base. With the single exception of fossil fuels, exports are low.

Development in the Arab world has been hampered by corruption, mismanagement and authoritarianism. Defeat in the Six Day War against Israel in 1967 had ramifications still felt to this day. It effectively ended the dream of pan-Arab nationalism, and preceded the phenomenon of political Islam and its violent cousin, the Jihadi movement.

To bring about reform, the Arabic-speaking world must look to similar regions in the world and try to emulate successful policies and unions. The Spanish-speaking world would be a useful model to begin with, being fairly analogous in terms of shared language, religion, etc. Latin American countries have made broad advances in areas such as public health and education in the later part of the 20th century, despite many suffering from dictatorship in the decades beforehand. Although there is still some way to go in Latin America, the prospect of war between states has diminished considerably, which is not the case in the Middle East, as various Arab states compete for influence over the region, interfering in each other's internal affairs. One reason for such improvements in Latin America is the fact that many South American nations have been in economic and political union with each other over the past two decades. Mercusor, which encompasses the South American nations to the east of the Andes, has proved remarkably effective at encouraging co-operation between nations that were once rivals. In 2008, the Latin American states established the Union of South American Nations in an effort to eventually create a political and monetary union in the mould of the European Union.

In order to secure a prosperous future, the Arab League in its present form must be disbanded and a new Greater Middle East and North Africa initiative must be realised, taking into account modern politicly reality by including Israel and other non-Arabic speaking key states, such as

Turkey, Iran, Malta and Cyprus. Such a suggestion is not as radical as it may initially seem. Both Jordan and Egypt recognise Israel. In 2007, the Arab League even sent a delegation to Israel. Although they speak different Arabic dialects, the north African states have very little else in common with the Arab segment of the Arab world so it would be prudent for North Africa to have its own forum, modelled on the GCC.

Only with realistic international union can the Arab world work together towards peace and prosperity, rather than using the current model: an externally devised grouping which is as much a forum for rivalry and conflict as it is for co-operation.

CHAPTER 11

THE ARAB MEDIA

The Arab Spring was a false dawn for democratic freedom. Although several authoritarian regimes in the Middle East have crumbled, freedom of expression remains particularly restricted in these countries where any kind of political and religious dissent is regarded as treachery. The media in countries like Egypt and Tunisia are navigating a dangerous path as they adapt to their new governments who may seek to tame the media, as their predecessors did. Egypt closed down 25 television outlets which opposed the military-backed government.

In terms of sheer number of broadcasters and publishers, the Arab media landscape is vast and confusing. In his book, *(Un) Civil War of Words*, Professor Mamoun Fandy refers to almost 700 satellite TV stations and argues that, despite the numerous stations competing against each other, the Arab media remains inherently political rather than commercial. That is, the Arab media is operated and controlled by various political, religious, and ethnic forces which use it as agitprop for their own ends.

Professor Fandy argues that because of the authoritarian setting in which they operate, the Arab media are very different to their Western counterparts and cannot be looked at in the same way. The Arab media can only be understood in terms of the social and political context in which they operate. Nearly all of these media outlets, affiliated to either government or opposition, are subject to rigorous oversight and restrictions by the Arab regimes; many simply serve as weapons in the foreign and domestic conflicts in which those nations are engaged. Professor Fandy also points out that Arab media are actually granted more freedom in occupied areas than under their own governments. It is accepted that reporting from the West Bank, Gaza Strip, and occupied Iraq was more vigorous and more critical of government than that of the bureaux in Damascus or Cairo.

Over the past 60 years, Arab regimes, aware of the power of the media, have used their newspapers, radio and TV stations to manipulate public opinion. Many Arab media outlets were traditionally based in Cairo and Lebanon. Following the Lebanese civil war in the early 1980s, many relocated to London. Unlike other foreign language or ethnically focussed newspapers printed in London, the London based Arabic media do not concern themselves with the quarter of a million Arabs who live in the UK. Poles, Pakistanis, etc, have newspapers concerned with their community, but Britain's Arab media tend to concern themselves with events in the Arab nations.

Throughout the 20th century political attitudes in the Arab world have changed and the Arab media have reflected this. Early in the 20th century there was a trend among the youth towards communism. During the 1930s and 1940s, many young Arabs came to admire European fascism. Of particular appeal was the anti-Semitism coming from Germany and the fact that the Axis powers were fighting the hated colonial powers, namely the British and the French.

Over the years, the dictatorships realised that censorship was of paramount importance, in order to inhibit the spread of seditious ideas. To this end, they monopolised the media and reserved the right to appoint its editors, all the while prohibiting other forms of political expression.

Co-option of the intelligentsia was also an important tactic. By bringing public intellectuals into the regimes, and providing them with a platform to speak, they would prove useful allies, and would have been far more damaging to the regime if they had remained outside it.

Throughout the second half of the 20th century, the Arab republics presented themselves as populist regimes, at the service of their people. As these governments were invariably dictatorships, it was necessary to manipulate public opinion in order to gain support from the populace, and marginalise opponents. The Arab Spring has changed the political dynamic, though the factions which now dominate simply exert their control in much the same way as the previous regimes did. For instance, Islamist input into the Arab media has greatly increased both inside and outside Egypt. Islamic TV stations have exploded across the Arab satellite networks since the early 1990s, playing host to various preachers and ideologues. The Arab regimes realise that in order to survive, the public needs a space in which to air its grievances, so the state media exists as a "safe, tame, virtual space" where certain individuals can express their views without threatening the established order.

After the Egyptian defeat to Israel in 1967, the secular Nasser established a radio station dedicated to recitation of the Quran, even though he had spent a great deal of effort establishing a secular regime, and courting communists in the region. Secular Arab dictators like Saddam Hussein and Colonel Gaddafi also understood the power and appeal of Islamic rhetoric, such as when Saddam famously added an "Allah Akbar" to the Iraqi tricolour flag or when Gadaffi televised the conversion to Islam of President Bokassa of the Central African Republic, apparently at his hands.

The Rise of the Saudi Media

Saudi Arabia is arguably the most powerful Arab state and certainly the wealthiest. Consequently, they have used the power afforded them by their petrodollars to spread their influence across the region, most potently through the Saudi-owned and operated media. The Saudi media empire began with the London-based daily newspapers *Asharq Al Awsat* (the Middle East) and *Al Hayat* (Life). *Asharq Al Awsat* was founded in 1978, and first made its name through its intense hostility to the Camp David Peace Accords. President Sadat was so incensed by the criticism that he publically lambasted the Cairo bureau chief during a press conference, accusing the paper of being a tool of Saudi propaganda. Since that time, the paper has become possibly the most influential in the region; by 2004 it had a circulation of around a quarter of a million, although circulation figures for these papers are notoriously difficult to calculate. The paper has a reputation for censoring journalists overtly critical of Saudi Arabia and for not reporting stories that reflect badly on Saudi Arabia, such as the homosexual Saudi Prince who murdered his servant in London in 2010. The paper was also forced to admit in the High Court in London in 2008 that it printed false stories concerning meetings between Qatari and Israeli government officials. The incident was one of a series in the great competition for regional influence between Qatar and Saudi Arabia, more of which will be discussed in more detail later.

Al Hayat is the newspaper's main competitor. Established in Lebanon in 1946, the Saudi Prince Khalid bin Sultan bought the paper in 1988, rebranded it and brought it to London. Under a diverse editorial team (still retaining many Lebanese Christians, as well as other minorities) the paper gained a reputation for iconoclasm and as a platform for viewpoints across the political spectrum, from secular liberals to hardline Islamists. Though famous for its scoops and its coverage, like its rival, the paper is never too critical of Saudi Arabia and discourages investigation into Saudi affairs. In spite of this, the paper has twice been banned in Saudi Arabia; once in 2002, after it printed an open letter from American intellectuals defending the moral foundation of the War on Terror, and again in 2007 after a series of articles criticising the Saudi government's response to a series of mysterious camel deaths. Professor Fandy also points out that *Al Hayat* employs a number of Lebanese journalists who have provided the paper with a great deal of anti-Syrian rhetoric. Such a position is fine for the paper to take as it does not conflict with the foreign policy of the Saudi government.

The satellite broadcaster MBC (Middle East Broadcasting Corporation) was founded in 1991, and was the first independent free to air 24-hour Arab satellite broadcaster. Officially, it is privately owned and its shareholders remain anonymous, though it is an open secret in Arab media circles that it is owned by the Saudi royal family. MBC is a broadcasting giant in the Middle East, and consists of around a dozen channels and websites, including 24 hour music channels, a channel dedicated to Hollywood films and a channel dedicated to women. One popular women's programme on MBC 1 is *Kalam Nawaem* (Sweet Talk) an Arabic version of "The View" a popular American format where four female presenters discuss women's issues for over an hour. The programme covers topics deemed so controversial in Saudi Arabia, such as women's suffrage and sexual relations, that MBC occasionally censors the programme itself.

The Saudis also fund a variety of religious television channels, the two most prominent of which are *Iqraa* (Read) and *Al Risala* (The message). These channels are sometimes subject to criticism for broadcasting radical and anti-Semitic content. Prior to the rise of Saudi broadcasters, the Arab media was dominated by the nationalist outlets belonging to the Arab republics. The religious angle of the Saudi media worked to counterbalance secular nationalism, an ideology with which Saudi Arabia had been in conflict for some time. They also served to promote the particular brand of Sunni Wahhabism to which Saudi Arabia seems so attached and intent on spreading throughout the Islamic world.

Over the past two decades the Saudi media have been tremendously successful, in part because of the inexhaustible chequebook from which they draw funds, but also because Arab Islamism has successfully portrayed Arab nationalism as a foreign ideology imposed by Western powers.

Al Jazeera and Al Arabiya

In recent years, Qatar's Al Jazeera has become the most popular news network in the Arab world, and the best-known globally. It has been so successful that it even launched its own English language version and spurred Saudi Arabia to develop a competitor, Al Arabiya. Al-Arabiya has also won praise for its investigative reporting. However, the channel has never been able to shake off the perception that it merely operates as the media operations wing of Saudi foreign policy. The dismissal of reporters for negative reporting on Gulf business interests (Emirates airline, for example) and for criticising the channel's editorial line has not helped in this respect. Nevertheless, Al Arabiya has made huge advances in the Arabic media since it was launched in 2003, and it reached a new level of international credibility with President Obama's interview in 2009.

However, Al Arabiya has yet to emerge from the shadow of its main competitor, Al Jazeera. Al Jazeera (The Island) was launched in 1996, largely by transplanting staff from the abandoned BBC Arabic TV station. The original BBC Arabic service was forced to close after the Saudi portion of its funding was withheld following the broadcast of a documentary on human rights, or lack thereof, in Saudi Arabia. After the BBC service closed, the Emir of Qatar stepped in, providing the new station with millions of dollars of funding and a base in Qatar. The creation of the network and its immense funding was a response by the Qataris to the domination of the Saudi media. Though ostensibly allies, Qatar has long feared being subsumed by Saudi Arabia and fiercely protects its independence. One of its tactics in this regard is the projection of soft power through Al Jazeera. Since its founding the network has won many admirers who respect its editorial independence and willingness to tackle controversial issues.

Al Jazeera made its name with a series of provocative reports on Arab governments, and still has a reputation for tenacious journalism. Although it has upset many governments – perhaps most famously that of the United States during the Iraq war and subsequent occupation – the channel will not run stories critical of its benefactors, the Qatari royal family.

Al Jazeera has also provided a platform for Islamist ideologues, and propagated Islamist politics throughout the region. For instance, Yusuf Al Qaradawi, possibly the most popular Islamist preacher in the world, is a frequent contributor to the twice weekly programme, Al Sharia wa al Haya (Sharia and Life). The programme is one of the network's most popular, and gives Qaradawi an audience of tens of millions. Al Jazeera's viewing figures are in the 40 and 60 million range.

Qaradawi is famously known as a self-appointed "global mufti," and uses the programme as an opportunity to reiterate many of the fatwas he issues with little regard to the traditional clerical bodies. These fatwas concern anything from wife beating (acceptable, but only if done lightly) to whether it is permissible to kill in legitimate struggle.

Qaradawi is a proponent of the Muslim Brotherhood in his native Egypt, however he actually lives in Qatar, and has done so since 1961, in exile from the Nasser regime. Most recently, Qaradawi used the programme to aggressively promote Egypt's Islamist-designed constitution. Qaradawi, like his sponsors the Qatari government, have wholeheartedly encouraged violent uprising during the conflicts associated with the Arab Spring. During the uprising in Libya, he issued a fatwa "To the officers and the soldiers who are able to kill Muammar Gaddafi, to whichever of them is able to shoot him with a bullet and to free the country and [God's] servants from him, I issue this fatwa: Do it." He also declared that it was permissible to kill civilians in Syria, if they were working for the Assad regime.

Al Jazeera and Al Arabiya are locked in a battle to undermine each other's national sponsor. Al Jazeera will frequently report negatively on Saudi Arabia, highlighting human rights abuses in the country and provide airtime to Saudi opposition figures. Saudi Arabia denies Al Jazeera staff access to Saudi Arabia and will also use its newspapers to attack Qatar. For instance, a 2005 American study showed Al Jazeera had a 65% audience share, compared with 34% for Al Arabiya. The study was subsequently attacked in *Asharq Al Awsat* as an incidence of pro-Al Jazeera bias.

Al Arabiya, on the other hand, encourages its reporters to undermine Qatar on air. Any story that shows the Qatari royal family in a negative light will do. Al Arabiya also tries to undermine Qatar in the court of Arab public opinion by highlighting Qatar's close relationship with the United States, and hinting at alleged contacts between Qatar and Israel, similar to the stories in the Saudi-owned newspapers.

The rivalry between the two is often expressed by their different coverage of the same events. In 2006, Al Jazeera described the Israel-Hezbollah war as "a pre-planned plot against Hezbollah," while Al Arabiya was far more critical of Hezbollah, calling Hezbollah's actions an "uncalculated risk." Saudi Arabia has consistently been opposed to the Shiite organisation in Lebanon, and the coverage of its news channel simply reflects this stance.

****

In decades past, many Arab journalists were pan-Arab nationalists and their output was consequently filtered through the perspectives of Nasserism, Baathism, Arab socialism, etc. Today, one of the pervading political outlooks is Islamism, and journalists likewise propagate different brands of political Islam through their work. Journalists are free to pursue their political agendas, as long as they do not interfere with or contradict that of their sponsors. The rise of pan-Arab satellite media has brought renewed questions of impartiality, considering the editorial slant of the broadcasters' sponsors, i.e. the Gulf States. Many liberals and intellectuals in the Arab world are denied meaningful airtime compared to Islamists, who suit the Gulf States' political agenda.

The Arab media has for a long time been subject to criticism for its professional integrity. The editorial outlooks of Arab publications and broadcasters are not only limited to the states and factions that control them but also the influence of powerful journalists within the staff.

There are many Islamist sympathisers within Al Jazeera, resulting in, for example, the network giving more prominence to statements by Hamas or Islamic Jihad, rather than Mahmoud Abbas, or other officials from the Palestinian Authority. The channel has also been a proponent of the Muslim Brotherhood in Egypt and Nahda (a similar Islamist movement) in Tunisia.

The Arabic media in general is more tolerant of Islamist government than its Western counterpart. Groups such as the Al Aqsa Martyrs Brigade or Hezbollah are often given more credence than in the West, and similarly there is less criticism of atrocities committed by these groups. Such organisations are universally described as terrorist within the Western media but many in the Arabic media see such groups simply as other political actors or rival combatants in war.

The national or ethnic background of journalists also leads to a bias in their work, which is amplified in the pan-Arab media landscape. Pan-Arab networks are often based in London or the Gulf and therefore import journalists from various Arab countries, and those journalists import their local prejudices.

Similarly, Palestinians are prominent throughout the Arab media, and as such, the Arab media devotes a great deal of airtime to issues pertaining to the Israeli-Palestinian conflict. Such subjects will not raise editorial ire because Arab regimes have traditionally seen the conflict as a useful outlet to direct public attention away from criticism of themselves. The third largest pan-Arab newspaper based in London, after *Asharq Al Awsat* and *Al Hayat*, is *Al Quds Al Arabi*, which was established by a group of Palestinians in London in 1989. *Al Quds* is far more rejectionist than the other two papers and often carries scathing Arab nationalist opinion pieces.

As has been said before, anti-Americanism is rife throughout the Arab world. One of the main ways in which criticism of America is vented is through the Arabic media. Rhetoric hostile to the United States is prevalent on the television, on the radio and in print. Curiously, such attitudes remain consistent regardless of the nation's foreign policy. Anti-Americanism is just as common in countries like Saudi Arabia or Egypt, which have been long time allies of the USA, as it is in countries like Syria, traditionally hostile to the United States.

Nearly all factions of Arab society are hostile to the USA. It is part of the popular anti-colonial narrative since the early 20th century, although the villains of the story used to be the British and the French. Arab nationalists blame the United States for undermining and ultimately causing the failure of local nationalisms: Nasserism and Baathism. Islamists resent the United States for the Western values which it represents and believe that it is engaged in some sort of civilisational conflict with Islam. Across the board, the United States is also hated for its unwavering support of Israel over the years. All these viewpoints are repeatedly aired, with the occasional regional variation, in the Arabic media.

The Arab regimes themselves, even those governments allied to the USA, are more than happy to permit anti-American rhetoric while the American government continually and publicly calls for democratisation of the region. The undemocratic Arab governments are naturally hostile to these calls and anti-Americanism is a useful tool to help portray democracy as some kind of foreign scheme, antithetical to Arab culture. Anti-Americanism, and anti-Westernism are also convenient narratives for Arab countries to use to deflect blame for their own failures. Many Arabs would rather see colonialism or neo-imperialism as responsible for their troubles, than blame their own corrupt and ineffectual governments.

Also, like the Palestinian issue, the USA is a safe topic and will often pass the scrutiny of the censors, unlike criticism aimed closer to home.

The Lebanese Media

Before many of the pan-Arab newspapers moved to London and the TV channels broadcast from Dubai, Beirut was very much a major hub of the Arabic media. Lebanon still has a huge influence on the media of the whole region, especially with regard to culture and literature. Lebanon was famous for its printing presses and publishers and acted as a haven for dissident writers across the Middle East who flourished in the more cosmopolitan and liberal environment of Beirut. Lebanon is still very much the centre of the Arabic literary world, hosting a major annual book fair. It is still home to dozens of publishers.

Lebanon is a fragmented society divided along sectarian lines. Each community, broadly divided into Christian, Sunni or Shia (though with plenty of smaller confessional groups) prefers political and social leadership exclusive to their religion. Political parties in Lebanon do not appeal to the public as a whole, only to the community they represent. Accordingly, the media is divided along religious lines, with Sunni, Shia or Christian TV stations or publications. Lebanon's faiths have often been in conflict with each other in the past, not least during Lebanon's civil war. When those groups are in conflict, their respective TV stations and newspapers dutifully commit themselves to the propaganda war being waged between the different sides.

The Lebanese media is not regulated by its government to the same extent as its Qatari, Saudi or Egyptian counterparts, and is described by Reporters Without Borders as the most free in the Arab world. However, much of the Lebanese media remains loyal to its owners, foreign or domestic.

For example, *Future TV*, one of the major Lebanese TV stations was founded by the late politician and businessman, Rafik Hariri. As such, the station has broadly followed its founder's mandate. Between 1992 and 1998, it substantially toned down its criticism of the government because Hariri was prime minister. The channel was also broadly pro-Syrian, like Hariri's government. When Hariri left power, the channel once more began to attack the government and was heavily critical of Hariri's successor, Selim Hoss. After the assassination of Hariri, which was largely blamed on the Syrians, the channel became one of Syria's most vocal critics in Lebanon.

The Egyptian Media

The Egyptian press came of age after the First World War when it became a forum for public debate of the various cultural and political issues of the time. The early 20th century was a time of many exciting new ideologies and their adherents began to debate with one another in the media, just as was happening in Europe at the time. Egypt was, and to some extent still is, the cultural centre of the Arab world. The Egyptian film industry accounts for around three quarters of all Arabic-language films ever produced. Cairo, once dubbed "the Hollywood of the Orient", still produces around 80 films a year.

The first major pan-Arab media outlet was *Voice of the Arabs*, an AM radio station operating out of Cairo, dedicated to spreading Nasser's Arab nationalist manifesto throughout the Arab world. When Nasserism was at its most popular, *Voice of the Arabs* was the Al Jazeera of its day. As well as lengthy diatribes against imperialism, the station also broadcast singers like Umm Kulthum who embodied Egyptian patriotic culture in the 20th century. Her radio concerts were so popular that Nasser would broadcast his speeches directly afterwards so as to achieve the highest possible audience.

Nasser gave the various anti-imperialist campaigns in the Arab world airtime on *Voice of the Arabs*. The Algerian anti-French movement, the FLN, were permitted to use the station broadcast to their compatriots. Likewise, the station agitated against the British in South Yemen and campaigned against Iraq when it joined the Baghdad Pact.

The first newspaper to be muzzled by Nasser was the Cairo daily, *El Misry*. In 1953, Nasser, displeased with one of its critical editors, levied a one million dollar fine on the paper. The fine was deliberately astronomical and the government knew the paper could not pay it. The paper was bankrupted and forced to close. By 1961 Nasser had seized control of all the newspapers in Egypt, ensuring that the government appointed its editors and its boards. The once proud liberal Egyptian media of the first half of the 20th century became a mouthpiece for whoever was in power.

Egypt, like many Arab countries, also controlled what the public consumed via its Ministry of Information. The ministry and the country's newspapers were so intimately linked that the editor-in-chief of *Al Ahram* from 1957 to 1974, Mohamed Hassanein Heikal, spent his last four years at *Al Ahram* working simultaneously as editor of the paper and minister of information.

Egypt's national media are directly owned and controlled by the state and it has long served as the primary method of communication between President and citizen. Unlike Qatar and Saudi Arabia, Egypt does have opposition-sponsored media but every station and publication is closely supervised and, where necessary, restricted by government supervisors. In any case, many private media interests are indirectly linked to the state since ownership of many businesses in Egypt is ultimately in the hands of a small wealthy elite with intimate ties to the state.

The Higher Press Council in Egypt is a government-appointed official body that grants licences to publishers in Egypt. It wields draconian authority, though its grip on the media has been less evident since the demise of Mubarak. As mentioned in a previous chapter, the Muslim Brotherhood knows that control of this body ultimately results in control of what Egyptians watch and read, and therefore what they think. When in power, they moved to control the Press Council; the Brotherhood and its sympathisers wanted to have the ultimate say over who is appointed the editor of an Egyptian newspaper.

The primary method of control is through licensing. All media outlets need a licence in order to operate. Should the newspaper or broadcaster begin to make contentious statements the authorities can simply withhold or revoke its licence. With no licence, the state can close down the outlet, as it has done before, persecuting journalists who go too far in criticising the established order. Neither are licences cheap. The costs start at a million Egyptian pounds (around £100,000 sterling) for daily newspapers. Foreign newspapers also need approval from the censors before being allowed into the country.

The Egyptian statute contains a plethora of press laws which ultimately void any constitutional freedom of speech. There are laws against insulting the President, exciting public opinion and spreading false news. In practice, the legal precedents are largely irrelevant, as the Egyptian government repeatedly showed willingness to use brutal tactics such as beating or kidnapping to keep recalcitrant journalists in line.

When unrest rocked Egypt, as it did in 1968 and 1977, the regime enforced a total media blackout in order to protect the regime. A media blackout is very much the nuclear option, for when a situation is beyond the control of the Ministry of Information to handle. In 2011, during the uprising that ultimately toppled Mubarak, a media blackout was considered ineffectual because many protesters were getting their news and organising via the Internet. In any case, the public lost confidence in the traditional media. To solve this problem, the government cut the country's Internet.

****

The Arab media can be roughly divided between outlets that are owned by political factions (state or otherwise) and the so called "independent" press. Very few outlets can be considered editorially independent. The media does not conceive of too many bold ideas, has been overly cautious, and will only indulge in veiled criticism of their home regimes. Many employees of news agencies doubled as informers for the state secret police. Likewise, the funding of media and the many columnists and commentators is never discussed in the open. Censorship still exists after the Arab Spring and it is naïve to assume otherwise.

Even the Arab newspapers and TV channels based in London are still under the patronage of various regimes and censorship still operates. However, states no longer have a monopoly on the media their people choose to consume. The process of freeing up the media began in the 1990s with the spread of pan-Arab satellite television and foreign satellite television. CNN, BBC World and MSNBC have been readily available for nearly two decades. The Internet has also swelled the selective flow of news and information within the Arab world into a flood. Facebook and Twitter are the best known, and definitely played a significant role in the Arab Spring revolutions, though they are not news services in the traditional sense. However, they helped enable the street protest movements to operate without leaders, in effect becoming "open source" uprisings. In many ways, these were the only open movements in closed societies and, unlike much of the media, the Internet prevented the movements from becoming community specific, tapping into a kind of collective consciousness.

As the regimes weathered the Arab Spring, many made considerable efforts to harass and ultimately silence critical bloggers. Bloggers can be difficult to trace, highly mobile and most of the time able to operate only with a laptop and a digital camera. These bloggers also blur the line between activist and journalist and are often associated with the new phenomenon of "citizen journalist."

These citizen journalists were able to provide the world with images of the brutality of their governments, often within minutes of an incident taking place. Imagery of shootings, beatings and riots causes immense damage to the reputations of countries, and provides the opposition with ample propaganda. In such an environment, the regimes will always be playing catch up.

Buying the Right Stories

For dictators, one of the problems with the pan-Arab media, is that they transcend national boundaries. Enforcing censorship through threats of brutality or the withdrawal of licences, the favourite tools of dictators, is generally either frowned upon or simply impossible in foreign territories. However, criticism of the Arab regimes has consistently been an off limits topic for Arabs and, as a result, many Arab journalists engage in self-censorship, even when abroad; arguably a far more powerful restriction than state censorship. Likewise, many eminent and perceptive Arab commentators and political scientists are blacklisted from certain media outlets as their views are seen as too radical or disruptive.

One other method available to the dictatorships was to buy positive stories about themselves, or negative stories about their enemies, by paying journalists to write them. Colonel Gaddafi and Saddam Hussein invested heavily in buying friendly journalists. The reporting of the events in Libya in 2011 revealed how many Arab media barons tiptoed around their stories until they felt safe.

The problem was not limited to the nationalist dictators. The monarchies of the Gulf do the same, although they use their considerable wealth and connections with Western society to slightly more subtle effect. As mentioned previously, many Gulf monarchies own controlling stakes in a number of transnational Arab media outlets and can depend on them to print or broadcast friendly stories. These governments are even able to influence the Western media by using American and British public relations companies as intermediaries. The Kuwaiti government famously employed Hill and Knowlton in Washington DC during the Iraqi occupation in 1990 and 1991. They planted favourable stories about Kuwait in the American and British media.

The Arabic language media based in London became a lucrative industry after the Lebanese civil war, despite the high costs involved. Its reporting and political leaning followed that of their generous and obscure financial backers, serving up old fashioned agitation and propaganda. Despite poor journalistic standards, being in London somehow gives these outlets an air of prestige. For decades, many Arab editors in London and the UAE grew rich on the patronage of Arab dictators. Some dictators even poured millions of pounds into establishing their own media newspapers and broadcasters. Some of these outlets had no significant circulation, and some didn't even bother with advertising. Employees in these concerns remained tight-lipped about what went on inside, especially as they often work cash in hand.

The Arab Spring caused problems for many of these editors as their government sponsors ended up in exile, in prison or dead. Many of these editors have a degree of credibility in the West via their additional careers as commentators on Arab affairs for English language newspapers and television channels.

The Nature of the Arab Media

Arabic language news and journalism differs greatly from its Western counterpart. Though the sets and photogenic presenters are clearly modelled on those of CNN or the BBC, the nature of the news is quite different. Whereas an interview with a politician on the evening news in the UK or the USA may last two or three minutes, Arab politicians like their interviews to go on far longer and they can often talk for up to two hours. Discussion programmes, in an effort to fill airtime, will also last as long as feature films. Also, deference and respect means that Arab politicians will be offended if they are not granted the same amount of time as their colleagues and rivals.

The Arab media is also far more concerned with the formalities of diplomacy, so meetings between ambassadors and foreign ministers will feature high on news agenda, where they would barely warrant a mention in a Western newspaper. Part of the reason for this is the authoritarian nature of government in the Middle East, which demands respect and attention from its subjects. Prestige is also of immense importance; high profile meetings are essential in news coverage. This kind of political vanity was highlighted in a comical incident in 2010 when it transpired that Egypt's state-owned *Al Ahram* doctored a photo of Hosni Mubarak in the company of President Obama and a few Middle Eastern leaders to make it look as if Mubarak was walking in front of the American President, rather than behind. The authorities did not realise that the power of the Internet would not only expose the fake but broadcast the trick.

As a result of such deference to officialdom, reporting in the Arab media is tedious. Statements, conferences and meetings are dutifully reported, but the implications or the causes of such events tend not to be investigated. Uniform significance is ascribed to all the activities of governments and their ministers. Events are made newsworthy by the presence of authority, rather than as a result of public interest.

The Arab media have traditionally had little or no interest in investigative journalism, although this has changed in recent years, after attempts by the likes of Al Jazeera to emulate investigative television formats popular in the West, such as the BBC's Panorama. However, in spite of this, major national corruption scandals are not touched upon. The Arab media used to not report on the tens of thousands detained in prisons without trial in any Arab country. In addition, certain documents, which would normally be publicly available in the West are not published due to the political sensitivities involved, the perfect example being the Camp David agreement in 1978.

Another tradition of the Arab media is a tendency to either mislead or exaggerate. For instance, the Egyptian media greatly exaggerated the British losses in the 1956 Suez war and Israeli losses in 1967 and 1973 wars.

The Arab Intelligentsia

Many Arab intellectuals have complained about the lack of intellectual freedom in the Arab media. The situation has reached a point where the governments no longer need to censor opinionated journalists and commentators because they are shouted down in the news studios. Debates are reduced to binary outcomes. For example, Abd Al Hamid Al

Ansari, the former dean of Islamic Law at Qatar University, complained on Bahraini television in 2008 that Arab news programmes regularly invite religious or extremist personalities, stating, "anyone who disagrees with them is considered a traitor or collaborator. When one guest is a nationalist, the other is considered a traitor or collaborator. When one guest is a religious figure, the other is considered deviant with false beliefs." Al Ansari also inferred that the persistent inflammatory rhetoric, constantly blaming foreign powers as the source of Arab problems, was a form of "media terrorism."

The problem has become more acute as Islamists acquire political influence, although, as the statement infers, the issue is also apparent with nationalist commentators as well. In any case, the Arab world can now count dozens of Islamist satellite channels, which will only give airtime to like-minded individuals.

The monopolisation of the debate is a deficit to contemporary understanding of culture in the Arab world. Despite the prevalence of retrograde governments, the Arab world is still rich in talented, cultured and intellectual personalities. However, they find it harder and harder to have a voice in the Arab media. For example, when the Egyptian liberal author Sayyid Al Qimni was awarded an Achievement in Social Sciences prize by the Egyptian ministry of culture in 2009, Egyptian Islamists immediately launched a hate campaign against him through the media. Qimni, an outspoken advocate of secularism and opponent of Islamic fundamentalism, would never have been awarded such a prize when the Islamists controlled the Egyptian government.

Politicisation and patronage has damaged the understanding of literary and academic culture. When Ayatollah Khomeini issued the famous fatwa against Salman Rushdie, not a single columnist or imam objected, nor did the media allow contrary voices to express their disdain. There were some – the Egyptian Nobel laureate Naguib Mahfouz, for example – but they were drowned out by the torrent of religious fervour.

In the past, the Arab media has had a selective approach to what it decides to report. Today, with the advent of the Internet and social media, it is becoming ever harder to keep acts of brutality or incidences of embarrassment out of the public eye. There have however, been plenty of ignoble events in the Arab world, widely talked about by the public which make it into the newspapers.

For example, in 1982, Rifaat al Assad, on the orders of his brother, Syrian President Hafez al Assad, massacred around 20,000 people (estimates range from a few thousand to double that) in Hama, after the Syrian Muslim Brotherhood took control of the city. It was perhaps the single bloodiest event in the history of the Middle East. The mere mention of the incident is taboo in Syria and the story was not reported or discussed in any of the major newspapers. Incidentally, in the late 1990s Rifaat al Assad founded the London-based pan-Arab satellite TV network, ANN (Arab News Network). Though ostensibly a news network, the channel follows the general pattern of serving as agitprop for its owner.

The seizure of the Grand Mosque of Mecca by Islamic militants in December 1979 lasted two weeks and 250 lives were lost. The 68 captured militants were subsequently executed. The Saudis instigated a total media blackout, even cutting Saudi Arabia's international phone lines to prevent the news from spreading. The blackout was eventually broken by a statement by the US State Department in Washington, much to the chagrin of the Saudis.

When Saddam Hussein invaded Kuwait in 1990, the Arab media was caught off guard. What resulted was a total media silence for 48 hours as, rather than report the news, the editors had to confirm the line they would take with their patrons and owners.

Coverage of Bahrain has been muted in the Arab satellite media. The silence on a channel like Al Jazeera is particularly conspicuous when the coverage of Syria and Egypt verges on the hysterical, with its wholehearted encouragement of the revolutionary movements.

Press Laws

Arab countries have press laws. They vary from country to country, but they all essentially entail restrictions on what journalists can write about. Press laws tend to be vague and all-encompassing, so they can be referenced arbitrarily to censor material, or even detain journalists. Yemen, for instance, has an "anything" fireshield within its press statutes, including:

- "Anything which prejudices the Islamic faith and its lofty principles or belittles religions or humanitarian creeds."

- "Anything which might cause tribal, sectarian, racial, regional or ancestral discrimination, or which might spread a spirit of dissent and division among the people or call on them to apostatise."

- "Anything which leads to the spread of ideas contrary to the principles of the Yemeni revolution, prejudicial to national unity or distorting the image of the Yemeni, Arab or Islamic heritage."

- "Anything which undermines the public, prejudices the dignity of individuals or the freedom of the individual by smears and defamation."

As is patently obvious from the text, such prohibitions can effectively outlaw whatever political material the government deems seditious. In Algeria, it is illegal to "defame" government officials or state institutions. Similarly, in Kuwait it is a criminal offence to publish material criticising the constitution, the Emir, Islam or to incite acts that offend public morality or religious sensibilities. Saudi Arabia contains within its statute the prohibition of material that either harms national security (many in the Saudi government consider the right of women to drive to be detrimental to national security) or that "detracts from a man's dignity."

****

Unlike in the West, the Arab media is not driven by profits; the Arab media does not make any profit. The smaller independent outlets are dependent on their owners and benefactors; they do not have the necessary audience to make money from either sales or advertising revenue. The media landscape in the Arab world is not a free market, with outlets often subject to banning or harassment. In recent years, satellite broadcasters have been subject to jamming, particularly in countries such as Iran and Syria, where governments have employed old Soviet technology to jam satellite broadcasts. In many ways, the private media follows the model set by the state media, of subsidy, the difference being that the state media receives state subsidies and the private media demands constant investment in order to survive. This is especially apparent for satellite broadcasters, as TV stations are notoriously expensive, requiring huge overheads and high running costs. Even Al Jazeera, which was recently voted the fifth most influential global brand (ahead of Microsoft and Coca Cola) has difficulty attracting advertisers, reportedly, after Saudi Arabia put pressure on businesses not to advertise on the channel. It is difficult to conceive of Al Jazeera surviving in its current form without its Qatari funding.

The question of training in the Arab press is a pertinent one. Many Arab journalists do not go through the process of journalistic training that their Western counterparts do. However, even with such training, Western journalists still make basic factual mistakes, so training is not a quick and easy solution to the problem of disinformation in the Arab world. Official sources of information in the Arab world are notoriously unreliable, and constantly engaged in cover-up and misdirection. The advent of the Internet and social media has also not necessarily improved the veracity of what is written in the media. Journalists may report rumour and conjecture on the Internet as fact.

The intellectual vacuum has also resulted in a lack of interesting or dynamic comment pieces in the Arabic media. The usual columnists use their weekly inches to pontificate about the dangers of Zionism, imperialism, secularism, etc. This lack of thoughtful opinion makers is also apparent in the lack of human interest stories in the Middle East. The Western media has perhaps become too obsessed with human interest, whereas the Arabic media devotes far more time to discussion of political issues. Likewise, interviews in Arabic newspapers tend to follow a straight question and answer format; the popular Western style of incorporating answers into extended prose is alien to Arabic journalism.

In terms of reach, number of stations and technological sophistication, the Arab media has evolved at a staggering rate in the last two decades. However, much of the content has changed little since the 1950s, when inflammatory rhetoric constantly blamed foreign powers for Arab problems and criticism of the home regimes was taboo. Despite the Arab Spring, the Arab media is still some way from becoming truly editorially independent and objective. In order to facilitate such a transformation, democratic freedoms must be acquired in Arabic countries themselves; press freedom often accompanies democracy. The media is also skewed by the wealthy individuals who fund it. So long as liberal and secular newspapers and TV stations are unable to match the funding available to the Islamist media outlets, such voices will struggle to be heard in an ever more crowded marketplace.

CHAPTER 12

ISRAEL – GEOPOLITICAL REALITY

There are moments in the life of nations and peoples when it is incumbent on those known for their wisdom and clarity of vision to overlook the past, with all its complexities and weighing memories, in a bold drive towards new horizons. Those who, like us, are shouldering the same responsibility entrusted to us, are the first who should have the courage to take fate-determining decisions which are in consonance with the circumstances. We must all rise above all forms of fanaticism, self-deception and obsolete theories of superiority. The most important thing is never to forget that infallibility is the prerogative of God alone.

President Sadat's Speech to the Knesset
20 November 1977.

When Sadat made peace with Israel in 1977, many of his fellow Arab leaders were shocked and furious. The Arab League's response was to expel Egypt in 1979. The other Arab leaders ordered the closure of the Arab League headquarters in Cairo and moved its staff to Tunisia. It was not until 1989 that the League re-admitted Egypt, now under Mubarak, and returned its headquarters to Cairo.

Egypt and Israel ratified a historic peace agreement in 1979, which has since been the bedrock of relations between the two nations. Jordan followed Egypt, by signing its own treaty to normalise relations with Israel in 1994, a free trade zone and industrial park in the area of Arava were agreed upon, border crossings opened and joint business ventures embarked upon.

Mauritania became the third Arab state to open full diplomatic relations with Israel in 1999. Mauritania, along with Tunisia and Morocco, had actually been pursuing diplomatic ties with Israel since 1994. That year, Israel opened a liaison office in the Moroccan capital Rabat, while Morocco reciprocated by opening its own office in Israel in early 1995. Mauritania initially went through the Spanish foreign ministry, by establishing a small presence at the Spanish embassy in Tel Aviv in 1995 and opened its own diplomatic mission in Tel Aviv the following year.

Diplomatic relations with the countries of the Maghreb are significant because Israel counts many North African émigrés among its citizens, who still retain an emotional attachment to their ancestral homelands. After the renewal of Palestinian terrorism in 2000, Morocco and Tunisia broke off diplomatic ties with Israel. Nevertheless, some commercial relations and tourism continue, as well as contacts in other fields.

The Gulf States showed no interest in opening relations with Israel until the 1990s. Unlike the Arab states to the north, they had no need of the financial inducements normally provided by the United States. Indeed, the oil blockade by the Gulf States in support of the 1973 war against Israel was one of the most effective tactics employed by the Arab side in the war. However, after the Oslo accords in 1993, the Gulf States made tentative moves towards opening relations with the Jewish state. After initial contact was made, there were low key visits by government ministers. In 1994, the Qatari foreign minister held a secret meeting with Israeli officials to discuss a $1 million gas deal. In 1996 Israel opened trade representation offices in Oman and Qatar to further develop non-political relations. However, after Palestinian terrorism began to reappear in 2000, followed by the second intifada of 2002, relations have distinctly cooled, and the office in Oman was closed.

Yet, relations between the Gulf and Israel are not completely sour. Though no Gulf country has ever established full relations with Israel, a leaked diplomatic cable in 2009 claimed that the then Israeli foreign minister, Tzipi Livni, had a "good working relationship" with the UAE foreign minister Abdullah Ibn Zayed. The cable went on to say that the two officials "would not do in public what they say behind closed doors," inferring that, at the highest level of government, the states are keen to co-operate but cannot afford to due to such massive hostility among their populations.

✱✱✱✱✱✱✱✱✱✱✱✱

Although the Arab League now attempts to present a united front on the issue of Israel, in reality, the matter is far more complicated. During the first Arab-Israeli war in 1948, the Muslims of North Africa and East Asia had little or no interest in the question of Jewish settlement in Palestine. Similarly, today, Israel has no real bearing on the doings of North African states, and even some of those close by. Despite the rhetoric, many Arabs have come to accept that Israel will remain in the Middle East. Although there are pronouncements to the contrary by groups such as Hamas and Hezbollah, Israel will not be defeated by armed struggle.

Arab media do not often report on prominent Palestinians travelling to Israel for whatever reason so, in the public mind, Israel remains a mysterious entity, alien to the Arabs. When a visit to Israel is reported, it is often to stain the reputation of prominent opposition politicians. For instance, when Mohamed ElBaradei was reported to have visited Israel, the news was splashed across Egypt's front pages, painting him as an untrustworthy Zionist. Such selective reporting is an important tool of political blackmail for Arab governments.

Many Arabs believe that since Israel essentially occupies the West Bank and Gaza Strip, Palestinians have no contact with Israel, though this is not the case. There are Palestinians on Israeli football teams and a Palestinian-Jewish Orchestra. Jehad Al Wazir, the head of the Palestine Monetary Authority, is in close contact with Israeli leaders and speaks at Israeli business conferences. Indeed Ismail Haniyeh, one of the two disputed Prime Ministers of the Palestinian National Authority, sent his sick granddaughter for treatment in an Israeli hospital rather than to Jordan or Syria – a story that was not covered in the Arab media. There are numerous other examples of Palestinians who regularly deal with Israel in their day to day lives.

Egyptians or Syrians are not permitted to do the same and, should any prominent Arab visit Israel or work with Israelis, even outside the region, it will be latched on to by the Arab media and used as ammunition for character assassination. Similarly, some in the global Jewish diaspora – the American Jewish peace lobby, for example, which has become increasingly critical of Israel's behaviour – are, if anything, over-reported by Arab media.

****

Jerusalem has changed hands many times over the last millennium. During the crusades it was ruled by Christians and Muslims, with each change of administration often following brutal massacres and bloodshed in the streets. Under Ottoman rule, Jerusalem was almost totally forgotten for 400 years. In the Ottoman Empire, only cities were recognised, sometimes ruled by Imperial vassal rulers. Palestine was therefore in the dominion of Jerusalem, and not a delineated territory. The surrounding area was actually part of Greater Syria, which encompassed what is today Palestine, Israel, Jordan, Lebanon and Syria.

Israel was in effect founded in 1897 by Jewish nationalists at the first Zionist Congress in Basel, Switzerland. The leaders of the movement quickly emerged in the form of the Hungarian Jewish journalist Theodore Herzl and the Russian Jewish chemist Chaim Weizmann.

Theodore Herzl spoke no Hebrew or Yiddish, put up a Christmas tree and did not bother to circumcise his son. However, having experienced anti-Semitism in Vienna and Paris, he decided that rather than aim for emancipation and acceptance, European Jews would have to remove themselves from European society and establish a new state in either Argentina or Palestine. "At Basel," he once said, "I founded the Jewish state – if I said this loudly there will be universal laughter."

Chaim Weizmann left Russia and spent 30 years living in Manchester, where his constituency MP was Arthur Balfour. As a scientist, he helped develop explosives during the First World War, and rose to prominence in British society. Weizmann lobbied Prime

Minister David Lloyd George and Foreign Secretary Arthur Balfour to allow the creation of a Jewish state in Palestine. Weizmann's contribution to the war effort was so successful that it spurred Balfour to issue the Balfour Declaration in 1917, pledging the British government to the establishment of a Jewish state in Palestine.

In 1902, after the fifth Zionist conference in which Herzel reported his audience with the Ottoman Sultan Abdul Hamid, a leading Islamic thinker named Rashid Rida wrote an article in *El Manar*, titled The Revival of a Nation after its Death. "We should scrutinise our leaders' behaviour and take note of the Jews," wrote Rida, "They do not languish in the 'blessing of the Torah' in order to succeed. They have preserved their language and religious unity despite their dispersion. They have supported one another, mastered modern art and sciences, and amassed capital which is the basis of power and strength in present times. Nothing prevents them from becoming the mightiest nation on earth except statehood, and they are striving towards this in a natural way, through great national organisation. Nations do not succeed except through organisation."

When the Zionist issue was raised in the Ottoman parliament in 1909, contributions were mixed and only 50 out of 288 deputies remained in the chamber which counted 66 Arabs as members. In September 1912, Kemal Ataturk, later the first Prime Minister of Turkey declared he did not fear "Zionist danger," and welcomed Jewish settlement in Palestine. He also advocated that Jews, Ottomans and foreigners should have the right to purchase land in Palestine.

Sheikh Ali Yousif, the nationalist editor of Cairo's *Al Muayyad* newspaper, wrote in the autumn of 1912, "it is not for us to look askance at them with jealousy, and vengeance because of their enlightenment, and progress...then we will lose a highly industrious element, so needed by us always, especially at this critical moment."

The idea of large numbers of Jews immigrating to Palestine had a mixed reception amongst the Arabs. Hussayn Al Hussayni, the head of the municipal council of Jerusalem, said in 1914 he "saw no danger in the Zionist movement", another prominent Arab, deputy for Jaffa Hafez Bey, said he believed that "Zionist immigration can be both harmful and useful." Many other Arab deputies saw Zionism as an unacceptable imposition on their land and spoke out against it at any opportunity.

Palestine became a British mandate after the First World War and following the dissolution of the Ottoman Empire. From 1918, the British granted Jews in Palestine the right to fly their flag and Hebrew was granted equal status in the territory.

In 1918, Sharif Hussein of Mecca wrote in the *Al Qibla* newspaper, "The resources of the country are still virgin soil and will be developed by the Jewish immigrants. One of the most amazing things until recent times was that the Palestinian used to leave his country, wandering over the high seas in every direction. His native soil could not retain a hold on him...At the same time, we have seen the Jews from foreign countries streaming to Palestine from Russia, Germany, Austria, Spain, and America. The cause of causes could not escape those who had a gift of deeper insight. They knew that the country was for its original sons for all their differences, a sacred and beloved homeland. The return of these exiles to their homeland will prove materially and spiritually an experimental school for their brethren who are with them in the fields, factories, trades and all things connected to the land."

Sharif Hussein, and his son Emir Faisal, the future King of Syria and Iraq, were two of the most prominent Arab leaders of the day who felt that the Zionists, far from being an enemy to Arab self determination, could in fact be a useful ally. At the time, both Jews and Arabs lacked their own independent states and it was felt that perhaps they could aid each other in their endeavour. Hussein and Faisal met Chaim Weizmann, President of World Zionist Organisation, in Aqaba (present day Jordan) in 1918 with a view to working together in the future.

In 1919, Emir Faisal and Chaim Weizmann met again during the discussions in Paris which eventually resulted in the Treaty of Versailles. At the time, Faisal was the only recognised Arab leader in the world, enjoying as he did the support of the British. Faisal agreed to support the Balfour Declaration, specifically a Jewish state in Palestine. He then wrote, "We Arabs, especially the educated among us, look with the deepest sympathy on the Zionist movement. Our delegation here in Paris is fully acquainted with the proposals submitted yesterday by the Zionist organisation to the Peace Conference, and we regard them as moderate and proper." The two concluded their discussions with the Weizmann-Faisal agreement, a formal declaration of co-operation that each would assist in the creation of Jewish and Arab states in the Middle East. The agreement never achieved its objectives, partly because Faisal's plan for an Arab state was scuppered by the Sykes-Picot agreement between the British and the French in which the two imperial powers carved up the Fertile Crescent between themselves.

Palestine was finally properly defined in 1920. By the early 1920s, the Jews in Palestine had elected their own Zionist Executive Council so that they could more effectively negotiate with Arab politicians and tribal leaders.

The World Zionist Organisation set up a Zionist Commission in Palestine which the British recognised as the Jewish Agency in Palestine in 1921. From 1919 to 1923, 40,000 Jews arrived in Palestine, mostly from Russia and the Ukraine, where Jews were subject to pogroms which left an estimated 100,000 dead. Palestine was under British control, though the British Mandate in Palestine was not formalised until 1923.

In 1921, the pro-Zionist Muslim National Association, led by Hassan Bey Shukri and Sheikh Hadeib from Heifa sent a telegram to the British government in support of the Balfour Declaration, though it was never reported in the Arab media. The first World Zionist Conference, which would have far reaching effects for the Arab world, was likewise only a small news item in the Arab media of the time.

One of the biggest opponents to Jewish settlement in Palestine was Hajj Amin Al Husseini, the Grand Mufti of Jerusalem, one of the most prominent anti-Zionist Arabs of the 1930s and 1940s. Husseini met with Adolf Hitler on 28 November 1941 and the two made moves towards an alliance. Husseini believed that, after winning the war, Hitler would establish an Arab state with himself, Husseini, at its head. Hitler never publicly recognised the claim for Arab independence but he did declare that the "Arabs were Germany's natural friends because they have the same enemies: Jews, English and communists." Husseini was very much a self-appointed leader who claimed to speak for the Arabs. He was also a virulent anti-Semite, and wholeheartedly approved of the Third Reich's policy towards the Jews. After the war, he was taken into French custody. The French refused various attempts by the British and Yugoslavs to extradite him for war crimes and he eventually found his way to Cairo, where he still carried some weight as a potential Arab leader. However, such was his reputation as a Nazi collaborator that he unwittingly became one of Zionism's greatest arguments for a state. His wartime activities ended up being presented as evidence to influence the United Nations vote on the future of Palestine.

Israel's Foundation

The head of the political department of the Jewish Agency and future prime minister of Israel, Golda Meir met King Abdullah of Jordan in early November 1947. "He soon made his position clear, that he would not join any Arab attack on the Jews. And he would always remain our friend," she later wrote. "After all, we had a common foe, the Mufti of Jerusalem Hajj Amin Al Husseini. Not only that, he also suggested we meet again after the UN vote."

When it was rumoured that Jordan would join the Arab armies and fight against the Jewish state, Meir asked him directly if that was indeed the case, "King Abdullah was astonished and hurt by my question," she recalled and asked her to remember three things, that he was a Bedouin and therefore a man of honour, that he was a King and therefore doubly an honourable man and, finally, he would never break a promise made to a woman."

On the eve of war, Meir met him again; she and her assistant disguised themselves as Arabs and travelled to Amman to meet the King. When she asked him again if he had broken his promise, he replied, "when I made that promise I thought I was in control of my destiny and could do what I thought right. But since then I have learned otherwise." The King had believed he could take over the whole of Palestine and incorporate it into an enlarged Jordan, promising Meir that the Jews would be treated well and given representation.

The British Mandate was due to end at midnight on 5 May 1948. Palestine became the responsibility of the United Nations when the British left. The British devised a partition plan which saw the territory divided between a Jewish and an Arab state.

On 15 May 1948, the Jews unilaterally declared the foundation of the state of Israel, 50 years to the day after the first Zionist Conference at Basel. The first prime minister of Israel, David Ben-Gurion, declared "We extend the hand of peace and good neighbourliness to all the states around us and to their peoples. The state of Israel is prepared to make its contribution in a concerted effort for the advancement of the entire Middle East."

At midnight, President Truman recognised Israel, followed by the Soviet Union on 18 May. The surrounding Arab nations immediately declared war on Israel, initiating the first Arab-Israeli war. By the end of the first week in June, the Egyptian army was closing in on Tel Aviv and Jerusalem and the Egyptian air force was in the sky above Tel Aviv. The Egyptians had sought an independent Palestinian state in Gaza and the Negev, though they were unable to do so without the help of the Jordanians. The Jordanian army was arguably the most capable of all the Arab armies, commanded by the British General, Glubb Pasha. However, after King Abdullah annexed the West Bank, the King ordered his generals to cease all combat operations, and most importantly, not to help the Egyptians.

Egypt had 18,000 troops in the war, making its army the largest and best supplied among the Arab forces. However, due to its lack of vehicles, it was forced to use the navy to move around. The Syrian and Iraqi armies were poorly trained, uncoordinated and made minor encroachments into the north of Palestine. In effect, the Arab-Israeli war was not a war between Israel and a massive Arab force; it was a series of smaller wars fought concurrently between the Israeli army and various Arab armies who were unwilling or unable to help each other.

On 15 October 1948 Israel surged into the south, encircling the Egyptian army. Again, King Abdullah made it clear to his generals that they were not to help the Egyptians. On 24 February 1949 Egypt and Israel signed an armistice agreement, making the borders of original Palestine the new line between Egypt and Israel. Israel lifted its siege around the village of Faluja, where the Egyptians were holed up and released its prisoners, who included Gamal Abdel Nasser, the future leader of Egypt. King Abdullah negotiated directly with the Israeli foreign minister and General Moshe Dayan. Jordan ended up with the West Bank. Jerusalem was left in limbo, controlled by both governments.

Exodus

Immediately after its creation, Israel sparked a mass movement of people both inside and outside its borders. The Arabs who left Israel are still considered refugees three or four generations later, and are one of the world's most widely known refugee problems. Since then, more conflict across the region has led to a vast explosion of refugee movements in the Middle East – most recently from Iraq, Sudan and Syria – which have been ignored by the Arab media, which only deems Palestinian refugees newsworthy. However, although many of these movements dwarf the Palestinian refugee movement in terms of numbers, none has approached its importance in Middle Eastern politics and culture.

At the same time as Palestinians fled Israel, over a million Jews left the Arab world for Israel. From 1948 to 1972, 265,000 Jews fled Morocco, 130,000 left Algeria, 125,000 left Iraq, 105,000 left Tunisia and 75,000 left Egypt. In total 1,011,800 fled Arab countries, mostly for Israel. These numbers are rarely reflected upon today and are not reported to the Arab public. Many of these countries had flourishing Jewish communities. In Iraq, for instance, the Jews were very much at the forefront of Iraqi politics, culture and business until a series of anti-Semitic policies instigated the year of Israel's foundation rapidly turned them into second class citizens. Jews still remain in Iraq, though they number less than 20, who are forced to keep their Jewish identities a secret.

From 1949 to 1967, 661,000 Palestinian refugees fled Israel, mostly to Gaza, the West Bank, Jordan and Lebanon, though they later spread throughout the Middle East and beyond. Many were forced out by informal Israeli militias, some fled the war, some were forced out by the new Israeli government and some just wanted to leave. From the 1950s onwards, the Palestinian refugees were used as pawns in the political manoeuvres of a new generation of Arab dictators.

The right of return of Palestinian refugees was enshrined by United Nations Resolution 194 in 1967, which essentially decreed that refugees who had left Israel in 1948 and 1967 had the right to return to their land and property. The resolution is immensely controversial as Israel asserts that it is not obliged to permit Palestinians to return to Israeli land. The right of return has become something of a rallying point around which Palestinian self-determination is asserted and an issue whose resolution will be a central tenet of any future peace negotiation. However, whilst Palestinians left Israel and Palestine in huge numbers during the first few decades of Israel's existence, some opted to stay.

The Arabs in Israel

The main legal distinction between Jewish and Arab citizens of Israel is that the Arabs are not required to serve in the Israeli army. This was to spare Arab citizens the need to take up arms against Arab states. Muslim Arabs are permitted to join the army, though they are subject to thorough background checks. That has not deterred many Arabs from opting to serve in the IDF; in 2010 1,473 volunteered for national service. There have been Arab Generals in the Israeli Defence Force (IDF), including Major General Hussain Fares, commander of Israel's border police and Major General Yosef Mishlav.

Other religious communities, such as the Druze and Circassian communities are subject to the draft. In 1948, many Druze volunteered to serve in the Israeli army in the Arab-Israeli war. Israeli Druze have repeatedly declared their solidarity with Israel, while distancing themselves from Arab and Islamic politics.

There are about one and a half million Arabs in Israel, which equates to just over 20% of the Israeli population. Based on current projections, this proportion will increase to 25% in 2025. Though they are citizens of Israel, for the most part they still regard themselves as Palestinian or Arab. As citizens of Israel they have the right to vote in, and stand for, the Israeli Knesset. Arabs have in fact been members of the Knesset since Amin Salim Jarjora, Seif el Din el Zoubi and Tawfik Toubi were elected in the first Knesset election in 1949. As of 2011, 13 of the 120 members of the Israeli parliament are Arabs. Nawaf Massalha was the first Muslim Arab minister in the Israeli government, appointed Deputy Minister for Health in 1992. In 2001, Salah Tarif, a Druze, was appointed the first non-Jewish full member of the Israeli cabinet as minister without portfolio. In 2007, Rateb Majadele, the first Arab Muslim cabinet minister, also without portfolio, was appointed.

Muslims, many of whom are Bedouin, make up about 82% of the entire Arab population in Israel, along with around 9% Druze, and 9% Christians. 110,000 Bedouin live in the Negev desert, 50,000 in Galilee, and 10,000 in central Israel. The Druze of the Golan Heights, which was captured in Syria in 1967 and annexed by Israel in 1981, are considered permanent residents under the Golan Heights Law.

Arabic is an official language of Israel, and following Supreme Court rulings in 1990, the government must provide information on public services in Arabic for its Arabic-speaking population. For example, highway signs in Israel are actually trilingual, with names printed in Hebrew, English and Arabic. However, in smaller Arab villages, there are no Arabic road signs to denote the name of the village.

Within Israel, most Arabs are functionally bilingual in both Hebrew and Arabic, like the Kurds of Iraq who speak both Arabic and Kurdish. Hebrew is compulsory in Arabic schools in Israel. The Israeli education system is divided into Hebrew and Arabic-speaking schools and, within the Arabic section, the Druze have autonomy. The Druze religion emphasises service to the country in which they live, rather than to a greater religious community. Druze politicians even serve the more right-wing Israeli parties, with Knesset members representing both Likud and Yisraeli Beitenu parties.

There are about 117,000 Christian Arabs in Israel. Those Christian Arabs who have been prominent in Arab political parties in Israel included Archbishop George Hakim, Emile Toma, Tawfik Toubi, Emile Habibi, and Azmi Bishara and Israeli Supreme Court judge Salim Joubran.

Israel lacks a written constitution, so the rights of citizens are guaranteed by a set of basic laws. These laws regarding human rights and liberty supposedly guarantee equal rights for all Israeli citizens. The economies in the West Bank and Gaza are tied to that of Israel, with huge mutual benefits which have raised the living standards of Palestinians above that of those non-oil producing states in the Middle East. Again, such information goes virtually unreported in the Arab media.

****

When Anwar Sadat made peace with Israel in 1977, he envisioned a sustained and healthy relationship which was never really allowed to take root. Though Egypt and Israel are at peace, Egyptians do not go on holiday to Israel, nor do Israelis holiday in Egypt in any large numbers. However, there is no reason why, for instance, Egypt's Coptic Christians cannot visit the Holy Places in Jerusalem when there is apparently normalisation between the two nations. Likewise, there is no reason why the Egyptian national football team cannot play the Israeli national football team. However, this has not taken place. In fact, Israel plays its international football in UEFA, the European confederation, as the Arab nations that surround it will not permit it to compete in their regional grouping.

There is much double-talk amongst Arab leaders when it comes to Israel. Publicly, they are dismissive of the Zionist state and idly talk of Palestinian aspirations to nationhood. However, privately, they are far more accommodating towards Israel and many see the benefits of opening diplomatic relations. It is common knowledge, for instance, that the United States looks favourably on Arab states normalising relations with Israel and there are considerable benefits to be gained in terms of aid. However, the fact remains that the old anti-Israeli and anti-Semitic rhetoric has permeated the Arab public. Consequently, many reactionary segments of the populace, in particular the Islamists, make it difficult for governments to make contact with Israel. In spite of this, in 2002, the Arab League proposed a peace plan whereby the majority of the Arab states would recognise Israel, if Israel would allow a Palestinian state to take shape in accordance with the 1967 borders.

The Arab Spring has been of considerable concern to Israel due to the success of Islamist movements in the new political landscape. In November 2011, Prime Minister Benjamin Netanyahu warned that the Arab Spring was turning into an "Islamic, anti-Western, anti-liberal, anti-Israeli and anti-democratic wave." In many ways Israel preferred its relationships with the old dictators because they had allowed it to cultivate either stable relationships or stalemates with all its regional neighbours. Despite the rhetoric, the old Arab regimes essentially left Israel alone.

One of the major issues of public concern is that of the gas pipeline from Egypt into Israel. The pipeline supplies gas to Jordan and Israel and critics charge that the gas is exported at a rate far below the market price. Between 11 February and 25 November 2011 the pipeline was attacked eight times by militants in Sinai. Egypt had a 20-year deal to export natural gas to Israel. Gas supplies to Israel were halted by Egypt in 2012 because Israel had allegedly breached its obligations by not paying for some months. Benjamin Netanyahu sought to diffuse worries that the peace treaty was under threat, claiming it was not a diplomatic incident, but rather "a business dispute between an Israeli company and the Egyptian company." Egyptian Ambassador Yasser Rida mirrored the Israeli line by labelling the incident a business dispute too, rather than a diplomatic incident.

Within Egypt, the education authority still does not recognise the new map of the Middle East. In Egyptian classrooms, the land is marked Palestine, not Israel. For many Egyptians, Israel still does not exist. There are still laws on the Egyptian statute that criminalise Zionism and, should any Egyptian citizen declare themselves a Zionist, they risk losing their citizenship. Young soldiers are still taught that Israel is the enemy of the Arabs and many state and civil institutions refuse to have any ties with Israel at all.

Ultimately, Israel will remain in the Middle East, and there is very little the surrounding Arab states can do to remove it from the map. They have repeatedly failed to overcome Israel. For many Arabs, Israel is a monster because they have been raised on a steady diet of bigotry and prejudices that blurs the line between criticism of Israel's behaviour and outright racial hatred. One day, the Arab nations will have to make peace with Israel, and Israel will have to grant some form of wider self-determination in the Occupied Territories. The obstacles to this are sizeable, particularly as the parties of God on both sides block any kind of deal. Nevertheless, the public at large will also have to overcome prejudices nurtured by governments for many decades.

CHAPTER 13

TURKEY
THE ONLY MUSLIM MIDDLE EASTERN DEMOCRACY

Turkey first experimented with parliamentary democracy towards the end of the Ottoman period, in 1877, but it was a brief flirtation. The first Grand National Assembly was dissolved a year later, after two elections, by Sultan Abdulhamid II. According to Bernard Lewis, Kemal Ataturk and his successors believed that "democracy is a strong medicine for their ailing country, which must be administered in a measured process. Too large and too sudden a dose can kill the patient."

When Ataturk took control of Turkey, the country was falling apart. The Ottoman Empire was crumbling and Ataturk was forced to engage in a vicious war for Turkish independence to push the allies out of Anatolia. When the war ended, the Republic of Turkey was established and recognised by the world. Ataturk was determined to bring progress and democracy to Turkey. Nearly a century later, his vision for Turkey proved prescient; Turkey is now one of the few functioning democracies in the Muslim world.

According to the Economist Intelligence Unit's Democracy Index for 2012, Turkey ranked 88th out of 167. It lagged behind other Muslim countries such as Bangladesh and Indonesia but was still ahead of other Middle Eastern countries, with the notable exception of Israel. Turkey is one of the most important Muslim states in the UN, a vital member of NATO and a rising industrial power. It is often labelled the crossroads where East meets West, and not without some justification; 90% of its territory lies in Asia, 10% in Europe. Its population is almost entirely Muslim, yet it seeks to join the European Union. It is furnished with the most successful secular constitution in the Middle East and has successfully emancipated its women, though there are still some severe problems with cultural gender discrimination in the east of the country.

The Arab revolt in the middle of the First World War effectively broke the Ottoman hold on the Middle East and seriously hampered its chances of survival as an Empire. The revolt was largely engineered by Britain at the then astronomical cost of £11 million and it forced Turkey into a drastic retreat from its Arab Muslim provinces. The dismemberment of the Empire by the European powers after the First World War was the final humiliation. The Turks no longer had any appetite for the old claims of Muslim supremacy or any interest in their old Arab dominions.

At the close of the First World War, Turkey was at the mercy of the victorious powers – chiefly Britain, France and Russia. Turkey paid a heavy price for being on the losing side as Britain and France divided its Arab provinces between themselves, while several satellite states were established on its northern borders that were well within the Russian (or Soviet) sphere of influence. Turkey did manage to chase the allies out of Anatolia itself, preserving Turkish territorial integrity.

Post imperial Turkey chose to look west, across the Bosphorus, not south to Damascus or Mecca. For Ataturk, the great reformer, progress meant Westernisation. He replaced the Arabic alphabet with the Latin one. Religion and the Sharia were totally exorcised from the state. Turkey's new legal system was based on secular, civil codes. Ataturk even outlawed the fez. Predictably, such acts angered the conservative Muslims at the time, but such was his power, he managed to bend Turkey to his will by sheer force of personality.

As the previous imperial power, Turkey was looked upon with hostility in the Arab world which deepened when Ataturk abolished the Caliphate, the official core of the Islamic world in the name of Turkish secularism. The distrust was compounded by Turkey's tolerance of Jewish immigration to the Middle East, and later, by its alliance with the state of Israel.

****

The Islamic world has proved resistant to democracy in recent decades, particularly the Arab states. Rather than the problem being intrinsic to Islam itself, it is because the social fabric of Islamic countries is very different to those of the West. The authoritarian regimes of the Middle East have damaged the political culture of the Arab countries. As a result, those states have found it difficult to fit into international groupings and blocs. Their own grouping, the Arab League, is a dysfunctional and ineffectual body.

Turkey shares much of its history with the Arab world. It is very much on the cusp of Arab land, sharing its border with both Syria and Iraq. Turkey has also managed to democratise itself and is readily accepted into the international fold, being part of NATO and one day perhaps a member of the European Union.

As the Egyptian leg of the Arab Spring showed some initial success, it was hoped that the generals in Egypt could emulate the Turkish experience and implement democratic transformation. The comparison was prescient since the Turkish military had played a pivotal role in stabilising Turkey, returning it to civilian rule after carrying out several coups d'état during the second half of the 20th century, the most important of these in 1961, 1971 and 1980. The events of 2013 in which the Egyptian army removed President Morsi bear a striking resemblance to these Turkish coups. At 73 million, Turkey's population is comparable in size to that of Egypt, at 82 million. Both countries are predominantly Sunni Muslim and both countries have significant minority populations. Turkey, as a model which achieved both democratisation and economic liberalisation within a few generations, had a great deal to teach Egypt.

The civil war in Syria changed the parameters of co-operation between Turkey and the Arab world, creating a new set of priorities. The Syrian refugee problem is proving a difficult issue for Turkey and there have been incidences of cross-border fire from Syria into Turkey. When the war broke out, Turkey made no attempt to prop up Syria, as Iran and Russia have done, or any secret of its accommodation with the Syrian opposition. Turkey has no wish to intervene militarily in Syria, though it has made it clear that it will do so if provoked.

Turkey has long had a fraught relationship with Syria. Until 1999, Syria was tactically supporting the Kurdistan Workers' Party (PKK), which had been engaged in armed insurrection against the Turkish government since 1984. The Kurds, who are based in the east of the country, have proved a difficult minority for Turkey. Only when the prospect of accession to the EU was raised did Turkey start making serious efforts to engage with its Kurdish minority.

Turkey has enjoyed full relations with Israel since 1949 and even boasts a thriving Turkish Jewish community. It is one of Israel's most important allies in the region, and a key military partner. The Israeli and Turkish air forces use each other's air space for training. Turkey imports Israeli armaments; annual trade between the two countries is worth over $4 billion.

Turkey could play a leading role in a new Greater Middle East that includes Israel. Despite its Muslim population, Turkish political culture has proved largely resistant to the anti-Israel reactionary politics of the Arab dictators. The driving force of modern politics in Turkey has been the quest for stability. Even Turkey's three major military coups d'état were executed in response to the country becoming unstable, both politically and economically. Three coups in the space of 20 years are testament to the difficulty of stabilising a large nation in such a troubled region, another lesson which Egypt will learn in the coming decades.

Staggering economic growth has turned the country into the economic powerhouse of the modern Middle East in recent years. From 2003 to 2009, economic growth averaged around 7% a year. Growth peaked at 9.2% in 2010, falling to 8.5% in 2011 and tumbling to 2.5% in 2012. In spite of the economic downtown in 2012, the economy is still expected to out-perform many of its rivals in the years leading up to 2020. In 2011, for instance, only China's economy grew at a faster rate, leading some commentators to dub Turkey the "China of Europe." In terms of number of billionaires, Istanbul ranks fourth among global financial capitals, behind New York, Moscow and London. Turkey's economic growth is all the more impressive given the fact that its achievement is self made, rather than by an accident of geography. Turkey was not blessed with vast reserves of oil and cannot depend on its fossil fuel exports for economic growth, unlike Iran, Iraq and the Gulf States. This actually puts Turkey in a superior position to the Gulf States, in spite of their immense wealth, as Turkey can count upon vast human resources and practical military manpower instead.

Turkey possesses a first world infrastructure, which is all the more conspicuous in a region in ruins. To the west, Greece, Turkey's longstanding competitor, has struggled to deal with economic catastrophe since 2008. To the south, war has torn Syria apart. Great railways once connected Istanbul to Baghdad and Damascus. War has left the Syrian and Iraqi portions of the railway unusable. Meanwhile, within Turkey itself, high speed railway lines link the country together.

In an effort not to provoke the ire of the European observers who would deny it entry into the EU, Turkey has also made dramatic improvements in human rights. When the leader of the PKK, Abdullah Ocalan, was captured in 1999, the initial rash sentence of death was promptly commuted because capital punishment is prohibited by the EU's charter of fundamental rights; its abolition is a requirement for EU entry. Though Turkey's gradual and grudging commitment to human rights may be a sacrifice it has made at the altar of economic development, the net result is the same, putting Turkey on the path towards modernity.

The Turkish Model for an Arab Spring

At the turn of the 21st century most Arabs took a dim view of Turkey. Seen as a puppet of the West and a bastion against Arab nationalist aspirations, Arabs ranked Turkey as their third most hated country, after the United States and Israel. By 2010, things had changed. Eighty-five per cent of Arabs had a strongly positive opinion of Turkey, amongst the highest of any country in the region. While Turkey had been a pariah state in the Arab world a decade before, it had transformed itself into almost a regional patriarch, looked upon as a benevolent friend to the Arab peoples.

The key change has been the administration of the Prime Minister of Turkey, Recep Tayyip Erdogan. Erdogan, prime minister since 2003, is chairman of the Justice and Development party, the centre-right, Islamist-leaning and largest political party in the Turkish parliament. Turkey's President since 2007, Abdullah Gul, belongs to the same party. Erdogan has combined a political platform that aggressively pursues economic growth alongside Islamic social conservatism. This has proved incredibly popular in Turkey, although it is not without its detractors, particularly the urban youth. The protests that enveloped the country following the proposed redevelopment of Istanbul's Gezi park illustrated this in 2013.

Erdogan's economic credentials are strong. Under his tenure, Turkish citizens have experienced a tangible improvement in their economic situation every year. Erdogan's government initiated Turkey's application to join the EU, brought Turkey's systemic problem with inflation under control and dramatically increased per capita income in Turkey.

Erdogan's Islamic conservatism, however, has been more problematic. In 2013 he banned alcohol advertising and restricted the sale of alcohol at night. He also controversially declared that a yogurt product named *ayran* was Turkey's national drink, rather than *raki*, the aniseed liquor favoured by Ataturk. His wife wears a *hijab*, which is hugely contentious in a country where secularism is irrevocably ingrained in the political culture and hijabs are forbidden in public office. On occasion, he has engaged in salvoes against Israel over their treatment of the Palestinians. He expelled the Israeli ambassador in response to the Gaza flotilla raid, which severely strained the alliance with Israel, though has proved immensely popular on the Arab street. Turkey has lost some respect in the West, particularly in forums such as NATO, for championing Islamic causes, which may ultimately damage its prospects for EU membership. For example, in 2009 President Abdullah Gul vetoed the appointment of the Danish NATO secretary general Anders Fogh Rasmussen after his defence of free speech in the Danish cartoon of Muhammad controversy of three years earlier. The crisis was only resolved after the intervention of President Obama and the assurance that Turkey would be granted membership of the European Defence Agency.

Turkey's high-profile diplomacy in the Middle East has also increased its standing among Arab nations. The principal author of Turkey's foreign policy under Erdogan has been Ahmet Davutoglu, Turkey's foreign minister since 2009 and former foreign policy adviser to Erdogan and President Gul. Davutoglu realised that the Middle East was going to play a pivotal role in world affairs in the future so he carefully positioned Turkey at the political heart of the region. Davutoglu has pursued a "Zero Problems Policy," designed to avoid alienating any of the country's neighbours. Turkey has managed to maintain good relations with countries like Israel and the United States on one hand, and Iran and Syria on the other. Turkey was acting as intermediary between Syria and Israel until 2009.

Thanks to the efforts of leaders such as Erdogan and Davutoglu, Turkey is poised to take a leading role in the re-Ottomanisation of the Middle East. The influence of the United States and Western Europe in the region is arguably at its lowest point for many decades. Israel seems more belligerent than the USA; Iran is trying to assert regional hegemony; the Gulf States, in particular Qatar, are using their vast financial resources to try and assert their diplomatic muscle. By maintaining good relations with all such parties, Turkey may in fact prove to be the victor and assert itself as a regional superpower.

****

The protest movements of the Arab Spring want to see their country modernise with economic development and democracy. Envy of the West is regarded as cultural betrayal within Arab countries but Muslim Turkey is an acceptable example to follow. Specifically, Erdogan's Justice and Development Party has proved to be a model which the Arab Islamists can copy in order to assert themselves. The Muslim Brotherhood's Freedom and Justice Party in Egypt was clearly modelled on the Turkish JDP (known as the AKP in Turkey).

Erdogan himself is extremely popular in Egypt, as he is in much of the Arab world. When he visited Egypt in September 2011, Time magazine wrote that he was received "like a rock star." His unwavering support for Palestinian self-determination has made him an unlikely champion of Arab nationalism. He carries far more weight on the issue than any of the old Arab dictators, particularly Mubarak. Such adulation on the part of the Arab public is bizarre, as Turkey's military links with Israel went far beyond anything Egypt and Jordan had with Israel. Even though these links were cut in 2009, they would be quietly restored after the countries agreed a return to full diplomatic relations in 2013. The fact that Turkey can maintain such an alliance with Israel and still be regarded as a champion of the Arab cause, shows just how successful the "Zero Problems" foreign policy has been.

The Turkish experience of Islamic democracy is often referred to as "The Turkish model," the implication being that other Muslim states in the Middle East can and should emulate Turkey's political system so as to create a stable democracy with an Islamic flavour. One of the main reasons for Turkey's democratic success is that her democratic system and institutions were not imposed upon the country by the victorious allied powers, nor put in place by the departing colonial powers, as happened with the mandate Arab states. The political culture in many Arab states is blighted by an inferiority complex and an overarching conspiratorial narrative defined by colonial subjugation. Turkish nationalism however, looks to within, and defines itself by asserting Turkey's nationhood, not in opposition to a colonial power.

Turkey is not a perfect progressive democratic nation by Western standards, still only managing the halfway point in the various global democracy indices. However, it is the best model of democracy in a Muslim Middle Eastern country and therefore a good starting point. Turkey's record of democratic elections, peaceful change-overs of government, women's rights and civil liberties is generally superior to that of any Arab nation.

The major difference between Turkey and the Arab Muslim world is secularism. The profundity of this schism remains to be seen and will only become apparent if political Islam proves to be an immovable obstacle in the path of democracy. In recent years secularism has become something of a dirty word in Arab political circles and its Arab adherents are often shouted down and ridiculed in the television studios. In the Arab world, secularism or *alamania* is synonymous with an anti-religious ideology. However, the term used in Turkey is derived from laicism, from the French *laïcité* which equates to separation and the principle of separating religious affairs from those of the state.

Erdogan has been able to promote a form of political Islam that does not intrude on the secular nature of the state. It has not been without some controversy, and indeed provoked mass demonstrations demanding the protection of the secular nature of Turkey. However, his party is seen by many in the West as a collection of Muslim democrats, moulded on the Christian Democrats of Europe.

Turkey will no doubt play a decisive role in the Middle East. Though countries such as the United Kingdom, France and Qatar have deliberately set out to increase their influence in the post-Arab Spring Middle East, Turkey will end up surpassing them all in terms of importance. This is because the Arab Spring policies of the aforementioned countries are predicated on picking winners, hoping they will become strategic partners in the future. As the events of 2012 and 2013 have proved, such long-range forecasting has proved difficult in the Middle East, particularly with regard to the Syrian civil war. Turkey, however, has merely continued the "Zero Problems" foreign policy it has maintained since the early 2000s, that of healthy relations with all its neighbours, regardless of political or religious stripe. Rather than exerting its military power, Turkey will continue to exert its soft power in the region. Ahmet Davutoglu even declared to the Turkish parliament: "We will manage the wave of change in the Middle East. Just as the ideal we have in our minds about Turkey, we have an ideal of a new Middle East. We will be the leader and the spokesperson of a new peaceful order, no matter what they say."

Ultimately, Arab countries will look to Turkey for strategic support in the region, and many Arab nations are already doing just that. Turkey has already superseded the United States as the preferred interlocutor for negotiations with Israel among states that have no relations with Israel. Despite recent problems with Israel undermining the relationship, such as the expulsion of ambassadors and suspension of military ties, Turkey remains committed to its relations with Israel, and likewise, the more experienced diplomats and politicians in Israel are well aware of just how important an ally Turkey is.

The SCAF in Egypt seemed to admire Turkey's political institutions; however they made no in-depth study of them or of Turkey's political system and its transition to democracy. As the democratic transformation drags on, there will be no shortage of Arab leaders looking to Turkey and learning from its institutions and political culture, rather than to those of Western Europe or the United States. The record of Turkey, with its string of military coups and rocky path towards democracy, dogged by frequent public demonstrations against the government, will be the one which the Arab states will follow.

The Arab Spring necessitated the involvement of the United Nations, as well as military intervention by the world's superpowers. Such outside interference is not a prudent way in which to build a sustainable democracy. Arab states need to take the initiative, and develop civil society without nudging from the larger Western powers. They need to learn by example, not instruction. Turkey will be the state to provide that example.

CHAPTER 14

THE COLONEL'S LEGACY

Sowing the Seeds of Dictatorship

A study of Nasser, his comrades and the 1952 coup d'état is key to understanding the daunting challenges that faced Egypt after the uprisings of 2011 and 2013. After he rose to power in the 1950s, Nasser instigated six decades of dictatorship which would become a model for repressive government throughout the Arab world.

Nasser was hailed by the state-controlled media as the leader who gave Egyptians their 'dignity' back; the regime defined itself in terms of a resistance to imperialism. That restored 'dignity' was fine in theory but it meant something different in practice; thousands of Egyptians were held in concentration camps, denied basic human rights and forced to live in squalor. Many simply disappeared.

Via his *Voice of the Arabs* radio station, he relentlessly promoted an Arab superiority in a manner that sometimes bordered on euphoria. Nasser and his Free Officers not only abolished the monarchy but also systematically dismantled Egyptian political culture by suppressing all organised politics except their own and rebuilding Egyptian institutions in their own image. The Muslim Brotherhood was spared the same fate, but only for a few years before they too were outlawed, their leaders imprisoned or hanged.

Some members of the old political factions were easily co-opted, switching their allegiance to the new rulers. Many of the intellectuals brought in to defend Nasser seamlessly transferred their loyalties to Sadat and Mubarak in the decades that followed, regardless of their policies or political direction becoming the backbone of the so-called 'deep state'.

From Nasser's era until today, Egypt's economy has served as a model of economic mismanagement and inefficiency. Egypt's budget first went into deficit in 1955 and has remained so until this day. Millions of Egyptians live in slums. Some were forced from their homes after Nasser began his grand urban modernisation projects; a few of these slums are literally cemeteries. Half a million Egyptians live in the City of the Dead, an old necropolis on the outskirts of Cairo.

More so than Sadat or Mubarak, Nasser eliminated all forms of opposition. Very rapidly, he turned Egypt into something resembling a fascist state. Rather than being a people's leader, as he desperately sought to portray himself, he ended up being exactly the sort of authoritarian despot he so railed against in his youth. The gap between the new ruling class and the vast majority of the population expanded rather than narrowed, leaving Egyptian politics in the hands of a small elite, personally connected to the President.

By 1955, three years after the Free Officers coup, Egyptian jails held just under 3,000 political prisoners. That number would increase to around 20,000 by the end of the Nasser era. No one really knows for sure just how many Egyptians were jailed for political reasons.

Nasser consistently exaggerated British influence and interference in the country, claiming it was the humiliation of the Egyptians. Egypt, however, was not a colony and nor was it under occupation. No foreign power attempted to abort the Free Officers coup. Nasser himself was a middle-ranking army officer who had hardly been humiliated by foreigners. In fact, the CIA initially encouraged the Free Officers, and gave Nasser plenty of covert support.

For all his ideological confusion, Nasser embarked on a wide range of projects designed to re-engineer society on both a macro and micro scale. Such efforts are rarely indulged, even in communist systems. These schemes were underpinned by a network of oppressive agencies: the army, police, prisons, propaganda bodies, administrative and judicial structures and Egypt's embassies abroad. Their sole purpose was to repress and stifle all expressions of independent popular initiative.

In spite of his ambitions, Nasser consistently failed to organise the public into an effective political force. This was apparent in the failure of the 'Liberation Rally,' abolished in 1956, and its successor the 'National Union,' dissolved in 1961, and the 'Arab Socialist Union,' disbanded in 1971.

From Nasser onwards, absolute control of Egypt lay with the President. Once Nasser was undisputed leader of the republic, he quickly set about formalising his position at its heart. For example, article 113 of the 1964 constitution stated "the President in collaboration with the government lays down the general policy of the state in all political, economic, social and administrative fields and supervises its execution."

Political control of the public was exercised by the secret police which controlled and broke up, if necessary, any unsanctioned political activity in the country. The political arena featured crass demagoguery and tedious ideological diatribes. Ultimately, every service of state was supervised by the President – education, agriculture and the media.

Nasser acquired a new cause, Arabism, for his revolutionary Egypt. This ideology led to a policy of interference and subversive activity within other Arab states which culminated in a massive military intervention in Yemen. Nasser devoted much of Egypt's media resources into spreading his anti-colonial ideology, making himself a figurehead of Arab and even third world colonial resistance. Cairo Radio broadcast throughout the Middle East and Africa in Swahili, Somali, Hausa, Arabic, English, French and Portuguese, each broadcast repeating the same anti-imperialist rhetoric, in varying cadences. The African states would prove somewhat more resistant to Nasser. Many did not bow to Egyptian pressure to sever their diplomatic relations with Israel.

Nasser's attempts at unifying the Arabs resulted in the ill thought-out United Arab Republic, where Syria and Egypt were merged into a single country from 1958 until 1961. Though the experiment was a failure, Nasser persisted in his pan-Arab ideals, invading Yemen and leaving 26,000 Egyptian soldiers dead. The Yemen war was so damaging to the Arab League it effectively finished it off as a credible organisation.

The Rise of a Dictator

In 1952, a small group of army officers deposed the King of Egypt, King Farouk. They declared Egypt a republic and took control of the country with their leader, General Muhammad Naguib, as President. In an unusual example of Cold War collaboration the coup was supported by both the CIA and the KGB. Both parties were keen to undo British influence in Egypt and in the region at large. Though Naguib was nominally in charge, the young Lieutenant Colonel Gamal Abdel Nasser held the real power among the Free Officers.

On 24 April 1952 the United States National Security Council approved policy 129/1 with respect to the Arab states and Israel, "for fullest use of special political measures to influence political change... into channels that will effect the least compromise of Western interests and offer maximum promise of stable non-communist regimes." The policy gave the CIA the clearance to subvert Middle Eastern governments and sponsor potential alternative governments so as to create allies for the Cold War.

Egypt became something of a test case for the USA. Nasser would ultimately prove to be one of the CIA's greatest failures for he was a man they could not control. Throughout 1952 the CIA was kept aware of what was going on in Egypt by maintaining contact with the main Free Officers, in particular with Nasser. The CIA dispatched the officer Miles Copeland to Cairo to help reorganise the Egyptian Intelligence service, as well as to conduct seminars on American business and diplomacy. He stayed in Cairo for two years, became a confidante of Nasser and a useful informal channel of communication between the Americans and the Egyptian President.

Besides Copeland, the USA sent dozens of military advisers to Egypt. The CIA turned to Reinhard Gehlen, a German ex-general, to supply some of the officers. Gehlen in turn sent Otto Skorzeny, one of Adolf Hitler's favoured special operations commandos, to Egypt. Skorzeny recruited other ex-Nazis to work in Egypt, including some who had actively participated in the Holocaust, such as Leopold Gleim, one-time head of the Gestapo department for Jewish affairs in Poland. James Eichelberger, the CIA's station chief in Cairo, provided intelligence to Nasser's internal security service. Later, the CIA sent Paul Linebarger, later famous as the science fiction writer Cordwainer Smith. Linebarger was a former OSS propagandist and expert on psychological warfare. He instructed the regime on how to discredit its enemies and promote itself through the media. Linebarger specifically advised the Egyptians on how to create anti-American propaganda aimed at maintaining themselves in power. The tactic was extremely short-sighted as the majority of Middle Eastern countries would use his techniques and anti-Americanism would become endemic to Arab culture. The practice has severely damaged American interests in the region and will continue to do so for the foreseeable future.

In February 1954, Nasser had his army units kidnap Naguib and then announced to the nation that the President had been relieved of his duties. Protests against the purging of Naguib erupted, and were supported by the Egyptian media. Nasser was forced to retreat and reinstate Naguib as President. But he appointed himself prime minister, and carefully manoeuvred his allies into the major positions of influence. His friend, Major Hakim Amr, was promoted to full general and became Commander of the Armed Forces, a role which until then belonged to Naguib. Some officers in the army began to worry about Nasser's increasing dominance of politics and the military and particularly about the nascent politicisation of the army that was based on loyalty to Nasser himself.

After the fiasco of Naguib's abduction, many senior officers tendered their resignations. However, they opened the way for Nasser to purge the army of disloyal officers. In October 1954, 38 ex-ministers and prime ministers and 26 prominent journalists and writers were barred from working for a decade. All political parties were dissolved and the government bureaucracy steadily dismantled. Bureaucrats and politicians were replaced by ardent Nasserists, mostly mid-ranking career army officers, who had never held civilian positions before.

Egypt's institutions were almost 100 years old when Nasser took power; a liberal class akin to those found in Europe had been taking shape. However, with the end of the monarchy came the end of almost every other organ of the state because each was brought under Nasser's command. The very super-structure of the state was destroyed and rebuilt; political parties, parliament, the judiciary, capitalism, banking, universities and the press were all controlled by the state. All organised political activity outside the purview of government was banned and the more resistant leaders imprisoned.

Nasser closely monitored his colleagues for any hint of dissent. He even used the latest bugging technology acquired from the CIA to listen in on their private conversations. After taking over the Ministry of Interior in 1953 he had access to all the classified information the government held on Egypt's political elite. Nasser retired or removed 40 senior and 100 junior police officers from the ministry. Such an action was an indicator of Nasser's future political tactics. Upon taking control of a ministry or institution, he would promptly purge it of all disloyal elements. When they came to power the Muslim Brotherhood's tactic of removing troublesome individuals from ministries they headed was identical to the tactic Nasser had employed some 60 years earlier.

Nasser made numerous speeches denouncing Western influence and colonialism, while at the same time presenting himself as Egypt's saviour. He also negotiated the British withdrawal from the Suez Canal, which the British did on condition that Sudan was granted self-determination rather than subsumed into Egypt. This was against the wishes of Naguib, who was half-Sudanese.

In his younger years, Nasser dabbled with the Muslim Brotherhood, but was more drawn to a newly formed proto-fascist party Misr El Fatat (Young Egypt). Nasser never quite trusted the Muslim Brotherhood, although they had supported the Free Officers in their coup to topple the monarchy.

After the Free Officers came to power, Nasser ordered a trial of the police officers accused of the fatal shooting of Hassan al-Banna, the founder of the Muslim Brotherhood, back in 1949. They received lengthy prison sentences. However, they were quietly released after a few months when Nasser fell out with the Brotherhood after 1954. The Muslim Brotherhood were angry with the Free Officers, and with Nasser in particular, as they had initially seen him as an ally to their cause. Nasser had grown close to Sayed Qutb, one of the Brotherhood's main ideologues, visiting Qutb at home to seek his advice on affairs of government. Sometimes the two would spend all day together.

When it became clear that Nasser had no intention of bringing about the Islamic state the Brotherhood wanted, they were furious with him. Nasser tried to bribe Qutb, offering him any position in government he wanted. Qutb turned him down. Nasser also set about building a civil organisation, Tahrir (Liberation) to compete with the Muslim Brotherhood on the streets, in particular by offering rival social programmes of the sort that had made the Brotherhood so popular among the poor.

On October 26, 1954 Nasser was the subject of an assassination attempt as he gave a speech in Alexandria. A Muslim Brother managed to get within 25 feet of Nasser and opened fire on him. Nasser survived and, remaining calm, declared, "My countrymen, my blood spills for you and for Egypt. I will live for your sake and die for the sake of your freedom and honour." The whole spectacle was broadcast on the radio, across the Middle East. It was a watershed moment for Nasser; his brush with death won him extraordinary popularity. He capitalised on the moment, deliberately employing Egypt's cultural elite to start building one of the Arab world's first personality cults. Singers like Umm Kulthum sang nationalist songs with Nasser as the hero and plays were produced denigrating his political opponents. General Naguib was officially dismissed as President on November 14, 1954 though he had hardly appeared in public since March that year.

The regime used the incident as a pretext for a massive crackdown against the Brotherhood. The Brotherhood's top leaders were imprisoned, including Qutb. In October 1954 Nasser informed an English journalist that he had 18,000 Muslim Brothers in custody.

Some years later, King Faisal of Saudi Arabia pressurised Nasser to release some of the Brothers he had imprisoned. Many of the released made their way to Saudi Arabia, where they were provided with lucrative jobs. Those Brothers expelled from Egypt included Said Ramadan, son-in-law of Hassan al-Banna and father of the Islamic thinker Tariq Ramadan, who made his way to Saudi Arabia, and Yusuf al Qaradawi who settled in Qatar.

Nasser was finally confirmed as President by a public referendum in 1956. Four years after a coup that became known as the Free Officers Revolution, the entire government, military and political culture of Egypt, was centred on one man, Gamal Abdel Nasser. His early political actions were confined to fiery speeches full of vague aspirations to national identity and the restoration of dignity. His political platform centred around a small political group of Egypt's middle class socialists with whom he kept in contact after the coup. It was from among this group that the first civilian ministers were appointed in an overwhelmingly militarised cabinet.

Initially, American policy was to keep Nasser in power. It was hoped that he could become a leader of the Muslim world ("the Muslim Billy Graham") whilst still remaining friendly to American interests. However, Nasser's anti-American propaganda, and sponsorship of the fedayeen (Palestinian militia) making raids into Israel was extremely unpopular with the American Congress. This made it impossible for Nasser to buy arms from the US, which would have been his first choice; Congress has to approve any multi-million dollar arms deals. Nasser, however, believed he could play the superpowers off against each other, while still remaining "non-aligned", one of the core principles of his foreign policy. He opted to buy Soviet arms from the Czechs in a $250 million deal, an astronomical sum of money at the time.

The move sent relations between the USA and Egypt into a downward spiral. In addition to the arms deal, Nasser's recognition of communist China prompted the US and UK to withdraw the funds they had promised for the building of the Aswan dam. In response, Nasser nationalised the Suez Canal, provoking the Suez war.

In 1956 the Eisenhower administration abandoned the idea of supporting Nasser and Arab nationalism, turning instead to Saudi Arabia, hoping King Saud could lead the Muslim world against communism. By 1957, relations with USA were at an all-time low. When Vice-President Richard Nixon toured the Middle East, he snubbed Nasser by not visiting Cairo. When President Eisenhower himself visited the region in 1959, Egypt was again absent from the itinerary. Nasser would later mock the Americans for trying to co-opt him and claimed that the funds to build the Cairo tower, an ornate lattice construction which is still Egypt's tallest building, were the result of a cash bribe of a million dollars with which the Americans tried to buy him.

The Ahmed Hussein Factor

Nasser's political understanding of the world was influenced by one person in particular, Ahmed Hussein. Nasser became aware of Hussein in his teens, watching him deliver his rousing speeches in Cairo. Some of Nasser's major speeches would plagiarise large chunks of Hussein's speeches. An ardent admirer of the fascist leader of Italy Benito Mussolini, Hussein was a young lawyer who had founded the Young Egypt Party, of which Nasser was an early member.

Hussein was virulently anti-British, referring to the British as an army of occupation, a theme which would run through Nasser's grandstand speeches. Hussein understood the value of propaganda and powerful oratory, techniques which were employed around the same time to great effect by the fascists of Europe. He had been born in 1911 and raised in Damietta, on the Nile Delta. Politically active throughout his youth, he joined various political organisations at school and claimed to have attended an anti-British demonstration as early as 1919, as a small child. In 1931, he campaigned for the Middle East Student Unions Conference and, in 1933, he helped found the Misr el Fatat society (Young Egypt). They adopted the slogan, "God, country and the King," and held broadly nationalist ideals, such as the expulsion of the British and unity with Sudan. The group affiliated themselves to fascist Italy, and tried to cultivate relations with the German embassy, though the Germans would later turn them down.

In 1937, Hussein visited Mussolini, and on his return established his own political paramilitary force, the Greenshirts, emulating the Blackshirts of Italy and Brownshirts in Germany. Later on Hussein turned against Italy, considering it a "backward" country.

Just before the Second World War, he published the newspaper *Al Galaa* (The Evacuation) and became a popular figure, admired by many in Egypt's political circles, from the King down. He was even admired by Ali Mahir Pasha, twice prime minister in the 1930s and again in the 1950s. Older Egyptians joined his party which had been a youth organisation. For his political charisma, he acquired the moniker *El Rayes* (The President).

His greatest legacy stems from November 1938 when his organisation announced its *Waa'd wa Methaaq* (Charter Promise). The charter was a programme of social reform which advocated revolution and the use of force as a means of bringing about political change. He even called for a military coup and adopted nationalist slogans like "Egypt above all," "Egypt is the mother of all cultures," and "We have educated humanity."

He blamed the British for Egypt's backwardness, attacked the rich for their opulence and promised to give the poor housing, schools and hospitals. Such a revolutionary platform was obviously similar to that of Nasser and the Free Officers. Nasser took direct inspiration from Hussein who was only a few years older than he was.

By 1950, the Young Egypt Party had become the Socialist Party. In a manifesto from the 1950s, Hussein called for the formation of the United Arab States, for the same kind of pan-Arab state Nasser would try to establish with the United Arab Republic. In July 1952, a few months before the Free Officers coup, Hussein was arrested. He was released after the coup in July. However, the new regime could not tolerate such a popular political figure and Hussein was again imprisoned and subjected to torture during the power struggle between Nasser and General Naguib. After he was released, he went into exile, roaming from Syria, to Lebanon, to London, to Sudan. From exile, he sent telegrams to Nasser, one of his early followers, warning him not to fall into the trap of tyranny and dictatorship.

****

State repression by the police really began in earnest a few months after Nasser assumed absolute power in late 1954. It essentially continued ever after in different forms and guises, until the downfall of Mubarak. The General Intelligence Services, informally known as the *Mukhabarat*, were the eyes with which he monitored the population and the stick which kept them in line. Nasser's prisons had no address, were headed by generals rather than governors and lay outside the bounds of the judicial system.

The Mukhabarat were also essential for controlling what people read and watched, with the ultimate aim of instructing Egyptians in what to do and think. As such, the media was intricately linked with the Mukhabarat. Large chunks of radio news bulletins were devoted to the great leader's work and global leadership. Even many years later, Nasser's speeches were broadcast daily on Libyan TV during the Gaddafi era, one of the favourites being an old speech announcing the nationalisation of the Suez Canal.

In 1960, Nasser nationalised the Egyptian press, bringing the media and printing under state control. Even with total state oversight, it was still important to terrorise the occasional editor in order to keep the rest in line. In 1965, Nasser had Mustapha Amin, the liberal editor of the *Akbar Al Youm* newspaper thrown in prison on charges of spying for the United States. The charges were never proved but Amin was publicly denounced as a traitor. His crime was to call for democratic reform and closer ties with the West. The allegation was particularly hypocritical as Nasser himself enjoyed close links with the CIA back in the early 1950s.

In 1954, Nasser appointed a 33 year-old army major, Kemal El Din Hussein, Minister of Social Affairs. Two years later he was made Minister of Education, giving him the power to appoint or dismiss the deans of university facilities. One of his predecessors was the prodigious intellectual literary giant, Taha Hussein. Whereas Taha Hussein was an author, journalist and professor of ancient literature, Kemal El Din Hussein was a soldier with a degree in military science. He fundamentally changed the educational curriculum, shifting the focus away from Egypt's historical heritage towards modern Nasserism. The schoolbooks were rewritten so as to portray Nasser as the hero of the Arab nations. In morning assembly, children would sing songs proclaiming love for the great leader instead of the national anthem. Partly as a result of his invasion of Egypt's schools and therefore the minds of Egypt's children, more than 40 years after his death, Nasser is still absolved of his obvious failures, which were blamed on treacherous provocateurs and foreign powers.

The universities themselves, so often hotbeds of political activism throughout the world, were brought firmly under the regime's control. Student union elections were suspended, like most forms of democratic expression in the country, and student demonstrations were banned. Nasser gutted Egypt's universities even before he was officially President, sacking about 100 professors and lecturers in 1954. Many of the purged professors left Egypt, some for the USA and Europe, others to lucrative posts in the newly founded universities in the oil-rich Gulf States.

Despite his outspoken affection for socialism, Nasser was wary of actually allowing genuine socialist politics to take root in Egypt. To that end, he initiated the vertical segmentation of the population by professional activity, in order to prevent them forming solidarity partnerships or unions on the basis of class interest. By compartment-alising society, he prevented any other political movements from forming which could potentially be a threat to his overall control of the country. In a charade of mass participation, the regime created its own pseudo-representative local and central bodies, all loyal to Nasser and Nasserism, though they generally failed to mobilise the masses to act against their own self-interest.

In the 1960s, the judiciary grew more and more outspoken about Nasser's disregard for the rule of law. In 1969 Nasser responded by dismissing more than 200 judges, annihilating the integrity of the judiciary in what became known as The Judges' Massacre. The victims included the entire board of the Judges' Club, the Egyptian judges' association, numerous lower court judges and members of the Public Prosecutor's office. Some judges were even put on trial, accused of spying for foreign powers. When the court found the judges not guilty and dismissed the case, Nasser defied the court, rearrested the judges, ordered a retrial and sacked the judges who presided over the case. Once again however, the judges were acquitted, although none of them was reinstated. Realising that the recalcitrant judiciary needed to be firmly under his control, Nasser set about co-opting it with vanity positions and privileges. Where necessary, Nasser also used a military court, presided over by army officers loyal to him, to bypass the civil judiciary.

Nasser also set about seizing control of Egypt's economy. Many private enterprises were confiscated by the state or simply shut down altogether. Macroeconomic policy was totally under his control. The fiscal budget was no longer even discussed in parliament.

Economic Meltdown – Nasser's Socialism

Before 1952, state industries were limited to the railway network, a petroleum refinery and some military factories. By 1963 the state owned everything, from buses and lorries to major shops and large houses. All were taken from their owners and re-allocated by the state. While the prevailing ambition during the era of the monarchy had been to Egyptianise the country, Nasser's ambition was to nationalise assets to create extra revenue, which dried up after a few years. By the 1960s, the economy was in retreat. Cotton exports were dwindling and hard currency reserves minimal. In a desperate attempt to turn the export situation around, Nasser rushed into a fresh round of nationalisation and confiscation of private assets.

Confiscation was common. After the war in Suez, the assets of thousands of Egyptian Jews were confiscated, shortly before they were expelled. Another practical solution to Egypt's low living standards was to order landlords to slash rents by 50 per cent. Consequently, property values plummeted, and many fell into disrepair and eventual decay. Likewise, when the government ordered bakeries to cut the price of bread, the quality of bread dropped overnight.

One of Nasser's major economic projects was the Tahrir (Liberation) province, an attempt to create a socialist utopian community to the west of the Nile Delta. The project was characteristic of those favoured by 20th century demagogues, a poorly thought-out attempt at social and economic engineering via the creation of a model community, which was in fact a poor facsimile of a kibbutz seeking to emulate Israeli success at "making the deserts bloom". The project was a particularly Nasserist aspiration; he insisted that no outside expertise be brought in, that only Arab technicians would supervise and direct the effort. The project was a complete failure; seeking to reclaim 200,000 *feddans* (roughly equivalent to one acre) of arable land from the desert, it barely managed 12,000, mostly poor quality soil, at a cost of £13 million (some estimates are much higher). Each feddan cost £1,000, at a time when a feddan of good quality land fetched around £70. Nasser wouldn't be drawn to confirm figures at the time and no accounts were ever published. When the mass corruption of the project's governor, former Free Officer Magdi Hassanein, was exposed Nasser protected him, rewarding his theft and mismanagement with an ambassadorial posting to Prague. In the meantime, the whole endeavour was quietly dropped from the news and excised from history.

Nasser's agrarian reforms were largely symbolic. Land reform sought to redistribute just over a quarter of a million acres of land that mostly belonged to 300 families, including the royal family. Initially land ownership was limited to 200 feddans (or 300, for fathers with two or more children), though this was reduced to 100 in 1961. Ultimately, only about 15% of Egyptian land was reallocated to the peasantry because peasants were only permitted to buy five feddans of redistributed land from the government.

Egypt's state driven economy was riddled with systemic problems that inevitably resulted in economic failure. One of the major problems was that Nasser created a clientalist state; he simply bought the support of Egyptians by providing them jobs, regardless of whether the state could accommodate them or not. In early 1967 Egypt sought the services of the British human resources firm Booz, Allen & Hamilton to analyse Egypt's civil service. The firm warned the government that the government needed no more than 200,000 employees, as opposed to the million on the books. Were such a state of over-employment to continue, they reported, administrative chaos would probably be the result. Bribery had become commonplace, the only means available to a citizen to get anything done.

Despite the regime's optimistic projections, agricultural productivity showed no improvement over the Nasser years. Cotton production in 1968 was roughly the same as it was in 1918. Wheat imports went from 15,000 tonnes in 1955, to 300,000 tonnes in 1956. A decade later that figure had reached 3 million tonnes. By 1968 the value of Egypt's food imports was equal to that of its cotton exports. Being forced to import its food was humiliating for Egypt, and a far cry from the days when Egypt had been the bread basket of the Roman Empire.

Confidence in banking was severely damaged when the Banque Misr (Egyptian Bank) was abruptly nationalised in 1960. The governor of the Central Bank expressed his concerns about the economic situation to Nasser, stating that it was not the government's place to invest in massive development projects without any other economic stimulus because it would simply lead to inflation and hurt the economy.

For all Nasser's talk of self sufficiency, in May 1962, Egypt was forced to go to the International Monetary Fund for an immediate injection of credit of E£20m, on condition that the government rein in expenditure and curb internal demand. However, the government had no intention of curbing demand, or cutting expenditure. Indeed, expenditure began to rise dramatically with the escalating involvement in Yemen. The result was an immediate currency devaluation, leading to a massive spike in inflation which the government attempted to suppress. As the balance of trade deficit continued to grow, and the government kept prices artificially low, the early 1960s saw more and more shortages of basic foodstuffs such as rice, bread and meat, while the black market expanded dramatically.

Nasser's political quarrels of the 1960s led the USA to suspend its wheat shipments to Egypt, forcing Egypt to use its foreign currency reserves for payments on the global market. In 1965/6, Egypt was importing E£55m worth of wheat alone, higher than Egypt's total exports to the West (£E52m). The monetary situation deteriorated so badly that four aeroplanes out of seven of Egypt's national fleet of aeroplanes were grounded. The government did not even have enough hard currency to buy necessary spare parts.

On the eve of the coup in 1952, Egypt's gold reserves stood at $40 million with an additional $46 million in hard currency. The estimated hard currency reserve was less than $3million in 1967. The previous year, Egypt's balance of trade deficit was about $400 million. This was a catastrophic problem; its gold and currency reserves were virtually exhausted and its loans unserviceable. It is actually rather difficult to document the economic chaos that must necessarily have taken place in the intervening years because viable statistics from Egypt in the 1950s are both difficult to come by and unreliable. The regime would announce and broadcast often irrational economic policies and grand state projects, while quietly centralising the Egyptian economic system and suppressing any honest auditing of accounts.

When Nasser died in 1970 the legal minimum wage was set at E£7.5 per month, a mere 10% above what it had been in 1950, without even taking inflation into account. Egypt had just been through two disastrous wars; the involvement in Yemen which cost thousands of lives, and the war against Israel in 1967 which lasted six days and cost Egypt the entire Sinai Peninsula. For all Nasser's promises of grandeur, he left his country $3 billion in debt.

The Pan-Arab Leader and Divider

When the Suez crisis erupted in 1956, Egypt was almost a bit part player. Britain, France and Israel swiftly overcame any domestic resistance and were only forced to withdraw after the enraged US President Eisenhower forced their retreat through the considerable financial leverage the US held over Britain and France as a result of the Marshall Plan and an oil embargo in concert with Saudi Arabia. However, Nasser was able to spin the crisis into a victory for Egypt himself and, by extension, Arab nationalism. Nasser was suddenly a superstar in the Arab world, and Arabs saw him as a leader who could actually deliver on their aspiration towards self-determination. Egypt's propaganda services were full of praise, glorifying Egypt's defeat of the two major colonial powers, and Israel to boot.

By 1957, the divided Syrian leadership was courting Nasser as a potential leader for Syria as well. Such efforts would eventually lead to Egypt and Syria becoming one country. The United Arab Republic was born on February 1, 1958. It was a hasty undertaking but pan-Arabists hoped it was the first step towards the creation of a pan-Arab superstate. However, by 1961, the union had disbanded, wracked by disharmony and rivalry. Syrian politicians were vexed by Nasser's unwillingness to share power as well as by Syria's diminished position in the partnership. Nasser retained the name United Arab Republic as Egypt's official title, even after the break-up of the union. It was not until after his death that Sadat changed Egypt's name once again to the Arab Republic of Egypt.

As Nasser began to spread his pan-Arabist ideals, he came into conflict with other Arab countries, especially the major monarchies of the region – Saudi Arabia and Jordan – who were wary of Nasser's ambitions towards the leadership of the Arab world. As a result, there were multiple attempts by Egyptian intelligence to assassinate Jordan's King Hussein. King Faisal of Saudi Arabia ordered the printing of millions of books by Sayd Qutb whom Nasser eventually hanged. Though Saudi promotion of Qutbism was initially instigated as a means to combat Arab nationalism, the pandemic of Islamism it unleashed would be felt into the next century.

Soon after coming to power, Nasser embroiled Egypt in Cold War politics, ostensibly siding with the Soviet Union. Despite portraying himself as a global statesman, Nasser only ever met the world's major leaders once, in 1960, when he attended a United Nations General Assembly summit as the head of the Egyptian delegation. There he met the likes of Eisenhower and Castro for the first time. The United States, which initially thought of Nasser as a potential ally in the region, supported Saudi Arabia as a counterweight to him. Nasser's nationalist politics and alliance with the Soviets were increasingly worrying the US.

In spite of his pan-Arab rhetoric, Nasser carefully set about undermining pan-Arab institutions, and his neighbours, in the region. Nasser was only interested in pan-Arabism if he could be in control. Soon after the Free Officers' coup, Nasser sent a trusted comrade, Major Salah Salem to the home of the Secretary General of the Arab League, Azzam Pasha, with a gun in his hand, demanding his immediate resignation. The Arab regimes did nothing to put a stop to Nasser's blatantly domineering behaviour.

Nasser's largest undertaking in the cause of pan-Arab nationalism, however, was the North Yemen civil war. Yemen was very much Nasser's Vietnam, indeed, the historian Michael Oran described Vietnam as America's Yemen. Nasser began by committing 5,000 troops to North Yemen in 1962 in an effort to sustain a republican coup d'état against the monarch, Iman Al Badr. The young Al Badr had survived the coup and was busy plotting to retake the country, with support from Jordan and Saudi Arabia. After the United Arab Republic fell apart, Egypt had to regain some of its prestige and, crucially, find new allies for Nasser's brand of pan-Arabism, in a region that was proving curiously resistant to Arab political unity. Also, South Yemen was occupied by the British whom Nasser was keen to evict. He believed he could do so once he had a foothold in North Yemen.

The war started badly for Nasser. Egyptian field commanders complained that they had not been issued with any topographical maps of the country. Yemen, at the foot of the Arabian Peninsula, is a rugged, mountainous country whose villages tend to be built at the top of steep hills and mountains, largely as a deterrent to invaders. The Egyptians also had to overcome the local tribal fighters, well known for their ferocity and familiarity with their own land. The Egyptian intelligence chief, Salah Nasr, later conceded that Egypt possessed virtually no information at all on Yemen. Egypt did not even have an embassy in Yemen, having abandoned the country in 1961.

Saudi Arabia was desperate not to allow Nasser a foothold in Yemen and so propped up the royalist resistance. Egypt was also in open conflict with the Saudis, sending warplanes on bombing raids in southern Saudi Arabia. Yemen was one of the first conflicts since the First World War in which chemical weapons were used. Reports of gas were scanty at first, but incidents became more regular as the war dragged on.

By 1965, Nasser had 70,000 troops in Yemen. Though they held the large parts of the South of the country, the North was still very much in the hands of the royalists, aside from the major cities. In many ways, the war in Yemen was the template which other asymmetric conflicts, such as Vietnam or post 2001 Afghanistan, would follow. A better armed and equipped army holding the cities, amid an impenetrable countryside held by smaller irregular forces. The royalists would make use of caves as bases, moving about with ease, committing guerrilla raids, wearing down the enemy. They inflicted massive casualties on the Egyptians, 26,000 by the end of the conflict.

By 1967, with Egyptian forces still bogged down in Yemen, Israel decided to launch a pre-emptive strike against Egypt, Jordan and Syria. In the end, it was the Israeli offensive against the three Arab states that united the Arab world, rather than anything Nasser said or did in the cause of Arab nationalism. The war was an unmitigated disaster for the Arab states, who all lost vast swathes of territory. Egypt alone lost 15,000 men, although the war did at least give Nasser a face-saving withdrawal from Yemen.

An Arab League summit in Khartoum hammered out a peace agreement between Egypt and Saudi Arabia. Egypt would withdraw from Yemen, and Saudi Arabia would stop funding the royalists. Eventually, Saudi Arabia recognised the republic. Even though the royalists still controlled vast swathes of territory, they had effectively lost and disbanded in 1970. Iman al Badr went to live in Britain, where he died in 1996, the last heir of the Hamidaddin dynasty.

The New Middle East Order after 1967 and the Rise of Saudi Arabia

Israel first occupied the Sinai Peninsula during the Suez crisis in 1956. Though Britain and France were forced to withdraw soon after taking control of the canal, Israel held on to Sinai until 1957. Nasser made a number of concessions to Israel in order to secure its withdrawal, concessions that were kept secret from the Egyptian people, including one allowing UN observers on the Egyptian side of the Israeli border, another demilitarising Sharm el Sheikh, free passage for Israeli shipping through the Gulf of Aqaba (Gulf of Eilat, as it is known in Israel), recognition of Egypt-Israel border and the use of Suez Canal, with a gentleman's agreement that Israeli ships not hoist their flag as they passed through.

From the mid 1960s, Nasser increasingly indulged in sabre-rattling against Israel as his propaganda machine hailed him as leader of the Arabs and champion of the Palestinian cause. In March 1966, Nasser declared, "We shall not enter Palestine with its soil covered in sand, we shall enter it with its soil saturated in blood." By 1967, the threats had become more direct, with Radio Cairo warning, "The existence of Israel has continued too long. We welcome the Israeli aggression. We welcome the battle we have long awaited. The peak hour has come. The battle has come in which we shall destroy Israel." In case there was any ambiguity, Nasser clarified the position on May 18, 1967 by stating, "Our basic objective will be the destruction of Israel. The Arab people want to fight."

That month, Nasser expelled the UN peacekeepers from Sinai and announced a blockade of the Straits of Tiran (at the southern end of the Gulf of Aqaba) to ships bound for Israel. The blockade, which effectively sealed off the port of Eilat, violated the Suez armistice agreement. Nasser's actions were immensely popular across the Arab world; there were pro-Nasser demonstrations in the major Arab cities, and Arab governments lined up to wholeheartedly endorse Nasser's actions, encouraged by the Soviet Union. However, such a provocation was viewed by Israel as an act of war, a war for which they were prepared and the Arabs were not. Egypt had tens of thousands of men tied down in Yemen, and the Arab armies were generally poorly trained and ill-equipped.

Early in the morning on 5 June 1967, Israel launched a massive airstrike against Egypt. The Israelis knew that if they survived the coming conflict, they would need air superiority. The Soviet-supplied Egyptian air force, which constituted over 400 warplanes, presented the greatest aerial threat. Egypt's poor air defences, some of which were de-activated so as to prevent an Egyptian general who was flying at the time from being shot down, were almost totally ineffectual. The Egyptian air force was virtually wiped out, with most planes destroyed on the ground. The

Israelis strafed the Egyptian runways, rendering them unusable for the remainder of the war.

Despite the catastrophic losses on the first day, Nasser claimed to the public and to King Hussein of Jordan that Egypt had scored a resounding victory against Israel. King Hussein, who had been reluctant to get involved, decided to attack Israel from the West Bank and the Syrians, also influenced by Nasser's lies, attacked from the north. The attacks were all failures and Israel launched stinging counter-attacks into the heart of enemy territory. Within six days, the Israeli army swept across Gaza, Sinai, the West Bank and the Golan Heights. The war was over, Israel had won a stunning victory and the surrounding Arab states were crippled. Even though the war had been initiated by Israel, and even though Israel had won a stunning victory, it still appeared the victim of Arab aggression and enjoyed sympathy on the world stage.

Nasser was unchanged. After the defeat, he abruptly appeared on television to offer his resignation in a dramatic speech. The resignation sparked pro-Nasser demonstrations across Egypt, to which Nasser responded by returning to power. Although he was supposed to have relinquished power for 48 hours, he still retained command of the police and the army. That summer, Nasser arrested 50 senior army officers who had fought in the war, on the pretext that they were plotting a coup against him.

The defeat in 1967 and Egypt's humiliating exit from Yemen fundamentally changed the balance of power in the Middle East. Nasser's pan-Arab project was in tatters. King Faisal of Saudi Arabia tried to assert his country's leading role in the region, capitalising on his Islamic credentials as the guardian of the two Holy Cities, Mecca and Medina. The Saudis would be rebuffed by the Ba'ath regimes in Syria and Iraq, though the Saudis would live to see the Iraqi Ba'ath regime annihilated by the United States and the Syrian branch of Ba'athism torn apart by civil war in the 21st century. In any case, the Ba'ath regimes had little to do with Arab nationalism or Arab self-determination, each having degenerated into self-perpetuating personality cults marked by brutal repression and absolute autocracy.

The Saudis would soon realise the power of the media, funding and setting up newspapers and satellite TV channels in London and the Gulf. These TV channels would also become far more effective tools for exercising soft power than Radio Cairo had ever been. The Saudis also had a far more effective ally in the region in the form of the United States, rather than the Soviet Union. The Arab nationalist regimes who stuck with the Soviet Union, as Nasser had done, would live to see Soviet funding dry up as the USSR collapsed in on itself. Even Nasser's successor Sadat realised that the United States was the more crucial ally and he famously re-orientated Egypt towards the USA. In spite of the 1973 war, another defeat to Israel packaged as a victory in Arab history books, it was the support of the USA which won Egypt back the Sinai Peninsula in the Camp David Accords of 1977. When Saddam Hussein invaded Kuwait in 1991, the USA engaged in a full-scale war to win it back for the Kuwaitis. Although the Gulf States are almost totally dependent on the United States for their defence, they have been able to maintain their territorial integrity, and their archaic monarchic governments.

****

Nasser's presidency was not without domestic opposition. In September 1965, the funeral of former Prime Minister Mustafa El Nahhas turned into a mass demonstration against the oppressive regime. Many were arrested and the coffin was removed from the cemetery by the police. Nasser faced his own 'Mubarak moment' in March 1968. The demonstrations began when students started a sit-in protest, enraged after the regime acquitted two air force officers charged with incompetence during the 1967 war, though two other officers were convicted. The protesters demanded tougher sentences for all four of them. The protests quickly spread across Cairo, Alexandria and Helwan. Demonstrators chanted "the police are the enemy of the people!" "Where is freedom Sadat?" "Dismiss this parliament of incompetents!" "Down with Heikal!" as well as "No socialism without freedom."

The government tried to direct the protests by using a trade union leader in their pay to assume leadership of the demonstrations, and hopefully calm them down. The plan did not work. The regime also shut down the Helwan to Cairo railway in another ineffective effort to stop the unrest from spreading. In Helwan, the police were forced to retreat, and protesters took over the town's police headquarters. The police later fought back and re-occupied the police station. Due to tight state censorship, figures of those killed or wounded were never released. In Cairo, the protesters besieged the parliament, and the main office of the state's *Al Ahram* newspaper. When the editor-in-chief, Mohamed Hassanein Heikal refused to appear before the demonstrators, they called him a coward and tried to set fire to the building. He was forced to flee through a secret door.

The protesters' demands were systematically played down and distorted by the media and state television. Army and police were deployed in strategic parts of the city where they fired tear gas and live rounds. The university campus was occupied for the first time. In retaliation, the university was closed for a month and several hundred students and workers were arrested and imprisoned on charges of sabotage.

The authorities systematically suppressed all information about the numerous popular demonstrations spreading across Egypt's towns and cities. Ultimately, the uprising failed due to a lack of coordination and the secret police were able to detain the ring-leaders.

Afterwards the regime activated its propaganda machine. Rigged elections were held, and Nasser made a series of democratic promises that were never fulfilled. It is ironic that some protesters carried Nasser's portrait during the 2011 uprising; Nasser brutally suppressed such civil unrest, and would have done theirs.

CHAPTER 15

THE MODERNISERS ISMAIL AND FUAD

Khedive Ismail

My country is no longer in Africa; we are now part of Europe.
It is therefore natural for us to abandon our former ways and to
adopt a new system adapted to our social conditions.

Kedhive Ismail, 1869

The grandson of Muhammad Ali, Khedive Ismail dreamed of Egypt as a France by the Nile, and of Cairo as his Paris. Tahrir Square was his Place de la Concorde, at the end of a boulevard that began at Abdeen Palace.

Ismail became the Khedive of Egypt in 1863. His elder brother and original heir to the kingdom had been drowned in a tragic railway accident as his railway carriage was pulled across the Nile in the days before railway bridges. Egypt was still nominally an Ottoman province. However, since the reign of Ismail's great grandfather Muhammed Ali, the governors of Egypt had run the country as a nominally independent state.

The young Ismail was among the first children of the 'Paris School', the generation of Egyptians sent to France for their education. Their European education shaped the outlook of leaders like Ismail, who saw themselves as having more in common with the monarchs and aristocrats of Europe than with the *beys* and *walis* of the Ottoman provinces. As

Khedive, Ismail continued the grand state building project of Muhammad Ali, the great rebel Viceroy of Egypt. However, Ismail gave the Egyptian state a cosmopolitan character, helping to create and develop Egypt's middle class and intelligentsia. It was a major challenge. Egypt's infrastructure was not much further advanced than it had been in medieval times.

Khedive Ismail had one major advantage over his predecessors in his mission to modernise Egypt: the Suez Canal. Stretching 100 miles from the Mediterranean to the Red Sea, the canal took a decade to build, finally opening in 1869. Though it was originally regarded as a fantasy by the Ottoman Sultan who permitted its construction, the canal would change the shape of communications and transport in the Middle East for decades, remaining a vital maritime link in the 21st century. After the Suez Canal was completed, Egypt suddenly became very much the centre of the Middle East, with Britain and France keeping a close eye on its affairs. Britain in particular, which had long had an interest in the region, saw the canal as of vital strategic importance, an essential component in the sea-route to India.

However, the interest of the Great Powers would cause major problems for Ismail. Like Muhammed Ali before him, he wanted to see an independent Egypt and so pursued an aggressive policy of economic development in order to diminish his dependence on the Europeans. However, throughout his rule, he paid little heed to the Europeans, who were displeased at his efforts to rule without their supervision. His attitude would eventually lead to his downfall.

Ismail ushered in an Egyptian cultural and intellectual renaissance, the architectural achievements of which are typified by his Ismaila Square, renamed Tahrir Square by the ruling military junta in 1952. In a daring leap forward, he launched a complex scheme of reform, re-fashioning centuries of tradition in Egypt's cities, towns and villages.

For the first time, he introduced municipal services to Egypt's population centres – piped water, canals, public transport, street lighting, gas supplies, bridges, modern European street designs and public squares. A hundred thousand Europeans were co-opted by the Khedive who used their skills to transform Egypt into a modern state. By the end of his reign, this commonly maligned and disregarded ruler had overseen a large number of improvements.

He even indulged in social engineering, the results of which had far reaching consequences. He introduced a proto-social welfare system, set up homes for widows and orphans and introduced a code of ethics for commerce and industry. At a time when the very prospect of educating women was taboo, he opened schools for girls in the major cities. He spent the then vast sum of £289,000 on judicial reform and founded the first Egyptian Chamber of Deputies which resembled a modern legislative chamber, something unknown in the Muslim world at the time.

His reign also saw attempts to revitalise Egypt's financial system. He founded the Anglo-Egyptian Bank in 1864. He also enticed thousands of European administrators to Egypt to manage the transformation. He introduced secular education. He launched major schemes to reform the slave trade, the constitution, the customs system and the post office. All these schemes stimulated commercial progress. In order that the economy would continue to prosper, he created industries for Egypt – the sugar industry, for example. At the same time, he had a taste for the opulent lifestyle of the European upper classes. He built palaces in which he lavishly entertained guests and, in an effort to import European cultural life to Egypt, he opened an opera house and a theatre.

The capital, Cairo, was greatly expanded. He built an entire new Paris-inspired quarter of the city. To the north, Alexandria in particular was redeveloped beyond recognition, into something resembling a cosmopolitan Mediterranean city.

Ismail also needed to link Egypt together. At that point Egyptians were still largely dependent on horses, carts and donkeys for transport. As far back as 1833, Muhammed Ali had considered building a railway to link Cairo with Suez. In 1854 one of Ismail's predecessors, Abbas I, had built the first railway in the Middle East, along Egypt's Mediterranean coast. The line was extended to Cairo and Suez a few years later.

Ismail greatly expanded the railway system by pushing it south, into Minya and Asyut. He also built up the lines in the north of the country, creating a modern rail network. In a very short space of time nearly all of Egypt's major cities were connected by railway lines.

Education and Culture

Ismail, who had been educated in Paris, tried to bring the education he had received in Europe to Egypt. As such, he introduced a structured system of public education, building upon what had been in place previously. In the new system, the young were taught about the other civilisations that surrounded them, rather than just about Egypt. By introducing formal education the literacy rate reached 7%. This may seem small by modern standards but was a great improvement considering that imperial Russia could only boast 4% literacy at the time.

Under Ismail's predecessor, Said Pasha, Egypt had a mere 185 schools. By 1875, there were nearly 5000. Khedive Ismail also established the first state-sponsored girls' schools. Up until that point, any parents who wanted to educate their daughters were forced to send them to foreign-run institutions. There had been European-sponsored girls' schools in Egypt since 1835 but they were strictly for non-Muslim girls. This would again be the case after Ismail's reign. State education for girls was abolished during the British occupation.

The drive to educate the population was not universally accepted. Many parents refused to have their children educated in the schools because many of the first teachers were Christians.

Another staple of European culture which Egypt badly needed was a national library. The Khedivial Library was the result of this drive. Established with the aid of Mustafa Riyad Pasha, one of the more reform-minded politicians of the day, the Khedivial Library was a major achievement and became a major centre of learning in Egypt. So committed was Riyad, that he donated revenues from his own lands to the building and maintenance of the library. Riyad was a popular minister of the day. However, unlike the Khedive, he did not simply seek to import European practices and institutions to Egypt, rather he realised that public education was one of the best ways of alleviating the endemic poverty of the masses. Riyad, a Circassian, would later become one of the most prominent Egyptian politicians of the late 19th century.

Such efforts extended into the field of Egypt's media which, at that period, was practically non-existent. The first Egyptian medical magazine appeared in 1865. In 1876, *Al Ahram* (The Pyramids) was established, one of the best-known newspapers in the Arab world. It is still Egypt's foremost state-owned newspaper.

In 1869, the Khedive opened Egypt's first opera house, part of a scheme to transplant European cultural institutions to Egypt. The Khedivial Opera House was very much influenced by Italian culture. The Khedive employed Italian architects to build it, and it opened with a performance of Verdi's *Rigoletto*. The Opera House was also the site of the world premiere of Verdi's *Aida* two years later, in 1871. It lasted for another century, until it burned down in 1971.

Slavery

In the 19th century, slavery was common throughout the Muslim world and Egypt was no exception. However, slavery in Egypt was not the massive industry it had been in East Africa or the Americas. Up until the early 19th century, Egypt was ruled by the slave warriors known as the Mamluks, who were still present in the military even after Muhammad Ali massacred their leaders in 1811. Even Khedive Ismail's predecessor, Said Pasha, recruited black slaves into the army

Eunuch slaves were the most expensive, used for watching over the harem. They were mostly captured Nubians or Abyssinians, and their castration was performed by Coptic priests in Asyut. The mortality rate caused by castration was 90%, hence the high market value of the eunuchs. The price of slaves varied from £10 to £100.

Most slaves, however, were female, part of the sex slave industry. Women and children were sold by poor parents who were unable to feed them and then bought for the pleasure by merchants and aristocrats. Some children would even volunteer for slavery in an attempt to provide for their families. On the occasions that these slave women produced a male child, it was perfectly possible that the child would grow into an influential member of society, if the father had a sufficiently high social rank. However, by the reign of Ismail, female sex slaves, or concubines, were part of an ever more anachronistic social hierarchy that was becoming irrelevant in the changing society of 19th century Egypt.

The early 19th century saw the abolitionist movement gain strength in Europe. The British abolished the slave trade in 1807, and slavery itself in 1833, and then began to pressurise other nations to do likewise. During his 1867 visit to London (accompanied by Nubar Pasha) Ismail was lobbied by the British to ban slavery. Ismail explained that he wanted to do so, but it was "a trade that has lasted 13 centuries and that it may take about 20 years to totally outlaw." That year, the Khedive gave an impassioned speech against slavery in Paris. However, European observers such as the British and Foreign Anti-Slavery Society lobbied the Khedive to actually abolish the trade itself. The British writer, Lady Duff Gordon, a resident of Egypt at the time, went further in her criticism, accusing the Khedive of hypocrisy for owning – as she claimed, perhaps slightly dubiously – 3,000 harem slaves as well as slaves in his army and on his sugar plantations.

Within Egypt, there was intense debate as to the morality and legality of slavery, with the arguments of both sides bolstered by quotes from the Quran. Public support for abolition was not high as the trade had been legitimised by successive Islamic governments for over 1300 years.

However, slavery was dying out in Egypt, even without European pressure to prohibit the trade. In 1840, it is estimated that there were between 22,000 and 30,000 slaves in Egypt, approximately 0.5% of the population of five million. These numbers were steadily in decline throughout the latter part of the 19th century. In 1877, against the objections of the Ulema, of the grand mosque at Al-Azhar and of the grand Mufti, Ismail signed the Anglo-Egyptian convention on slavery outlawing the trade in all territories subject to Egyptian rule. A manumission office was opened, to oversee the freeing of Egyptian slaves. From 1877 to 1889, around 1,500 slaves a year were passed through the office, with that number shrinking to 153 in 1905.

Slavery remained institutionalised in the Ottoman Empire. Though the Empire officially ended slavery in 1847, the practice continued because there was no penalty for owning slaves. Ismail did not end slavery; however, he did bring about many of the measures which ultimately ended the practice. There was no great act of emancipation. Rather slavery seemed to drift out of fashion in Egypt as society changed, in part due to Ismail's other reforms which made it redundant.

****

In spite of his sluggish efforts to abolish the slave trade at home, slavery provided a justification for the Khedive to extend his influence upstream of the Nile, something that he had long intended to do. In 1869, Ismail sent the British explorer Samuel Baker into central Africa with a contingent of 1700 men with the objective of suppressing the slave trade, as well as to open Africa up to trade with Egypt. On his expedition, Baker established the province of Equatoria. Subject to Egyptian rule, it encompassed parts of today's southern Sudan and northern Uganda.

Ismail would send a number of expeditions up the Nile. After Baker, he sent the famous British soldier Charles Gordon along the river, later appointing him Governor-General of Khartoum. In 1874, Ismail sent Charles Pomeroy Stone, a Union general from the American Civil War to map central Africa and assert the Khedive's control over Sudan. In one audience with American officers, Ismail told them that he preferred to use Americans as the United States had no colonial interest in Egypt.

These expeditions, of which there were quite a few, proved extremely expensive. Like many elements of Ismail's reign, they incurred huge debts for Egypt.

One of Ismail's main domestic allies was Nubar Pasha. Born Nubar Nubarian, the politician was an Ottoman of Armenian descent, whose father had married into the Egyptian elite. Nubar was a career diplomat who, like the Khedive, had been educated in France. The two were on friendly terms before Ismail's accession as Khedive, and once in power, the Khedive used him to win approval for his ambitious projects from the Sultan in Constantinople. Nubar Pasha was prime minister towards the end of Ismail's reign and would serve as premier twice more in his career.

Nubar was another keen reformer, and there is plenty of evidence that he cared deeply for his adoptive country. He was particularly unhappy that the corvee system of labour was still used in Egypt for public works projects in which labour could be demanded of the local population, without proper compensation or wages.

Ultimately, Nubar would prove too adept at his job and would plunge Egypt deep in debt. He had negotiated various large loans as a means of funding Ismail's many major developments and welfare reforms for the poor. These loans would prove too large for Egypt to handle and the debt made the Khedive's position untenable.

The British MP, Steven Cave, was sent by the British to Egypt in 1875. In his report of 1876 he wrote that there was hardly a city or province that had not received substantial benefit from the government. However, all these reforms came at a great price. Egypt was crippled by its debt. After the initial burst of development, there was barely any money left to maintain these projects, particularly the railway. In spite of this, Cave reported that Egypt was still solvent, although he recommended that the British establish a commission to oversee Egypt's finances.

The debts climbed to £98m. When government expenditure was audited, there was £5.48 million missing, most likely spent on the army or the Khedivial palaces. The French and the British, who were flexing their colonial muscles over Egypt, determined that Ismail had to be removed. Much of Egypt's debt was owed to Europe so the nation became a target for European investment. The British and the French deemed that control of the country was essential, particularly in the light of Egypt's strategic importance and their distrust of the Ottomans. The Khedive was exiled to Italy at first, spending his last years in Constantinople and died there in 1895.

Ismail was succeeded by his eldest son, Tewfik. However, the British Lord Cromer became the de facto ruler of Egypt, establishing a system whereby Britain effectively governed the country with the consent of a puppet ruler. It was a system which endured until the uprising of 1919, which resulted in a unilateral declaration of independence in 1922.

King Fuad

Fuad, the son of Khedive Ismail, oversaw a great deal of change for Egypt, from the writing of its first constitution to the creation of its first secular university, established when Fuad was still a prince. Fuad applied much of his considerable energy to developing Egypt's intellectual and scientific institutions. Art, music, theatre, cinema and sports all flourished, so much so that the period is still remembered with nostalgia.

By the beginning of the 20th century, Egypt's middle class was beginning to show a degree of social and political maturity. The Egyptian national project seemed to reflect Western modernity and culture, particularly with regard to the nation's interactions with Europe. Egypt's major cities, particularly Alexandria and Cairo, grew into cosmopolitan regional hubs for culture, commerce and tourism.

The roaring '20s did not pass Egypt by; the country became a fashionable hangout for Europe's rich and famous. The discovery of Tutankhamen's tomb by the Englishman Howard Carter in 1922 sparked massive worldwide interest in Egypt's ancient history. The explosion of Egyptology also gave rise to Pharaonism, a secular ideology advocating Egypt's independence from Islamic culture, and its important place in Mediterranean civilisation.

Fuad, like his father before him, spent much of his youth in Europe. Educated in Paris and Vienna, as a young man he settled in Italy where his deposed father Khedive Ismail was living. Fuad was fond of Italy, and served in its military, reaching the rank of captain. The young prince spoke several languages and was well-versed in European politics and culture, reportedly becoming close to the King of Italy.

Being the seventh son of the deposed Khedive, it was thought unlikely that he would ever claim the Egyptian throne. However, upon the death of his older brother, Hussein Kemal, the title passed to him by way of Hussein's son, who declined the position. In 1917, at the age of 49, Fuad ascended the throne of Egypt, assuming the title of Sultan. In 1923, a year after Egypt's independence from Britain, Fuad substituted the epithet Sultan for King. After the implementation of the 1923 constitution, Fuad became the first constitutional monarch in Islamic history.

Fuad was a cautious King and no risk-taker. His European outlook and education helped him focus on building a secular, modern state. However, despite his obvious care for the Egyptian masses, he was never quite comfortable with them. Though fluent in several languages, his Arabic was underdeveloped.

Fuad had studied political economy and legislation and closely followed events in British India. Prince Fuad returned to Egypt in 1902, called by Khedive Abbas II to be an adviser. Like his father before him, Fuad was a moderniser, determined to strengthen Egypt's state institutions. Unlike his father, he knew that vast debts spelt disaster for Egypt. He determined that the government must take in more in revenue than it spent.

One of King Fuad's first prime ministers was the nationalist leader Saad Zaghloul. Zaghloul was a leading figure in the Wafd Party, immensely popular and a keen reformer. The King and Zaghloul complemented each other. Whilst the King played at high diplomacy and supervised the reformation of institutions, Zaghloul mobilised the masses behind the government and lent Egypt's reforms a popular credibility, so that they were seen as more than just European imports. Zaghloul's popularity stemmed from his staunchly nationalist credentials and the fact that he had spent years in exile. However, the relationship between Fuad and Zaghloul soon deteriorated.

At the time, much of Egypt's business and government was still managed by foreigners. Fuad embarked on a programme of Egyptianising the higher circles of power in the country. In 1927, he issued a decree insisting that at least one Egyptian must be on the board of local companies, and at least 25% of employees should be Egyptians.

In spite of the declaration of independence in 1922, Egypt's relationship with Britain was never properly defined during Fuad's reign. The delicate balance of Egyptian independence collapsed in 1924 when the British Governor General of Sudan, Lee Stack, was assassinated on a drive through Cairo. Seven Egyptian students dressed like *effendi* (i.e. in Western clothes) pulled out revolvers as his car drove past them and peppered it with bullets. The British were furious, demanding a public apology and that the killers be held to account and Egyptian troops withdrawn from Sudan. Zaghloul refused and was forced to resign, raising the question of whether Egypt was indeed independent any more, or whether it remained a British protectorate.

In that year's elections, the Wafd Party was defeated by a coalition of liberal and unionist parties, as well as independents. The Wafd Party would win elections again in 1926. However, both King Fuad and the British resolutely refused to allow Zaghloul to become Prime Minister again.

In 1927, King Fuad went on a four and a half month tour of Europe accompanied by his Prime Minister Sarwat Pasha and a team of ministers, perhaps the most important visit by an Egyptian leader in the 20th century. In the course of the trip, he visited industrial, financial and educational institutions and met with various political leaders. Fuad was afforded a full state visit to Britain, during which King George V paid him two informal visits at the Egyptian Embassy. A few days later, he was invited to a garden party at Buckingham Palace, a rare occurrence in the protocol of the day. He travelled to Liverpool to see the cotton mills and to Manchester to see the university, where he offered professors teaching jobs at Cairo University.

While on the Italian leg of his visit, Saad Zaghloul died. The King ordered the nationalist politician, at times an ally and at times an enemy, a full military funeral.

In 1928, Fuad dismissed the Prime Minister Mustapha Nahas who had assumed leadership of the Wafd Party after Zaghloul's death. Nahas tried to sign into effect a law that would make it illegal for the King to rule without parliament, which Fuad believed would give the Wafd Party absolute political power. In 1930, the King – unhappy with the agitation of the Wafd Party – dismissed Nahas, abrogated the constitution and ruled as an autocrat with pliant ministers to do his bidding. He justified the decision as being taken on the grounds of concern that anti-British agitation would lead the British to re-occupy Egypt. In 1935, thanks to huge popular support for Nahas and the Wafd Party, Fuad restored the 1935 constitution. The Wafd Party was re-elected.

During his rule, trade unions were established and greatly expanded, matching the professional associations of the West. One of the main advocates of trade unionism in Egypt was Fuad's cousin, Abbas Halim. The two cousins were not political allies and fought continually during Fuad's reign. Halim, who became a prominent member of the Wafd Party was known for his campaigns for labour rights, and efforts to improve working conditions. He even tried to create an Egyptian Labour Party. The animosity between Halim and Fuad was so great that Fuad actually crossed his name off a list of royal family members.

Fuad also tried to reform education in Egypt. In 1908, when he was still a prince, Fuad was instrumental in the establishment of Cairo University, the first secular university in Egypt. State universities had begun to appear in Western colonies such as India as well as in eastern countries such as Japan. The idea that Egypt should have its own civil institution of higher education was gaining momentum; such an institution was seen as an essential component of a modern nation state. Fuad's foreign ancestry and upbringing was used against the project by traditionalists, who saw the civil university as a foreign invention. Yet, Fuad's foreign connections were essential in the early stages of the university; he managed to get a number of Italian professors to come and teach in Cairo.

Of course, Egypt did already have a university, the world famous Islamic centre of learning, Al-Azhar. Fuad and Zaghloul, who briefly served as minister for education, tried to change the status of Al-Azhar. Al-Azhar is probably the most famous and respected Islamic institution in the world. It operates as a mosque but also as a university, founded by the Fatimids in 970. Fuad tried to develop it into a modern theological institution. He issued a decree splitting the university into three separate departments – Arabic, Sharia and theology – and introduced formal written exams as a means of attaining a degree, as opposed to simply being at the university for the requisite number of years. Al-Azhar was also a bastion of traditionalism, a quality which Zaghloul and Fuad wanted to preserve, acting as a counterweight to modern Islamic militancy, which was in its infancy at the time. Modern Muslim militancy would become manifest after Zaghloul's death with the founding of the Muslim Brotherhood in 1928, and the Young Men's Muslim Association and Islamic Guidance Association, both founded in 1927.

One of the most pertinent questions in the Muslim world was the question of who should assume the title of Caliph. Ataturk had abolished the Caliphate in 1924; at that point it was merely a ceremonial title for the Ottoman Sultan. In 1926, a congress met at Al-Azhar to discuss who should be made Caliph. King Fuad was a candidate, as was Sharif Hussein of Mecca (who had already proclaimed himself Caliph). Meanwhile, in the Sudan, the Mahdi named himself Caliph. Though King Fuad publicly denied that he wanted the post, Egyptian state newspapers began to extol the virtues of King Fuad as Caliph and it has been suggested that Fuad used Egypt's Ulema of religious clerics to promote his claim. The Wafd Party were opposed to the idea of King Fuad becoming Caliph; they feared a religious title would afford him even more temporal power. In the end, the conference at Al-Azhar was inconclusive. It degenerated into a scramble by advocates of the competing Arab sovereigns to receive the appointment for their patrons.

In the early 20th century, women's rights were a priority in Egypt. The prevailing belief was that if some form of greater female emancipation could be achieved it would be another step on the path towards progress and modernity. King Fuad encouraged female education and, in 1923, universal primary education was made compulsory.

Fuad did not, however, ban polygamy. Nor did he bring about the vote for women, something that was still rare in Europe at the time. In 1927, a committee formed by the Egyptian cabinet recommended the abolition of polygamy, though Fuad refused to actually make it illegal. The traditionalists were still opposed to stifling age-old religious customs.

Health

As King, Fuad spent a great deal of time concentrating on the health of the nation. Most of Egypt's major hospitals were built during his reign and he also ensured that medical schools were brought up to European standards. One of the major problems of the day was inflammation of the eye. One of the consequences in children was blindness. Fuad established centres for medical research to combat this menace and its root cause, trachoma.

In 1927, the King's personal physician, Mohammed Shahin, outlined an ambitious 16-point plan for public health. One of his greatest concerns was rural health. At the time, the majority of Egypt's population still lived in the countryside and healthcare was generally poor. Shahin called for the introduction of clean water supplies to Egypt and for basic codes of hygiene to be practised across the country. His plan also required that new roads be built to ease the overcrowding of small villages and for the state to organise refuse collection.

Shahin also helped introduce basic sanitary guidelines into Egypt's newspapers and schoolbooks. Small commands such as "wash your hands before and after you eat," were simple maxims, yet went a long way to improving the basic health of the nation. Shahin was an early advocate of vaccination, urging smallpox inoculations every seven years.

Shahin tried to combat tropical disease and expanded public health programmes in the cities and provinces. Aware of the sluggishness in the system for anyone in need of first aid, he masterminded an expansion of hospital emergency services and set up an ambulance service.

Three weeks before he died, in 1936, King Fuad founded Egypt's first Ministry of Public Health, with Shahin at its head. Healthcare in Egypt was still a long way off European standards but these reforms made public health a topic of concern for Egypt's politicians, in a way which it had not been since the first state-sponsored health programmes were introduced by Muhammad Ali a century previously. State provision of public health was particularly important for Egypt's status as an independent entity, since the British had used Egyptians' disregard for the health of its masses as justification for their occupation and governance.

Fuad also believed that if Egypt was to become a truly modern and independent state then it had better have a modern military. In 1930, Fuad established the first Egyptian air force, known as the Egyptian Army Air Force. Initially, it was almost entirely supported by the British and headed by a Canadian officer, Victor Hubert Tait. Tait was very much the father of the Egyptian air force and King Fuad was so impressed by him that he granted him the Order of the Nile and the rank of *Kamaichin* (lieutenant colonel). Two hundred Egyptian army officers volunteered to be pilots. After rigorous testing, the field was narrowed down to three, who were subsequently trained by the British.

The Egyptian air force was initially deployed to curb drug smuggling, particularly in the form of the hashish trade from Lebanon, Palestine and Greece. Unlike alcohol which was subject to religious taboo, narcotics like hashish and opium were neither stigmatised nor prohibited. It is estimated that there were half a million drug addicts in Egypt in 1929, mostly using opium or hashish. Smuggling via the Suez Canal was common, as was the use of camels from Palestine. Alexandria's harbour was the second main transit port by which drugs entered the country. King Fuad took a firm stand against narcotics, campaigning against the hashish trade internationally and tasking his new air force with targeting drug smugglers. Fuad worked to cut the supply rather than to criminalise its use, in order not to drive it underground.

King Fuad died in 1936, shortly after signing another treaty with the United Kingdom to affirm Egypt's independence. He was succeeded by his 16 year-old son, Farouk. The young King had neither the experience nor gumption to stand up to Mustafa El Nahhas in the way that his father had done. In the resulting years, the Wafd Party would totally dominate Egyptian politics, though political life was punctuated by the Second

World War. Ultimately, Farouk would be forced to abdicate during the July revolution in 1952, passing the throne to his infant son Fuad, who would live as a King without a crown, in exile.

CHAPTER 16

THE LANDSCAPE

The spectacular falls of Mubarak and Ben Ali in rapid succession preceded a short lived period of euphoria in the Arab world. Reminiscent of the fall of the Iron Curtain some two decades earlier, the Arab Spring was supposed to usher in a new era of democratic freedom and development in the Middle East.

However, the Islamist ascent to power proved a disappointment. The new governments had no plans for nation building, and the factionalism and bickering which had come to characterise Arab politics got worse, not better. It was the second time in just under a century that the Arab world had undergone such political emancipation. At the close of the First World War, the Arabic-speaking provinces of the Ottoman Empire were liberated as the Empire collapsed. However, that too was a false dawn because – just as in 2011 – there was no benign or capable leadership to drive political change.

Throughout the 20th century, the Arab world was consumed by coups and counter-coups, some of which dared to call themselves revolutionary. In reality, they offered little more than petty personal rule and dictatorship. Commentators and seasoned Western observers understood that the simmering discontent of the Arab peoples would inevitably lead to some sort of backlash, though they did not know when or how it might happen. The regimes ignored the warnings, promising their people that only they could deliver prosperity, and promising the West that only they could combat terrorism.

The Arab Spring and its subsequent fallout was characterised by indecision and confusion on the part of the outside world, particularly the West. After carefully crafting relations with regional despots, the Western countries had no idea what to do when the democracy they had been calling for finally arrived. This bewilderment was matched by general Arab mistrust of the West. Foreign policy and the public image of the outside world were still based upon unrealistic assumptions and expectations, especially where the United States and Israel were concerned. Public judgment had been influenced by decades of crude media propaganda and paranoid cafe rumours.

Behaviour, attitudes and history differ enormously within the Muslim world. Practices broadly accepted in one country might be regarded as taboo in another. Likewise, judicial punishments such as limb amputation are not actually widespread across the Muslim world. Political attitudes also vary greatly. The crushing of the city of Hama by Hafez al Assad in 1982, or the killing of hundreds in the Kaaba incident of 1979 in Saudi Arabia would not have happened in countries such as Egypt or Tunisia, where neither the public nor the political leadership would have stood for that degree of brutality.

So far, many Arab regimes have successfully weathered the Arab Spring, and do not face any credible threat of imminent political change. In part, these countries took a variety of short term precautionary measures to prevent uprisings on the scale of Tunisia, Egypt or Syria. However, these countries are still in denial about the prospects for democratic change, and the anger within their own populations. Even Saudi Arabia, a country of incredible wealth, has faced its own problems with internal dissent, which it has dealt with by completely covering up any outward signs of social unrest. The government then spent billions on domestic projects, and sent troops to crush the uprising in Bahrain, leaving its domestic critics in no doubt as to what may happen if a protest movement managed to spread across the country.

What came after Spring?

The tactics of the protest movements which proved so successful – the use of the Internet, no specific ideology and a reluctance to support existing opposition leaders or elect new ones – were actually the main brakes on democratic change once the old regimes had been toppled. Although the masses had poured out onto the street, it was the Islamists, who had been quietly organising for decades, who won the subsequent political battle.

Elsewhere, the Syrian and Libyan versions of the Arab Spring deteriorated into civil war when the protest movements came up against leaders who were not willing to stand down, but were content to use military force to crush the demonstrations. In Syria, estimates vary, but around 150,000 lives were lost in just over two years of conflict. In addition to the loss of life, there has been substantial destruction of the country's infrastructure. What began as protests had become a sectarian conflict; the Assad regime broadly represents the interests of the Alawite community. Within Syria, a general disregard for human rights, which was first manifest as torture and summary executions, has degenerated into massacres, discrediting the regime and the opposition alike. The conflict began to spill over into neighbouring Lebanon and Iraq, both countries afflicted with their own sectarian problems.

The conflict also took on an international dimension, with the Gulf – namely, Saudi Arabia and Qatar – and the West supporting the rebels, while Hezbollah, Iran and Russia were firmly behind the regime. The vested interests of these foreign powers and the presence of foreign fighters from around the region, fighting on both sides, will complicate any political solution.

The Tunisian uprising which began in late 2010 was perhaps the most dramatic of the Arab Spring. It cost 338 lives and ended when President Ben Ali stepped down, three weeks and six days after the protests began. After Ben Ali fled the country, Tunisia has been governed by a coalition of several parties, the Islamist Nahda party being by far the largest. Though economic disenfranchisement was one of the primary causes of the uprising, the economy declined throughout 2011, with output falling and unemployment rising. The economy improved in 2012, but this was largely due to industries like tourism and mining returning to pre-revolutionary levels rather than any tangible development. The Islamists in power, following a pattern that would repeat itself throughout the post-Arab Spring Middle East, concerned themselves with enacting socially and religiously conservative legislation, rather than working on the faltering economy. Although there had been a nominal lifting of censorship in the wake of the uprising, the Islamist government has repeatedly sought to curtail freedom of expression, often for offending Islamic sensibilities.

The Nahda party lost a great deal of confidence among the electorate for failing to halt the economic decline. In January 2013, there were reports that Tunisia's treasury reserves were empty, that the government could not even cover operational expenses. The government denied this, even though the reports issued from its own news agencies.

Looking to the southern tip of the Arab world, the brief flowering of the Arab Spring in Yemen was partially resolved by handing power to the Vice President, Mansur Hadi, who stood unopposed in a referendum to determine President Saleh's successor. Certain areas within Yemen declared themselves to be Sharia-compliant, setting up their own courts with their own medieval prohibitions and retributive justice. Despite the opportunity to reform in Yemen, the country is still saddled with tribal structures of power, albeit with cosmetic political adjustments. The economy is also in a very grave state and there is a serious north/south divide in Yemen, with very credible rumblings of secession in the south. Such problems have been endemic to Yemen for decades, as the government has failed to exert its authority on a tribal country where the general public holds more weapons than the government.

The example of Bahrain is indicative of a political schism within the Middle East. While the petroleum-exporting countries of the Gulf have wholeheartedly supported the calls for popular uprising in the nationalist republics, they have remained staunch allies of the ruling Sunni Khalifa dynasty in Bahrain who have had to deal with their own recalcitrant population's call for democratic change. Since the popular movement comes from a predominantly Shiite population, there are also hints of a miniature Cold War as Saudi Arabia and Iran jostle for influence.

Sudan is too weak, dysfunctional and divided to have its own Arab Spring. Indeed, while the rest of the Arab world was engaged in political change, Sudan was actively splitting in two, as the South seceded from the North.

In North Africa Algeria had already had its Arab Spring, some 20 years earlier. The Algerian civil war between Islamists and the government cost some 100,000 lives, traumatising the country and blunting its appetite for more change. The regime has readjusted, creating a degree of stability under its 75-year-old President.

The Palestinian territories can be considered the most thriving Arab land amid the chaos, as it remains the world's highest per capita aid recipient, due to generous handouts and overlapping donation schemes. The government of Benjamin Netanyahu in Israel is reluctant to restart negotiations that may lead to Palestinian self-determination, making a Palestinian state seem a distant prospect. Practically however, the Palestinians have to work with Israelis, with many Palestinian parents opting to teach their children Hebrew alongside Arabic. The interaction between Palestinians and Israelis is generally ignored by the regional Arabic media, which has thrived on anti-Israeli and anti-Jewish rhetoric since the foundation of the state.

Peace between Israel and Palestine and the Arab world at large seems far out of reach at present. Arabs will not forget the Israeli treatment of Palestinians. However, many in the Middle East forget that several hundred thousand Jews were expelled from Arab countries after the creation of Israel. In essence, the story of Israel and Palestine is a quest for refugee rights, with each side claiming the moral high ground. Consequently, there have been many lost opportunities for peace between the Arab world and the Jewish state.

Failure

A variety of explanations have been advanced as reasons for the failure of these uprisings to live up to the initial hype. Possible answers were the rigidity of the existing regime, the so-called 'deep state', and the reactionary strands of Islam, all of which were incapable to progress.

The economic pressures resulting from incompetence, corruption, cronyism and poor administration have forced many of the Arab middle classes to leave their countries over the past five decades, mostly to the West. Many of these migrants were younger men, which led to severe social dislocation, devastating the civil polity of the Arab world.

From the 1970s, the middle classes of the Arab world, particularly in Egypt, diverged. The two strands both had cultural aspirations, though they looked to different parts of the world to fulfil them, partly directed by patterns of immigration. Some Egyptians went to work in the oil states of the Gulf, exposed to the Islamic social conservatism inherent in such societies. In parallel, was the traditional Westernised middle class which several decades ago would have emulated and developed the fashions and ideas of Britain or France and today looks to the United States.

The Arab regimes conspired to prevent promising political leaders achieving any kind of popular support. Politicians were frequently blacklisted or, in some cases, imprisoned and so denied any kind of meaningful public platform.

The popular comparison with Eastern Europe is not strictly fair as the conditions which surrounded the end of the communist regimes in the late 1980s were different from the Middle East of today. The Arab world did have weak economies and entrenched dictators; however, the communist leaders in countries such as Poland resigned themselves to the inevitability of reform once it became apparent that the Soviet Union would no longer support them. In the Arab world on the other hand, many Arab leaders tried to cling to power and some, such as the Khalifas in Bahrain and the Assads in Syria, knew they could count on their foreign benefactors to support them come what may.

The Arab regimes in turn responded with violence and denial. When the Soviet Union collapsed, the communist regimes of the satellite states did not engage in sustained civil conflict in order to remain in power. Religious organisations, such as the Catholic Church in Eastern Europe, undertook broadly non-political roles, as opposed to many of the Arab world's Islamist clergy, who used the Arab Spring to impose their understanding of the Sharia.

The fall of the Iron Curtain, and the wider democratisation of the Third World was part of a wave of democratisation that spread across the world from the 1980s. This wave spread through South America, Asia and Africa, though it seemed to bypass the Arab world. It followed a period of political emancipation which had been ongoing since the end of the Second World War, when imperial possessions turned from colonies into nation states.

The intellectual elites of the Arab world did not bother to ask themselves which aspect of their politics and culture had inhibited their democratic progress. Indeed, when the issue of the democratic deficit is discussed in the Arab media, regional problems of that kind are often blamed on outside forces, particularly the West and Israel. Islamists are often able to capitalise on this paranoia and present democracy and personal freedom as concepts alien to the domain of Islam.

The resistance to democratic change is all the more illogical given the fact that the idea of an Arab renaissance has been central to political thinking in the Arab world for many decades. The Egyptian dictators, Nasser, Sadat and Mubarak, traded on such rhetoric but they refused to take account of public grievances.

Change could have only come from the outside, often with the support of major powers with their own complex interests in the Middle East, or by integrating expatriates untainted by political quarrels, who have the necessary knowledge and expertise to bring about reform.

Western interest in a stable Middle East increased dramatically after the terror attacks of 2001. In many ways, the attacks were a Year Zero for Western observers. In the years following 2001, the West, particularly the United States, tried to rethink their strategies in the region. In February 2002 President Bush presented "The Greater Middle East Initiative," calling for democratic and economic reform. It was widely attacked by state-sponsored Arab media, variously described as a 'Bush dictate,' or 'American imperialism.' As has been mentioned before, the Arab media will invariably treat any American interventions or suggestions in the region with severe hostility.

Bush called for the emergence of civil society in the Arab world, whilst also declaring that reform should come from within. The Arab regimes were uninterested, more concerned with building their dynastic legacies. The United States therefore sought to bypass the regimes and the usual diplomatic channels, with their policy of 'direct public diplomacy.' In this manner, they began funding civil organisations in countries like Egypt, raising the ire of the respective governments.

Another major problem for the regimes is that they had been promising democracy for years. Egypt had lived under a strange hybrid form of democratic authoritarianism for over a decade previously, holding predetermined elections and propagating meaningless democratic slogans. The explosion of broadcast media, the vast majority under the watchful gaze of the state, even allowed a degree of criticism of the regime.

The authoritarian regimes slowly lost their grip on the public as they began to stagnate. The prevalence of social networking made it difficult for the governments to censor the media and arrest agitators. In part, this was because of the incompetence of the security services which had always relied on their monopoly of violence to break up protest movements. They simply did not understand how to use the technology being used against them. The potential for every mobile telephone to become a news camera with footage broadcast to the world within minutes made it ever harder for the state to cover up the brutality of its security forces.

Egypt

Vast, teeming, cosmopolitan Cairo is known to the Arabs as "the mother of the world," *Umm Eldonia*. Egyptian influence on greater Arab culture goes back centuries. Egyptians were the main educators of the region in the first part of the 20th century, when there were hardly any schools at all in vast swathes of the Arab world. Most Arabic cinema is made in Egypt. Egyptian leaders such as Nasser were famous across the entire Middle East. In the mid 20th century, Egypt seemed to dictate the political culture of the region. The Egyptian political elite had the chance to develop a modern political culture and set an example for the wider Middle East. In the aftermath of the uprising of 2011, Egypt was admired throughout the region and the world at large, like Poland while it was breaking free of Soviet influence.

Western observers regularly contend that Egypt has never had democracy, but that isn't really the case. From 1923 to 1952, there was a workable democratic government in Egypt. Initially, this arrangement, basically a constitutional monarchy, was abused by the powerful reformer, King Fuad. It was an attempt to create a liberal political system based upon the rule of law in emulation of Europe. However, the all-important constitution of 1923, a benchmark in the Arab world, was eventually abrogated by successive governments. The situation changed when the 16-year-old King Farouk came to power and the elected politicians were able to run the government without being regularly overruled by the King. Though the democracy was not perfect by any means, it was definitely comparable to the systems operating in Europe at the time, some of which degenerated into fascist dictatorship.

Egyptians account for roughly a third of the Arab peoples. Anger was simmering across a region where politics is dominated by the pursuit of the perks of power, a pursuit that had become particularly apparent in Egypt. Managing the system of hidden allowances, backdoor commissions and bribery, which had developed from the days of Nasser to Mubarak, had become an art. Corruption was widely accepted as the norm and was not a source of shame; on the contrary, it was admired.

In the 1980s, the Minister of Interior once light-heartedly taunted police officers when they asked him for a pay rise, "none of you ever spend your salaries for the abundance of bribes, I know." Many Egyptians admired the interior minister, General Zaki Badr for his brash frankness. Mubarak expressed the same sentiment by telling a decorator that he earned more than the President because his salary was fixed at E£5000 a month (£500). Such unrealistic payscales meant that patronage and embezzlement was the only way in which Egyptian politicians could earn a decent living. It was a similar state of affairs in state jobs, commerce, university posts etc.

Promotion was based on personal relationships rather than merit. In such an environment, loyalty, rather than ability became a prized asset, as initially Mubarak, and later his son and wife, sought ministers they could rely on. No matter how corrupt a politician may have been, an appearance of outright piety was necessary. This was particularly apparent during Sadat's reign. Under him, the Islamists became his cheerleaders, writing books proclaiming admiration for the President or his wife.

Hosni Mubarak was a hybrid leader, not a dictator nor a democrat. His final years in power were marred by the fact he was clearly not interested in governing the country any more, increasingly leaving day to day rule to his ministers or his son Gamal. This lack of interest was particularly apparent after the death of his young grandson, and his own diagnosis with intestinal cancer. He dramatically cut back on public appearances. In many ways, Mubarak is a classical Egyptian Muslim. As he entered old age, he became less materialistic and more conciliatory, letting Islamists out of prisons, allowing political parties to form and easing censorship of the media. However, one issue which remained taboo was corruption. Books about corruption in Egypt were published abroad and never allowed to circulate within the country or even be translated into Arabic.

He began to look frailer and, in a vain attempt to hide his fragility, used make-up for his interviews and dyed his greying hair black. The more he let the media speak its mind, the more antagonistic it became, attacking him and his regime. He allowed the lower levels of government to act as they pleased too. Consequently, Gamal and the clique that surrounded him would lash out at the nascent political opposition, trying to shut the Brotherhood out of the political process, which made the public lose even more confidence in the crumbling government.

Towards the end of his rule, Mubarak's regime began to resemble a dynasty with his wife and son wielding ever more power, appointing ministers and ambassadors in key Western capitals as well as determining state policy. Mubarak deliberately left the post of Vice-President vacant so that his son could slot in at the right time, perhaps after "spontaneous" public demand. Mubarak marginalised the generals, shutting them out of political decision-making as he prepared his son for leadership. To secure the regime, the Mubaraks preferred to depend on the police and other internal security forces, rather than on the military. Consequently, the generals were uneasy about Gamal's grooming for the presidency. This was a departure from the days of Nasser, when the President's power-base was centred on the army, the secret police and the state media.

The last round of Egyptian politicians before the uprising of 2011 thought it fashionable to compare themselves to British politicians. Gamal Mubarak was fond of the former Prime Minister Tony Blair. Mrs Mubarak copied Mrs Thatcher's taste in clothing and her mannerisms. Every young Arab leader's wife thought of herself as an Arab Princess Diana, copying her haircuts and dresses. Their empty aspirations only served as a political veneer, providing ample ammunition for tweeters and bloggers to expose their vanity.

When Mubarak was deposed, political prisoners – Islamists mostly – numbered in the hundreds rather than in the thousands, as they had under Nasser and Sadat. Such a figure is indicative of the fact that Nasser was a far more stern and authoritarian dictator than Mubarak, yet the Egyptian media and the public at large still regard Nasser as the national hero, and

Mubarak as a corrupt villain. In truth, many of the grievances laid at Mubarak's door could more accurately be blamed on those he had delegated to run the country, namely on his son and his wife.

Gamal was known in international political circles, and received in major capitals as the heir-apparent. Mubarak never formally made Gamal his successor, though it would have followed the precedent set by the Assad family in Syria. It was clear that various other Arab leaders were contemplating the same arrangement, in particular Colonel Gaddafi and Ali Abdullah Saleh of Yemen. Mubarak slowly succumbed to his son's ambitions, which alienated the top ranks of the army, as well as the media and the public in general. Nonetheless Mubarak continued to feel safe as President, remaining in the position for nearly a third of a century, a longer term than his two predecessors put together.

The discontent and unrest which eventually became the uprising of 2011 had roots going way back beyond the events in Tunisia. The Egyptian general strike of 2008 was very much a proto-revolution. Beginning on April 6 of that year, a date from which a major Egyptian revolutionary movement derives its name, the strike used social media engines like Facebook, Twitter and text messaging to organise itself beyond the gaze of government scrutiny. The government response left two dead. The call for a larger strike a month later went unheeded after the Muslim Brotherhood promised to support it.

When the uprising began, the military made a conscious decision not to prop up the government. After years of marginalising the military, the elite at the heart of government had no one to turn to when things got tough. During the height of the protests, the army tanks rolled into Tahrir Square without ammunition and so did not fire a shot. The police fled, and the army were suddenly responsible for policing the streets. Despite the army's presence, there was a general breakdown in law and order. A mob stormed the ministry of interior, the intelligence headquarters, the National Democratic Party headquarters and many police stations. Many of the buildings were then subject to arson attacks. Even the Egyptian Museum was not immune to vandalism; it was broken into and some ancient mummies destroyed.

The Egyptian government swiftly dismissed these protests out of hand. At the beginning, the Egyptian Interior Minister Habib El Adly did not even think it necessary to consult other government ministers on a plan of action. It was a decision he would later regret as he was put on trial and imprisoned a few weeks later.

After 18 days of demonstrations, the most senior generals persuaded Mubarak to relinquish power with the least possible humiliation. Mubarak declined the offer to leave the country. He and his sons, Gamal. and Alaa, were subsequently arrested, as were most of the other hated figures within their ruling clique. Parliament was promptly dissolved.

Despite the subsequent success of the Islamists, young secular men and women were very much the driving force of the uprising. Being media-savvy, they also found it much easier to gain outside support for the uprising. However, with no visible leadership, it was difficult to determine just who would take control of the country. The Muslim Brotherhood only joined in the uprising when the regime was already badly damaged and it had reached a point of no return. The Brothers would soon claim leadership of the uprising, as the secular leadership were caught unprepared and opportunists from years past competed to win a share of the leadership. The Brothers were not the only Islamists to impose themselves in Egypt; there were many other factions – Salafists, moderates, conservatives, etc.

The generals in the Supreme Council of the Armed Forces who ended up running the country were not clear about their responsibilities or roles once Mubarak was out of office. Their discipline and initial popularity reflected a general desire for peaceful reform.

But the SCAF became complacent, with long daily meetings which got them nowhere. The whispers of plots and conspiracies between them resulted in a SCAF which did not trust itself. Neither did they trust the liberals and the secularists who were marginalised. Nor did the secularists and the liberals trust the SCAF, seeing them as a continuation of the regime they had only just toppled. Such was the case when the SCAF rounded up NGO workers, putting them on trial for crimes against the state. Many assumed that the SCAF and the Brotherhood had some sort of deal, as they were the only two political units that co-operated in the wake of the uprising.

The SCAF had power, but they were unable to exercise it or help put Egypt on the path to democracy and freedom. They co-opted 'elderly figures' from the Mubarak regime, who were deemed untainted but were generally useless, such as the Prime Minister Essam Sharif. The generals were hyper alert to what each other was up to, particularly if anyone was meeting US officials. There were constant rumours, even within the SCAF itself, that the United States favoured General Anan. These turned out to be false. By the end of their time in power, the SCAF lost the confidence of most Egyptians, and were likewise abandoned by Egypt's foreign allies, most importantly, the United States. The Islamists, with the tacit support of some SCAF generals, were given an opportunity to fill a political vacuum. The media was divided, many outlets supporting the Brotherhood and most spouting the anti-Israel and anti-US rhetoric. Accusations of foreign meddling in Egypt's internal affairs only helped the Brotherhood, by portraying secular civil society as a branch of American espionage.

The United States rightly tried to persuade the SCAF to create a political environment conducive to democracy. However, the SCAF became paranoid and considered any advice to be interference in their internal affairs. The SCAF had little foreign policy experience, nor did they feel it necessary to get advice in the complicated world of diplomacy. Their communication with the outside world was minimal, and based on military rather than political experience, mainly derived from intelligence reports.

The generals' revisions of the provisional constitution were flawed and contradictory but ultimately irrelevant as they had made no effort to enforce its provisions. There was no objective assessment of their purpose in power. Since such a situation had never really happened before, their role was left ambiguous, undefined and secret. The public assumed that their intention was to ensure that the future President was a military puppet, particularly since they were so crucial in getting the President to stand down, and in the light of their clumsy attempts to protect the military from presidential oversight.

For many decades, Mubarak and his predecessors treated the professional class with contempt. Little changed. The generals also failed to co-opt this class by dealing with the Brotherhood at the expense of the liberals. Intellectuals and secularists, silenced and marginalised, gave way to Islamists and their sympathisers who already dominated most of the professional syndicates and unions due to widespread apathy and very low turnouts among their members for elections.

Fundamentally, the generals thought they understood the Brotherhood and Islamists better than any of the other groups that make up Egypt's fractured civil society. Many Islamists had been arrested, interrogated, imprisoned or put under surveillance. Consequently, the government had reams of classified information relating to the Islamists, which they felt they could use to their advantage.

******

Egypt's first parliamentary elections ended with the dissolution of parliament. The Islamist dissolution was blown out of proportion by the SCAF and the Muslim Brotherhood alike. The parliamentary elections were a sham and would not stand up to the scrutiny of a court. The chamber turned into something resembling a lunatic asylum with members shouting religious slogans, rather than debating political issues. When the high court dissolved the parliament, the Muslim Brotherhood cleverly shifted the blame onto the SCAF, which remained, as usual, silent. The silence only incriminated them further.

The Muslim Brotherhood ultimately triumphed with the election of Mohammed Morsi as President in 2012. The Brotherhood promptly set about undoing the influence of the generals. After the Rafah border incident in which Gazan militants killed 16 Egyptian policemen Morsi swiftly dismissed the Head of General Intelligence, opening the first wound in the body of the SCAF.

Soon after the Rafah incident, Morsi ordered Field Marshal Tantawi, the head of the SCAF, to retire. It was a shock to some and a relief to others. The Field Marshal was content that his past would not be examined and, upon receiving the Order of the Nile, Egypt's highest honour, seems assured of respect and protection from prosecution. When the remaining senior generals were sacked, the influence of the SCAF diminished.

Upon his election, Mohammed Morsi began antagonising the United States, appealing to the prejudices of the Egyptian electorate. However, he has refrained from cutting Egypt's ties with the USA, probably in consideration of the huge amount of aid the United States gives Egypt. This aid was extremely unpopular with conservative elements of the US Congress, who do not believe American money should go to an Islamist government.

The two reliable US allies at the top of the military, General Sami Anan and Field Marshal Tantawi, were gone. The potential problem was that a severe shake-up of military top brass would slowly undermine Egypt's special status with the US, a major ally in the region and, in turn, jeopardise the peace treaty with Israel. The relationship received a further blow when an anti-American mob burned vehicles on the street, shouting "Obama Obama, we are all Osama," in the same week that the United States ambassador to Libya was murdered by Islamist militants. Relations with the United Kingdom also deteriorated. The new government propagated rumours that the billions of pounds Mubarak had embezzled were held in British banks and that the British government was unwilling to repatriate the money.

Though the Brotherhood government promised to uphold the peace treaty with Israel, they increasingly used the language of Hamas, referring to Israel as the "Zionist entity," a derogatory term used by Arab governments who do not recognise Israel.

The economy continued to decline after President Morsi came to power. Egypt is still heavily dependent on foreign aid and has failed to become part of the economic boom enjoyed by other developing countries such as India or Turkey. Egypt's tourism industry has struggled to recover. Egypt's economic failure is a sign of the catastrophic economic mismanagement the country has endured over the years, and which Morsi was unable to reverse. The continued failure of the economy served as a primary rallying point for opposition to Morsi. It signalled the incompetence of the Muslim Brotherhood, their lack of a credible economic plan.

******

It seems that neither protesters nor governments have learned the lessons of the Arab Spring. After months of hope and anticipation, it culminated in civil wars and widespread political alienation, and ultimately had little positive impact worldwide. In part, this is because of the Islamist domination which followed.

In a wider context, political Islam is a global problem. There are no heavyweight Islamic thinkers. There are a few ideologues who appeal to broad sections of society but there are few progressive theorists. The history of Islamism is essentially an 80 year-long power struggle.

Islamist televangelists dominate the airwaves across the Middle East, turning family homes into venues for Islamist ranting. A common misconception, particularly in the West, is that these people are a passing phenomenon. In fact, they are the entire region's strongest opposition movement. Political resistance in the Middle East will tend to take an Islamist form, as is clearly demonstrated by the conflicts in Syria, Iraq, Afghanistan and Pakistan.

Even the non-violent ends of the movement consistently express support and admiration for violent Islamist factions. The blind Sheikh, Omar Abdul Rahman, possibly the principal ideological director of Islamist terror in the 1980s and 1990s, is revered by large sections of the Egyptian public as well as the Muslim Brotherhood, who regard his release from prison in the United States as a long-term foreign policy goal.

Political Islam carries with it many problems. For instance, it has traditionally been hostile to women's rights. Women, despite being broadly disenfranchised in the Arab world, were not significant players in the Arab Spring. In fact, women's rights have been generally eroded in the countries which experienced political upheaval, as secular principles have been subsumed by Islamism.

The wider movement of political Islam is conducting a campaign of bullying the professional and intellectual classes of the Arab world into acquiescence. One of the strengths of the Islamists is that it does not require a great deal of thought among its adherents. The fact that ideology can be described as divine means that it doesn't need to be argued and reasoned in the way that secular liberalism does.

A Muslim who practises the daily rituals may not be a particularly religious or spiritual person, as these admonitions are often an obligatory requirement rather than a personal choice. Many people who simply consider themselves Muslims, though of no particular political stripe, can be convinced to adopt certain political positions, in accordance with the ideology of the local Islamists who enjoy the support of local imams.

It is important, however, not to lump all forms of political Islam together. Political Islam means different things to different people within and outside the Arab world. The sluggish, even retrograde, pace of democracy is not necessarily a problem of Islamic culture. Muslim countries such as Turkey, Bangladesh and Indonesia have comparatively advanced democratic systems when compared to the Arab world.

The history of political Islam is inconsistent, and the movement has generally lacked the maturity of other ideologies. Though it claims to be beholden to ancient traditions, it has in fact been adapted, and at various points fabricated, to serve various interests at various times. For centuries now, the hadith of the Prophet Muhammad have been manipulated to suit the political interests of the time.

A problem with Islamism as a workable political ideology is that it proclaims to be rooted in the past. However, the conquests and divisions in the time of the first four Caliphs need to be put into context. There are many examples of tyrannical Caliphs, with the establishment of an Islamic empire by the Umayyads and their impact on the direction of Islam still very apparent in the schism between Sunni and Shiite.

The Islamist movement is fragmented between the more conservative and moderate strands. Although they broadly share the same ideology more conservative Salafists are engaged in a dispute with the Muslim Brotherhood for not being Islamist enough. Conservative Islamist imams are a special category of political climbers. Despite being clerics, they could expect lucrative jobs in the oil producing Gulf States. They have broad-ranging regional political influence, using religion as a tool to achieve political ends.

Though Saudi Arabia may be home to Wahhabism, Egypt is the real home of political Islam. The Muslim Brotherhood, which has offshoots in just about every Arab state, was formed there. Groups like Gama'a al Islamiyya and Egyptian Islamic Jihad, the models which nearly every other Islamist terror organisation seeks to emulate, began in Egypt. Sayyid Qutb, the ideological forefather of modern Islamism, whose books were printed and distributed by Saudi Arabia, was an Egyptian. Egyptian Islamism is the benchmark by which Arab Islamists are measured.

Egyptian Islamists straddled a difficult line between prohibition and official acceptance during the Mubarak years. They praised the President when it suited them, and made themselves more attractive to the government than the secular democrats when it came to making deals. The roots of this collaboration can be traced back to the 1940s when both the army and proto-Islamists, including the early Brotherhood, co-operated in their fight against the occupying British forces and liberal politicians, who were then far more prominent in government.

The vast majority of Islamists share the desire to make the Sharia the principal source of legislation. However, many Islamists wish to see Islamic courts operating as the de jure legal system, which will necessarily lead to a two-tier judicicary. Naturally, when the Muslim Brotherhood came to power, they prioritised the legal system within the constitution, making the Sharia the basis for all law in the country.

In the face of the Islamist onslaught, the liberal movements struggled to make headway in post-Arab Spring politics. The liberal movements, more concerned with their own individual standing rather than the advancement of a coherent political plan, needed to re-evaluate their political priorities. Many street protesters do not trust any available political figures and regard any sort of talk of compromise as treachery.

The liberal movement today lacks the kind of intellectual heavyweights who, in years gone by, were respected right across society. A century previously, Egypt produced great thinkers such as Taha Hussein or Qasim Amin. However, it is difficult to see any of the intellectual personalities of today commanding such moral authority. Government control of the printed word and the broadcast media has not produced an environment conducive to free discussion, and the Arab world has witnessed a general decline in the role of the public intellectual.

When in power, the Muslim Brotherhood failed to control the army, which would prove a fatal mistake. The army was the only credible challenge to the Brotherhood's authority, and it knew it. With time that could have changed. Brotherhood members had been forbidden from enlisting in the army, though there were moves by the Brotherhood to have more of their sympathisers within military ranks.

In many Arab states, senior generals were politically divided and slow to grasp the gravity of the changes facing their countries. The military are often the arbiters of political succession in countries afflicted by political turmoil. It was the military who forced General Pinochet from power in Chile when he lost the popular plebiscite. In Turkey, the military has intervened three times when it believed the government was ignoring the secular mandate of the Turkish political project. The Turkish model could have been one which Egypt, Tunisia and Syria could have emulated, albeit with some modifications.

Arab politicians are doomed to repeat the mistakes of the past, romanticising poverty, rather than ending it. The famous Egyptian filmmaker, Youssef Chahine, once said, "Every one wants to emigrate from poverty." In that respect, things have not changed in Egypt. The brain-drain began in the 1950s and reached several million in the 1970s, coinciding with the explosion in the price of oil. The country still suffers from the brain-drain, as its best and brightest move to the West and the Gulf, chasing salaries Egyptian companies simply cannot compete with.

Egypt's nationalist leftists – like those in Syria, Iraq and Lebanon – tended to be self-serving and failed to bring about the living standards which they had advocated. While not so powerful today, Arab nationalism and leftism really were the dominant ideologies of Arab politics in the mid 20th century. Their monopoly of the media left no room for liberals and liberalism, preventing them from taking root. The Arab media is still broadly controlled and operated by illiberal interests who prefer to accommodate Islamist polemicists rather than secular liberals.

The Copts

One important but seldom discussed group in Egypt are the Copts, Egypt's indigenous Christian minority. The Copts account for roughly 10% of the population, about 8-10 million people. There is no official record of how many Copts emigrated from Egypt during the past 40 years but it could have been over a million. Many emigrated to the United States, Canada and Australia, creating their own autonomous organisations, out of sight of the Egyptian government. There, they lobbied their adoptive governments about abuse of Coptic rights, raising the ire of the Egyptian state. This kind of external criticism was particularly apparent during the 1970s, when it used to infuriate President Sadat. The Copts became a political embarrassment during Mubarak's visits to the US, just as they were when Sadat visited President Carter. The Coptic Pope, Shenouda III, became a political as much as a religious leader, his visits turned into high profile trips, replete with closed gatherings and meetings.

The Copts have been angry for some time, as a result of their general disenfranchisement from political life in Egypt and their poor treatment by bigoted policemen or state officials. This anger turned to fear after the fall of Mubarak, as Christians saw the People's Assembly become dominated by Islamists, and the constitution itself become Islamised. Not only were none of the key positions of government held by Copts, but they were all held by Islamists. With the Islamists in power, the Copts were terrified they would become second class citizens, and there was even talk of bringing back the *gizya*, the Quranic tax on non-believers dating back to the earliest days of Islam. The global Coptic diaspora was vociferous in its fury, particularly in the United States, and recently in the UK, where it has well-established pressure groups.

In order to build, or even renovate a church, the Copts had to seek a presidential permit. This prohibition dates back to the Hamayouni Decree of 1856. In turn, this doctrine goes back to the Covenant of Omar. Drawn up during the Islamic conquest of Jerusalem, it prevented Christians from building churches in Islamic lands. However, in Europe and the United States, the Copts are not subject to such restrictions. There, the Coptic community acquires disused churches, or builds new ones for the Coptic congregations of the US, UK and Canada.

The late Pope Shenouda III, who died in 2012, was vital in connecting the Coptic community in Egypt with the wider diaspora. He frequently travelled to visit Coptic communities and met with senior foreign politicians in the process.

Though Copts were a common feature of the Wafd Party at the beginning of the 20th century, they have been sidelined from government since 1952. None of Nasser's Free Officers or members of his Revolutionary Command were Copts. Despite their numbers, the Copts were not elected to a single seat in the 2000 parliamentary elections. In the 2005 elections, only one Coptic MP was elected, Dr Youssef Boutros Ghali, who had long been part of the elite at the heart of government. There was not one Coptic provincial governor. No Copt was ever trusted with the important portfolios of Interior, Defence, Justice, Foreign or Information. The heads of intelligence and the army are always Muslims.

The President had the right to appoint 10 additional members to parliament to balance the composition of the assembly. These appointees would invariably include several Copts. However, such appointees were second class representatives, not having a constituency and, as they are indebted for their elevation, they do the bidding of the regime.

By consistently marginalising the Copts, a schism has emerged in Coptic society, which must be healed if society is to develop harmoniously. Involving Copts in the higher positions of government may even help to safeguard against excesses of the regime. Bringing Copts into politics will lead to a more inclusive society and go some way towards introducing pluralism to the Egyptian state.

With Copts kept outside of the political mainstream, it has been easy for conspiracy theories to arise. There have been rumours of nefarious plots concocted by Copts to steal away Muslim women, or perhaps construct their own state on Egyptian land. Such paranoia can quickly lead to violence. There are numerous incidences of intimidation of individual Copts, and many stories of forced abductions. The Copts have long complained of unwillingness of the police to investigate such matters.

Several hundred Copts have lost their lives in sectarian violence over the past four decades in Egypt. There have been riots, Coptic homes and businesses set alight, terror attacks on Coptic churches. On New Years Day 2011, less than a month before the beginning of the uprising, 23 Copts were killed and 97 injured after the Two Saints Church in Alexandria was bombed.

The Copts have their own satellite channels, their answer to the explosion of Islamic TV stations; they trade insults over the airwaves. Copts have their own businesses, and sometimes have their own schools, associated with the Church. They are generally better educated and enjoy a higher living standard than their Muslim compatriots. However, the minority integrates less and less with the Muslim majority, in part due to the hostility they experience on a daily basis simply for being Christian.

There are some Copts, especially in the US, who are known to harbour strong anti-Muslim views, as was evident from a YouTube video promoting a supposed movie titled, "Innocence of Muslims", the producer of which was revealed to be a Copt named Abenob Nakoula Bassely.

Clips of the crude film, which portrayed the Prophet as a womaniser, thug and child molester, circulated on the Internet triggering outrage worldwide. Protests in response to the film clip turned violent in many parts of the world, leading to scores of deaths. It was initially suggested that the murder of US Ambassador to Libya, Chris Stevens, and other

US diplomatic staff, were the result of mob violence over the film. The cast of the low-budget film clip, who were grossly misled about the purpose of the film, faced death threats from various groups.

Egypt's Coptic Orthodox church was quick to condemn the insults to Islam and also condemned the Copts abroad who financed the film.

CHAPTER 17

MORSI AND THE GENERAL

I could write volumes on the lack of intelligence on the part of the Brotherhood, and on the corruption of both religion and politics, but this is another battle that requires different tools. We are losing this battle before it has even begun. Those who claim to be the freedom fighters, and have been denouncing the fascism and discrimination of the Brotherhood are now contributing to the building of sympathy towards them. They are a disgrace to the principles of freedom which they claim to stand for.

Dr Bassem Youssef
Host of *The Program* and *America in Arabic*

Mubarak and his family may have been humiliated, and so too the Brotherhood. But the old order survived. The revolution was deliberately orphaned.

Bernard Lewis

By June 2013, the people of Egypt had had enough of Islamist government. Millions poured out onto the street for protests timed to coincide with the first anniversary of President Morsi's ascent to power. The army, led by Minister of Defence General Fattah El Sisi announced that Morsi had 48 hours to sort out his differences with the opposition or they would take power. Sisi, and his colleagues at the top end of the army must have known that there was no way that either the

Brotherhood, nor the street opposition movement, which had adopted the moniker, *Tamurod* (Rebellion), would enter into any dialogue. In any case, even if President Morsi had opted to enter discussions, which of the hundreds of thousands of protesters crowding Tahrir Square could he have talked to?

In the preceding months General Sisi had actually dropped some hints that the army would be willing to take control of the country. Over the course of Morsi's first year of the presidency, he had been unable to reverse the general breakdown in law and order that had begun with the toppling of Mubarak. Sporadic protests continued across the country, driven by ideological opposition to the Muslim Brotherhood and severe economic problems.

A few hours after the deadline passed, the army took control of the state television building and closed down Brotherhood-affiliated channels. Sisi appeared on television, announcing that Morsi was no longer in power. Egypt's top judge, Adly Mahmud Mansour, was presented as interim leader and the constitution suspended. There would be another parliamentary election. A military backed civilian government was in place within 24 hours and a committee of 50 was chosen to draft a new constitution.

The ousting of Morsi triggered widespread political turbulence. The Muslim Brotherhood and its allies staged two sit-ins to demand Morsi's reinstatement, restoration of the constitution and the return of the Islamist-dominated legislative council. Nearly two thousand protesters were shot and the Brotherhood's leadership, along with thousands of rank and file members, were rounded up by the new "authority", which caused tension both inside Egypt and in the wider world. General Sisi claimed a mandate based on the millions protesting against Morsi and the critical leadership vacuum.

ElBaradei, who could have been a part of the solution for Egypt, was co-opted by the military during the popular protests and installed as Vice President, but as the military swept away the Islamists with huge loss of life, ElBaradei was forced to flee to Vienna under media accusations that he was a spy and an agent of the Zionists and US. He resigned as Vice President because he "couldn't bear the responsibility" for decisions he disagreed with. The British Foreign Secretary expressed concern about the loss of Mohamed ElBaradei from the interim government, calling it a "blow" and a "bad sign" that reflected Britain's own concerns over violence and force used to clear protests.

The self-serving intellectuals of the Mubarak era had never been a substitute for a genuine civil society – poor education and the loss of trust left nothing to fall back on, fuelling violence and conflict. The post 1952 structures of state remained in place, with some of those who served under Mubarak recycled, especially in the media, foreign ministry and of course the senior figures in the military. The military were supported by the state-run media machine and "independent" satellite TV and newspapers that were known for their service to Mubarak. Opposition outlets were outlawed.

The security forces, and General Sisi in particular, have been lionised by state and private media, who denounce the Brotherhood as terrorists and have labelled other liberal groups as fifth columnists. General Sisi has little or no political experience and very little was known about him before he ousted Morsi.

The bloody confrontations shifted sympathy towards the protesters and triggered US condemnation and even led the US to revise its aid policies towards Egypt. President Obama is trying hard to avoid the political repercussions of US aid being used to support Egypt's military.

Senator McCain, a man who is not known to mince words, has called the generals' ousting of Morsi a coup, and detaining him is likely to further fuel the debate about general Sisi's intentions. The danger is that Morsi will slowly become the victim in the eyes of the Western media and the military the villain.

The British media have become increasingly anti-coup and frequently refer to Morsi as the first freely-elected President in Egypt, while the anti-Islamist media has been in a non-stop hysteria, portraying the former head of military intelligence as a hero, paving the way for him to become President.

General Sisi is in a difficult position, on the one hand keeping Morsi for too long will lose him vital support in the West, but on the other releasing him will make him a hero to a sizeable section of society and give him the opportunity to give damaging interviews to domestic and international media.

Morsi was kept in custody in an undisclosed location and received no visitors for four weeks until he met EU foreign policy chief Lady Ashton who spent two hours with Morsi inside a military facility, where he was also visited by an African Union delegation. Curiously, the Arab League Secretary General (a former Egyptian foreign minister) is absent from the whole drama, but nothing surprises with such a dysfunctional and divisive organisation.

The government lacks coherence and General Sisi, interim President Mansour, and interim Prime Minister Al Biblawi have never worked together. Sisi has the charisma of General Musharraf and is hailed by the left-leaning media as the new Nasser, whereas the interim President, Adel Mansour, is a political lightweight. Neither of the two have domestic or foreign political acumen. Appointing a technocrat government and the media hyping the general is counterproductive. So far they have failed to impress foreign visitors from the EU or the White House.

Sisi sought immunity for the military within the new constitution, as he believed it was the backbone of the state and, in light of the current circumstances, would continue to be for at least 15 years.

He also retained the power to try civilians by military courts, which, in effect, reinforced the army's status as a state within a state. The Supreme Council of the Armed Forces retained the power to approve the choice of defence minister for a period of eight years from the time the constitution passed into law. It also bans any party founded on "a religious basis".

The constitution laid out new eligibility requirements for high office which were designed to exclude a tranche of untainted, valuable individuals like ElBaradei and others with real practical experience of the workings of democracy and civil society, further marginalising those who would have benefited Egypt most.

A law has been introduced criminalising protests by requiring citizens to secure police permission for protests at least three days in advance. It imposes jail sentences of up to seven years and fines of up to 300,000 Egyptian pounds ($43,600 – a full 10 years' salary of the average employee) upon protesters who carry weapons, explosives, ammunition or fireworks, wear masks or block roads. Those who organise protests without permission will be fined between 10,000 and 30,000 Egyptian pounds.

Egypt's new constitution reinvented Nasser's law allowing the military to arrest and try civilians in military courts – and police used the new law's extraordinary powers to reject or allow protests to frustrate the would-be protesters.

The UN has called the new law "seriously flawed", while Amnesty International, Human Rights Watch and 19 Egyptian human rights groups have said it threatens the right to protest.

In November 2013 the court in Alexandria rushed in handing down a prison sentence of 11 years to a group of young female Morsi supporters – including juveniles as young as 15 – and ordering the detention of two dozen secular activists, all for participating in protests. This is a regime that has learned very little from the past. Images from the courtroom in Alexandria showed 21 young female defendants wearing the prison mandatory issue white headscarves and white prison uniforms, handcuffed to each other in a metal cage – it was a public relations disaster. Handcuffing and jailing these young girls brought them sympathy the world over. Human rights organisations and the UN condemned the heavy-handed court action.

The blogger Alaa Abdul Fattah was arrested and his wife beaten as he took part in a protest outside the Shura council in November 2013. The arrest orders for Ahmed Maher, head of the April 6 youth movement, and Alaa Abdul Fattah were given after they joined demonstrations outside parliament. Protesters were calling for the repeal of a new law that restricted freedom and banned demonstrations unauthorised by police.

Mr Abdul Fattah played a leading role in the 2011 uprising that toppled Mubarak. The new law effectively served the same purpose as the recently expired state of emergency. The fragile legal system is swamped by endless political and civil lawsuits.

There have been two gruesome incidents that are likely to haunt the General – nearly 2,000 people have been shot in clashes between security forces and supporters of ousted President Morsi, and 36 prisoners cooked alive after tear gas and a bomb went off inside an unbearably crowded prison van.

The Dilemma for President Obama and the West

On many occasions the US and European governments condemned the Egyptian authorities for human rights abuses, harsh prison sentencing and the stifling of free speech. The over zealous response from Egypt's interim President was a statement rejecting Mr Obama's words as, "not based on fact". He claimed they would serve to "embolden armed groups".

Jen Psaki of the US State Department expressed concern over the "methods" used to disperse the "peaceful" protesters and attributed the violence to the new anti-demonstration law. "The United States is concerned by the troubling effects of Egypt's recently passed demonstrations law," she said. "Peaceful demonstrators need to have a means to express their views."

Psaki pointed to reports that demonstrators were "beaten and dropped in the desert by authorities". "We reiterate the concerns we share with civil society representatives inside Egypt that the demonstrations law is restrictive and does not meet international standards," she said. "Limiting freedom of assembly, association and expression will not move Egypt's political transition forward."

The Generals' relations with the US have been frosty all along – from Field Marshal Tantawi down to General Sisi. This was clear from a meeting organised by the author and Lord Soley held in the House of Lords in London for General Mowafi, head of General Intelligence, to meet some MPs on his return from Washington. The General was clearly received badly in the US. Furthermore, the former Field Marshal refused to take a call from President Obama, which shows how out of touch the generals are with the real world. The softly spoken General Mowafi was concerned most with Qatari interference in Egypt and the support of NGOs with huge funds.

The US policy was misunderstood by the Generals and the Brotherhood alike, and the regime's public posturing does not reflect the deep anxiety underneath the facade of euphoria that has gripped the Egyptian media since ousting Morsi. Ending 60 years of autocratic rule is something, but the real challenge is addressing the political and economic turmoil, and ending endemic corruption.

Egypt requires fundamental social, political and economic vision on a grand scale. Reversing the structural damage of the last six decades is way beyond the country's resources and imagination. The only parallel is the West-led Marshal plan post WW2. The mere injection of a few billion dollars here and there from the oil-rich Arab states only serves as a palliative measure. Stabilisation of the Middle East will come from the US and Europe whose long-term interests are at stake should Egypt become a Pakistan by the Nile.

The West is facing a protracted dilemma as it becomes embroiled in the chaos and confusion at public and leadership levels. The EU is the biggest non-military donor to Egypt.

William Hague, the British Foreign Secretary, acknowledged: "Our influence may be limited – it is a proudly independent country – and there may be years of turbulence in Egypt and other countries going through this profound debate about the nature of democracy and the role of religion in their society. We have to do our best to promote democratic institutions and political dialogue and to keep faith with the majority of Egyptians who just want a peaceful and stable country."

The US weighs up Egypt's strategic importance in the context of the Middle East as a whole, where regional interests are complicated by a mix of religion and politics. The breakthrough agreement between Iran and the so-called P5+1 nations in Geneva caused turbulence within Arab regimes. The foreign policies of the George W Bush era have reached a stage of realisation where Turkey and Iran will have a leading role. Germany has asked for the release of Morsi, as has Sweden, which shares the view that the army should not interfere in politics.

Britain, France and Australia's call for a UN Security Council meeting was twisted by the Egyptian media, who blamed Turkey for instigating the meeting – the Turkish ambassador was later expelled.

The Post-Morsi Media Frenzy

Like many of its sister Arab countries Egypt is not a tax revenue state due to institutional corruption. It is still run as a city-state where 90% of the public lives in a miserable peasantry and thus the relation between citizens and state is vague and ill defined. Public services like health, education and transport are very basic and crumbling. Media euphoria masks realities on the ground.

Anti-US rhetoric from El Farein TV and other media outlets claims that Obama is "stupid" and "brainless" and even that Obama's younger sibling is a Brotherhood supporter.

The military's real intention in stepping in and ousting Morsi will entirely depend on how credible democratic change will satisfy the public at large. The public trial of Morsi proved more of a farce than the drama of pushing Mubarak into the court cage on his sick bed.

There is a great deal of disinformation and wild rumours from the main opponents. The slow pace in weeding out key old regime elements in the state machinery would ultimately abort any genuine steps towards secular democracy.

The Arab media is openly taking sides, with little objectivity. The two Gulf-based satellite TV stations pour in huge resources to support one side against the other. Al Jazeera TV and Qatar put their weight behind the Brothers, while Al Arabia TV and its financiers, Saudi Arabia, are supporting the military-backed civilian interim administration. A plethora of Islamist TV stations and newspapers, known as Islamist agitprop, were shut down by the military. Cairo-based journalist Hugh Miles has said that "the battle over the media is a key factor in the struggle for power in Egypt and almost every Arabic-language channel viewed as sympathetic to the Muslim Brotherhood has long since been shut down."

In an interview with Egypt's Al-Masry Al-Youm, Foreign Minister Nabil Fahmi said Al Jazeera was one of the reasons for worsening ties between the two states.

Almost three years have passed since the fall of the Mubarak regime, yet no credible leadership has been allowed to emerge. The media is firmly in the hands of the "deep state". The fall of political Islam in Egypt will have ramifications on Islamists all over the Arab world.

Amr Moussa, the 76-year-old former Mubarak minister and Arab League chief, was chosen as a safe pair of hands to lead the 50-member committee for writing the constitution. Moussa was popular for his stand against Israel and anti-Jew remarks that earned him a short-lived folklore song, "I love Amr Moussa and I hate Israel", which was distributed on cassettes. He is a typical old-era man, a smooth talker with a gift for political manoeuvring. Moussa will be accepted by the Arab monarchies that are fearful of getting caught by Arab upheaval inside their own countries.

Another alarming development is the resurfacing of the old silver-spoon leftists of the Mubarak era – the intelligentsia projecting nostalgic pictures of their first great patron Colonel Nasser along with pictures of

General Sisi as the new Nasser. This is the patron-client mind-set that typically attracts hangers-on. The 90-year-old Nasser propaganda minister Mohamed Heikal was happy to advise the new regime. The meddlers and opportunists are out in full force jostling for positions. Egypt is back to the 1952 scenario – "cake for take" as once described by the head of CIA office in Cairo just after the Second World War.

Calling it a second revolution is rather debatable when some 3,000 people were killed, thousands incarcerated in prisons and opposition voices silenced. The political vacuum may yet again be filled with the wrong elements.

Reading the Crystal Ball

In Egypt and the Arab world, where there is no tradition of free thought, political and religious moulding from infant school to university is so structured as to stunt creativity and new ideas. Copy-cat agitation is the only alternative. Egypt needs those with specialist training at the helm to fix a broken country and move it towards democracy in the broader sense rather than simply so-called free elections.

The latest constitution put the cart before the horse by stipulating presidential elections before parliamentary elections, under a different voting system, with two-thirds of the seats allotted to individual candidates and one third to party lists – reversing the proportions in the last polls, which Islamist parties won. It drastically weakens the political party system so that no party would ever be able to win enough seats to form a government, nor a meaningful political manifesto, Islamist or secular. No party can win elections outright or in a coalition, which fragments Egyptian democracy and pushes it towards the old totalitarian system. The primary intention of such a lopsided constitution is to stop the Brotherhood and its political wing the FJP and other parties from winning elections or forming a government.

The deeply flawed new constitution will equally undermine the political party system and democracy as a whole, leaving the old "deep state" as the sole beneficiary under the patronage of the generals.

The Brotherhood's success is partially due to political manipulation intended to give the public and the West two choices: the Brotherhood or the Old System. The well-funded and organised Brotherhood was able to outflank the liberals and almost succeeded in infiltrating the military. They moved from strength to strength by controlling the parliament, Shura council and the presidency but the Generals watched them closely. The military preferred dealing with Islamists as they have huge intelligence files about most of them, which made them easy to manipulate which was not true of law-abiding secular candidates, as the case of ElBaradei proved. The net losers in the post-Mubarak era were the secular citizens, as the real contest has always been between the Islamists and the Generals.

The ousting of Morsi was a tough decision and indicting him adds another twist as imprisoning Morsi and his aides inevitably raises questions. The army has its political cover in the huge protests that preceded President Morsi's ousting. The army-backed new government has now outlined a roadmap leading to fresh elections in 2014.

The media and the Generals wish to ignore Morsi, in Borg ElArab prison in the desert near Alexandria, and ElBaradei, self exiled in the gardens of Vienna. The media-savvy Brotherhood has turned Morsi into an icon victimised by the "deep state".

The purpose of the original uprising has been forgotten – the new constitution drafting committee is led by one of Mubarak's senior ministers and General Sisi, the real political power, is an ex Mubarak man too.

The Arab Spring has been a great disappointment and failure for many reasons. Democracy requires genuine political parties but in the current system self-interest is paramount and neither side is able to digest the concepts of compromise and trust. There is a false assumption that mere street agitations against autocracy would automatically herald democracy. The conditions that produced figures like Mandela, Gandhi or Aung San Suu Kyi do not exist on the ground. The return of the military in the form of Sisi could have been predicted three years ago.

The military-backed civilian interim administration is gravely lacking the political acumen to reconcile a divided society or avert confrontation with the US and EU. The UN Secretary General has been careful and even-handed in his warnings that have put the interim administration on the defensive.

Fifty years ago Egypt was self-sufficient in food; now it is the world's largest importer of food grains. Large private landowners have abandoned traditional cultivation of food staples in favour of cash crops for export. Last year the state spent $5.5 billion subsidising wheat, sugar, rice and cooking oil for public consumption. It also subsidises butane gas used for cooking and petrol. The International Monetary Fund (IMF) and the World Bank required big cuts in subsidies.

Egypt's population has more than doubled since then, and may expand by another 15 million in the next decade. That would mean that Egypt needs an extra 2.7 million tons of wheat a year by 2022.

The oil producing monarchies have pumped in $12 billion to support the military backed government and try to avert economic collapse. Western mediation and political pressure – probably the only plausible option – is likely to be viewed by both entrenched sides as unwarranted interference.

A significant section of the media (mostly from the Mubarak era), with questionable financial backers, are putting their resources into manipulating and polarising public opinion – even rebranding 1950s nationalist and xenophobic songs, propaganda pieces about Nasser as a "hero", and linking them with General Sisi, the second hero and the only hope for Egypt.

The old regime cronies resurfaced to manipulate and hijack the liberal movement, exploiting their hold of the media for decades fuelling more tension in the street.

The shooting of some 1,000 people and the political handling of the five-week Islamist sit-in were a blow for democracy. The way authorities broke up Muslim Brotherhood protest camps in the Egyptian capital, with the loss of some 2,000 lives, complicated Egypt's reconciliation and directly undermined the hopes of General Sisi, interim President Mansour and interim Prime Minister Biblawi to steer Egypt towards democracy.

Egypt now has three power rivals: the military-backed government, the Islamists and, in a distant third, the subdued liberals.

Political Islam started in Egypt and spread throughout the Islamic world as a Cold War project. Badly discredited in the decades since, it is now fighting for its fate in the country where it started. There is no predictable pattern now as Egypt and the region travel on an uncharted path of many twists and turns.

****

Celebrating the Third Anniversary of Mubarak's Downfall

Celebrating the third anniversary of Mubarak's downfall was a tale of two cities. In one, exclusively for those who supported General Sisi, Tahrir Square was made secure – with tanks and armoured vehicles blocking the square's feeding avenues, armed helicopters hovering above and snipers on the roof tops. The interim Prime Minister Hazem Biblawi made a brief appearance but did not speak or mingle with members of the crowd as dozens of officers in army-issue dark glasses tightly surrounded him. Flags and Sisi posters were in abundance. State and "private" TV stations merged into one, as did the print media, a sinister return to Nasser and Mubarak era practice.

Outside the square was a totally different picture. The army, police and armed helicopters chased off the opposition groups with sticks and bullets. Dozens were killed, hundreds wounded and several hundred arrested in different parts of the country. The media promptly blamed the deaths on the Brotherhood and criticised the foreign media for "misreporting".

The scene at Cairo's main Zenhom morgue was heartbreaking, with post mortems hurriedly conducted and bodies collected by relatives. Mutilated bodies of young men and women were taken out in makeshift open coffins for burial. Coroner or judicial reviews are seldom carried out, and records of such examinations are of dubious quality.

The next day the interim President, Adly Mansour, gave a speech on TV declaring a change of road map by bringing the presidential election before parliamentary election, a clear move to pave the way for General Sisi – in effect handing him the executive and legislative power, which may well alter the whole future parliamentary set up. The state and "private" media columnists have made it abundantly clear ever since Morsi's ousting that they are longing for another Nasser, whose gigantic Cairo police HQ was badly damaged by a car bomb two days earlier. As if the General had read the media's mind, he paid a visit to Nasser's grave, ostensibly housed in its own mosque, and later revealed a dream from his youth of his destiny to lead Egypt. The media "opinion makers" were already living in a fantasy, idolising Sisi and uncovering plots, concocted by the West (especially US and Israel), conspiring against their country and trying to assassinate its saviour General Sisi.

Would this old-fashioned 1950s propaganda square with the Internet age? Or has the state power, especially in the censored Middle East setting, lost its absolute monopoly on what people should hear and read? The media men of the pre-2011 era and the oligarchs who bank roll these outlets certainly succeeded in splitting the country with their scare-mongering tactics.

President Morsi and the Brotherhood unquestionably lost popular support, but they were not totally discredited. A significant role was played by Naguib Sawiris, a billionaire businessman of Coptic background who owns the popular "private" ONTV channel (established in 2009). He provided the anti-Morsi movement "Tamarod" with tens of millions of dollars, a colossal sum by Egyptian standards, and engineered the controversial 30 million signatures on an anti-Morsi petition. There are also allegations of a billion dollars in unpaid tax, which arose recently and is gaining traction in the public domain. The euphoria and emotional flood of patriotism is no substitute for emergence of mature politicians with a belief in good governance.

Egypt faces a multitude of challenges. There are deep internal divisions and economic meltdown is a continuing problem – one that could be exacerbated by a drop in electricity output and agriculture if the Ethiopian dam causes the Nile's water level to drop.

During a luncheon organised by the Egyptian ambassador Ashraf El Kholey at his residence in London, to which the author and a few academics and members of the House of Parliament were invited to meet the interim presidency adviser Dr Mostafa Higazy, Dr Higazy was questioned about the two elephants in the room: Morsi in Borg El Arab prison Alexandria and ElBaradei watching the unfolding drama from his residence in Vienna. He was also asked about the fate of the thousands in prisons, the Rabaa adwaia massacre judicial investigation and how good governance can take roots in such an environment, and his response was vague and short. Dr Higazy was still more tight-lipped when questions were asked about the military and Sisi in particular.

The last six months saw the killing of some 2,600 young men and women in a country not used to such a scale of political violence.

Thousands more, including children, bear scars, or lost eyes or limbs. It will be difficult for Sisi and the military to assume power without further polarisation and loss of life. The US and EU have expressed disapproval, which has been glossed over by the media and conveniently ignored in the corridors of power. The subsequent trials of Morsi, in a cage and soundproof glass box to muffle his voice, with foreign media forbidden from attending has raised serious human rights issues in Egypt and abroad.

BIBLIOGRAPHY

Abdul-Ghafoor, Abu Ziyaad ibn Mahmood ibn (translator): *Islamic Fatawa Regarding the Muslim Child*, 2007

Aburish, Said K.: *The Rise, Corruption and Coming Fall of the House of Saud*, 1994

Ahmed, Akbar S.: *Jinnah, Pakistan and Islamic Identity: The Search for Saladin*, 1997

Al-Abbad, Abdul-Muhsin: *Muslim Unification at Time of Crisis*, 2007

Al-Fauzan, Saleh bin Fauzan: *Rulings Pertaining To Muslim Women*, 2002

Al-Hashimi, Dr Muhammad Ali: *The Ideal Muslim Society: As Defined in the Qur'an and Sunnah*, 2007

Al-Hashimi, Muhammad Ali: *The Ideal Muslimah*, 2003

Al-Musnad, Muhammad bin Abdul-Aziz: *Islamic Fatawa Regarding Women*, 1996

Al-Othaimeen, Sheikh Mohammad bin Salih and Sheikh Abdullah bin Abdul Rahman Al-Jibreen: *Fatwa On: Fasting Zakat and Taraweeh*, 1996

Asher, Michael: *Lawrence: The Uncrowned King of Arabia*, 1998

Bacon, Josephine, Martin Gilbert consultant editor: *The Illustrated Atlas of Jewish Civilization: 4000 Years of Jewish History*, 2003

Benjamin, Daniel and Steven Simon: *The Next Attack: The Globalization of Jihad*, 2005

Blum, William: *Rogue State* (third edition), 2005

Boardman, John, Jasper Griffin and Oswyn Murray: *The Oxford History of the Roman World*, 1986

Bryson, Thomas A.: *American Diplomatic Relations with the Middle East, 1784-1975: A Survey*, 1977

Bulloch, John: *Final Conflict: War in the Lebanon*, 1983

Burke, Jason: *Al-Qaeda: The True Story of Radical Islam*, 2003

Campbell, Alastair: *The Blair Years: Extracts from the Alastair Campbell Diaries*, 2007

Catherwood, Christopher: *Winston's Folly: Imperialism and the Creation of Modern Iraq*, 2004

Chatterjee, Pratap: *Iraq, Inc.: A Profitable Occupation*, 2004

Chomsky, Noam: *Middle East Illusions*, 2003

Clarke, John Henrik: *Christopher Columbus and the Afrikan Holocaust: Slavery and the Rise of European Capitalism*, 1993

Cockburn, Andrew and Patrick Cockburn: *Saddam Hussein: An American Obsession*, 2000

Curtis, Mark: *Secret Affairs: Britain's Collusion with Radical Islam*, 2010

Darwish, Adel: *Anti-Americanism in the Arabic Language Media*

Diamond, Larry, Marc F. Plattner and Daniel Brumberg (eds): *Islam and Democracy in the Middle East*, 2003

Dreyfuss, Robert: *Devil's Game: How the United States Helped Unleash Fundamentalist Islam*, 2005

Dupuy, Colonel T. N.: *Elusive Victory: The Arab-Israeli Wars 1947-1974*, 1978

Dwyer, Philip: *Napoleon: The Path to Power 1769-1799*, 2007

Eban, Abba: *Abba Eban: An Autobiography*, 1977

Emery, Walter B.: *Archaic Egypt: Culture And Civilization in Egypt Five Thousand Years Ago*, 1961

Fandy, Professor Mamoun: *(Un)Civil War of Words: Media and Politics in The Arab World*, 2007

Flower, Raymond: *Napoleon To Nasser: The Story Of Modern Egypt*, 1972

Freely, John: *Istanbul: The Imperial City*, 1998

Friedman, Thomas: *Longitudes and Attitudes: Exploring the World Before and After September 11*, 2002

Fromkin, David: *A Peace to End All Peace: The Fall of the Ottoman Empire and the Creation of the Modern Middle East*, 1989

Fullick, Roy and Geoffrey Powell: *Suez: The Double War*, 1979

Gambetta, Diego: *Making Sense of Suicide Missions*, 2005

Gilbert, Martin: *In Ishmael's House: A History of Jews in Muslim Lands*, 2010

Gilbert, Martin: *Israel: A History*, 1999

Gilbert, Martin: *The Routledge Historical Atlas of Jerusalem*, 2008

Glubb, Sir John Bagot (Glubb Pasha): *A Soldier with the Arabs*, 1957

Goldmann, Nahum: *The Jewish Paradox*, 1978

Grayzel, Solomon: *A History of the Jews; From the Destruction of Judah in 586 BC to the Present Arab-Israeli Conflict*, 1947

Guide for U.S. Forces Serving in Iraq 1943, War And Navy Departments, 2008

Hackett, Ian: *Transcending Terror: A History of our Spiritual Quest and the Challenge of the New Millennium*, 2004

Haseeb, Khair el-Din, Saad el-Din Ibrahim, Ali Nassar, Ibrahim Saad el-Din and Ali el-Din Hilal: *The Future of the Arab Nation: Challenges and Options*, 1991

Heggy, Tarek: *The Arab Cocoon: Progress and Modernity in Arab Societies*, 2009

Heggy, Tarek: *The Arab Culture: Enchained*, 2009

Heggy, Tarek: *The Fall of Socialism*, 2009

Held, Colbert C.: *Middle East Patterns: Places, Peoples and Politics*, 2006

Herm, Gerhard (translated by Caroline Hillier): *The Phoenicians*, 1975

Herzog, Chaim and Shlomo Gazit: *The Arab-Israeli Wars: War and Peace in the Middle East*, 2005

Hindley, Geoffrey: *Saladin Hero of Islam*

Hitti, Philip K., preface by Walid Khalidi: *History of the Arabs* revised tenth edition

Holland, Tom: *In the Shadow of the Sword; The Battle for Global Empire and the End of the Ancient World*, 2012

Holt, P. M.: *Political and Social Change in Modern Egypt: Historical Studies from the Ottoman Conquest to the United Arab Republic*, 1968

Hourani, Albert: *A History of the Arab Peoples*, 1991

Huntington, Samuel P.: *The Clash of Civilizations and the Remaking of World Order*, 1997

Hussein, Mahmoud: *Class Conflict in Egypt: 1945-1970*, 1973

Hussein, Taha: *Al-Ayam* (Stream of Days), Arabic, 1933

Hussein, Taha: *El Fitna El-Kobra* (The Great strife after prophet Muhammad's Death), Arabic, 1947

Hussein, Taha: *Fe-Shier Jahi* (On Pre-Islamic Poetry), Arabic, 1926

Hussein, Taha: T*he Future of Culture in Egypt*, 1938

Hykel, Mohammed Hussein: *Memories on Egyptian Politics 1937-1952*, Arabic

International Affairs: Volume 84 Number 5, Chatham House, 5 September 2008

Jayyusi, Salma Khadra: *The Legacy of Muslim Spain*, Volume 2

Johnson, Paul: *The History of the Jews*, 1987

Jok, Jok Madut: *Sudan: Race, Religion and Violence*, 2007

Judt, Tony: *Postwar: A History of Europe Since 1945*, 2005

Karsh, Efraim and Inari Karsh: *Empires Of The Sand: Struggle For Mastery in the Middle East 1789-1923*, 1999

Karsh, Efraim: *The Arab-Israeli Conflict: The Palestine War 1948*, 2002

Kedourie, Elie: *Politics in the Middle East*, 1992

Keegan, John: *Intelligence in War: Knowledge of the Enemy From Napoleon to Al-Qaeda*, 2003

Kennedy, Gavin: *The Military in the Third World*, 1974

Kennedy, Hugh: *The Court of the Caliphs: When Baghdad Ruled the Muslim World*, 2004

Kennedy, Hugh: *The Great Arab Conquests: How the Spread of Islam Changed the World we Live in*, 2008

Kepel, Gilles (preface by Bernard Lewis): *Muslim Extremism in Egypt: The Prophet and Pharaoh*, 1985

Khan, Kamillah: *Niqab: A Seal on the Debate*, 2008

Khattab, Huda: *Bent Rib: A Journey through Women's Issues in Islam*, 2007

Kienle, Eberhard: *A Grand Delusion: Democracy and Economic Reform in Egypt*, 2000

Kiernan, Thomas: *The Arabs: Their History, Aims and Challenge to the Industrialized World*, 1978

Kyle, Keith: *Suez: Britain's End of Empire in the Middle East*, 2003

Laqueur, Walter: *No End to War: Terrorism in the Twenty-First Century*, 2003

Lee, Christopher: *Nelson and Napoleon: The Long Haul to Trafalgar*, 2005

Lewis, Bernard: *From Babel to Dragomans: Interpreting the Middle East*, 2005

Lewis, Bernard: *What Went Wrong? Western Impact and the Middle Eastern Response*, 2002

Lloyd, Selwyn: *Suez 1956: A Personal Account*, 1978

MacArdle, Meredith, Trudy Gold and (consultant): *The Timechart History of Jewish Civilization*, 2010

Mango, Andrew: *The Turks Today: Turkey After Ataturk*, 2004

Marriott, Sir John A. R.: *The Eastern Question: An Historical Study in European Diplomacy* (fourth edition), 1940

Meir, Golda: *My Life*, 1975

Miles, Hugh: *Al-Jazeera: How Arab TV News Challenged the World*, 2005

Mitchell, Timothy: *Rule of Experts: Egypt, Techno-Politics, Modernity*, 2002

Montefiore, Simon Sebag: *Jerusalem: The Biography*, 2011

Morkot, Robert: *Egypt: Land of the Pharaohs*, 2005

Murray, Margaret A.: *The Splendour That Was Egypt: A General survey of Egyptian Culture and Civilization*, 1951

Nixon, Richard: *The Memoirs of Richard Nixon*, 1978

Nutting, Anthony: *Nasser*, 1972

Nye, Joseph S.: *Soft Power: The Means to Success in World Politics*, 2005

Oliver, Haneef James: *The Wahhabi' Myth: Dispelling Prevalent Fallacies and the Fictitious Link with Bin Laden*, 2004

Oren, Michael B.: *Power, Faith and Fantasy: America in the Middle East 1776 to the Present*, 2007

Orwell, George: *Nineteen Eighty-Four*, 1949

Orwell, George: *Shooting an Elephant and Other Essays*, 2003

Phillips, Melanie: *Londonistan: How Britain is Creating a Terror State Within*, 2006

Rees, Laurence: *Auschwitz: The Nazis and the Final Solution*, 2005

Reid, Donald Malcolm: *Cairo University and the Making of Modern Egypt*, 1990

Rikhye, Major General Indar Jit: *The Sinai Blunder*, 1980

Roberts, Paul: *The End Of Oil; The Decline of the Petroleum Economy and the Rise of a New Energy Order*, 2004

Rodenbeck, Max: *Cairo: The City Victorious*, 1998

Rogan, Eugene: *The Arabs: A History*, 2009

Rose, Norman: *A Senseless, Squalid War: Voices from Palestine 1890s-1948*, 2010

Saleem, Amr Abdul-Munim: *Important Lessons for Muslim Women*, 2005

Saleem, Musa: *The Muslims and the New World Order*, 1993

Shahid, Muhammad Haneef: *Why Islam is Our Only Choice*, 1996

Silverman, David P.: *Ancient Egypt*, 1997

Stevens, Georgiana G. ed.: *The United States and the Middle East*, 1964

Synnott, Hilary: *Bad Days in Basra: My Turbulent Time as Britain's Man in Southern Iraq*, 2008

Unger, Craig: *House of Bush, House of Saud: The Secret Relationship Between the World's two Most Powerful Dynasties*, 2004

Vatikiotid, P. J.: *The Modern History of Egypt*

Wells, Colin: *Understanding Saudi Arabia*, 2003

Woodward, Bob: *Bush At War*, 2002

Wright, Lawrence: *The Looming Tower: Al-Qaeda's Road To 9/11*, 2006

Wright, Peter (with Paul Greengrass): *Spycatcher*, 1987

INDEX